Mallika

Doctoral Research Trends in Library and Information Science in India

By the Same Author

- **Research Methods in Social Sciences**
- **Special Libraries in the Electronic Environment**

Doctoral Research Trends in Library and Information Science in India

Shashi Prabha Singh
Professor & Former Head
Department of Library & Information Science
University of Delhi, Delhi

SYNERGY
SYNERGY BOOKS INDIA
New Delhi

First Edition 2014

ISBN: 978-93-82059-24-0

Synergy Books India
24/4800 Ansari Road, Darya Ganj
New Delhi-110002
Phone: 011-23268786, 23257264
Fax: 011-23281315
E-Mail: synergybooksindia@gmail.com
bookwell@vsnl.net

DEDICATED TO

MY REVERED BROTHER

DR S K SHARMA

(1942-2013)

Contents

Acknowledgements

This book would have not seen the light of the day without the invaluable support of the large number of professional friends and colleagues. Usually acknowledgements are given for intellectual contributions used in writings, but here it is for the sincere and earnest help extended by my professional friends and colleagues for providing the Ph D data of their departments. Frankly speaking, initially I thought, being a professional, collecting such data would not be that difficult, but very soon, I realized how difficult could be the job of collecting the data which was neither maintained by majority of the departments, nor had there been any systematic efforts in this direction. Leaving few departments, in majority of the cases, such data has to be compiled by doing personal efforts. Therefore, each of such professional colleague deserves individual thanks. Before I express my gratitude to all those who helped in collecting and sending the data, I would like to convey my heartfelt thanks to Prof Krishan Kumar for his invaluable comments, suggestions, encouragement and guidance extended in this whole endeavour. Prof. P B Mangla, Prof J L Sardana, Prof C R Karisiddappa, Prof P S G Kumar and Prof M P Satija for their creative writings on this subject which motivated me for writing this book and proved to be foundation to initiate and complete this work.

I feel indebted to express my sincere gratitude to all those professional friends and colleagues who took pains in collating and providing me the required data. Though, the number of such colleagues is too large, but their continued help and support motivates me to acknowledge them individually by their name. They are- Prof S L Sangam, Prof Sangita Gupta, Prof Alaka Buragohain, Prof Priti Mahajan, Prof Kaiser M Khan, Prof D Rajyalakshmi, Prof K C Sahoo, Prof P K Rath, Prof A Amudhavali, Prof S M Shafi, Prof Brajesh Tiwari, Prof Masoom Raza, Prof Amrit Pal Kaur, Prof K C Panda, Prof P K Panigrahi, Prof Ratna Bandyopadhyay, Prof Lalitha Aswath, Prof N Lahkar, Prof K S Raghavan, Prof K L Mahawar, Prof Neela J Deshpande, Prof Trishanjit Kaur, Prof M Nagarajan, Prof Dinesh Gupta, Prof Manoj Joshi, Prof Hemant Sharma, Prof Urmila Thakkar, Prof Jaideep Sharma, Prof B S Nigam, Prof. P. Padhi, Prof K Padmini, Prof Rochana Srivastava, Dr Pawan Kumar Gupta, Dr Shalini L Lihitkar, Dr Dalbir Singh, Dr Shyama Rajaram, Dr Vaishali Choukhande, Dr A P Singh, Dr Suparna Sen Gupta, Dr T D Tilwani, Dr U C Sharma, Dr Pushpanjali Jena, Dr K C Das, Dr M P Singh, Dr Naushad Ali P M, Dr Dimple Patel, Dr Sankaran Namoodiripad, Dr A G Ganesan, Dr Ally Sornam, Dr Mangala Hirwade, Dr Patibha Gokhale and Dr Sonal Singh. There are few other friends who also deserve special thanks namely, Dr Sarita Jain for her academic inputs during this study and the regular moral support; Shri O P Sachdeva for his constant support during this venture, Dr Tariq Ashraf for his all time kind help and all round academic and moral support, Dr Sangita Kaul for extending her time to time support and help by providing all required material from DELNET. My colleagues in the department, Dr R K Bhatt, Dr K P Singh, Dr Meera and Mr Manish Kumar deserve thanks for extending their support. Special thanks are due to my friend, Prof R S R Varalakshmi who not only guided me but also provided great support in collecting the data of various LIS Schools of South India which was an extremely arduous task. I wish to convey my sincere thanks to Dr Praveen Babbar for extending his constant help in this endeavour by managing and analysing the huge database developed for this work. It was not possible to systematize this vast data without his unstinted and untiring support. Last but not the least, I express my sincere thanks to my husband, Mr N P Singh and daughters, Dr Geetanjali Sahi and Dr Anupriya Singh Sukhija for their continuous encouragement and moral support. Without their cooperation, this work would not been possible. My very very special loving words are also due to my two little angels (grand daughters), Anushree and Dhriti, as a mere thought of their cute playful smile boosted my energy to complete this work.

Preface

Research is the most important intellectual activity in the higher education system which provides dependable solutions to the problems being manifested in various fields of knowledge. Research generates new knowledge and is directly responsible for the progress as well as social and economic development of a country. It has been regarded as a determinant force in supporting the economic performance and shaping a sustainable future of the society. According to former President of India, Dr A. P. J Abdul Kalam (2008), "the importance of research cannot be underestimated today when it has emerged as the driving force in the process of self-reliance in all cutting-edge technologies. In certain universities, research has been the main contributor and guiding force in realising its core competence". In other words, research would be a way to harness and find means to cater the social and economic needs of the world.

Library and Information Science (LIS) research in India is a post independence phenomenon, and the credit for starting it goes to Dr S R Ranganathan who had sown the seeds of research at University of Delhi by moving a proposal for Ph D programme in 1948. The proposal was well accepted by the university authorities and the first candidate for Ph D in LIS was registered in the Department of Library & Information Science, University of Delhi in 1952 and was awarded Ph D degree in 1957. At that time, University of Delhi was the only university in whole of British Commonwealth having full-fledged Library Science Department and offering the Ph D programme in LIS. During that time many scholars were awarded Ph D in library science related topics from other departments also. However, with the steady progress in LIS education and research, the number of LIS departments offering Ph D started increasing. Today there are around 83 LIS departments in India which are conducting regular Ph D programme. In addition, there are around 10 distance education departments offering Ph D programme in LIS.

Till 1993, Association of Indian Universities was publishing an annual bibliography of doctoral dissertations in Sciences and Social Sciences which was covering Library Science also but with its closure in 1993, a serious gap in bibliographical control of research in LIS for the library professionals and researchers was created. Though few books and some articles were published from time to time, presenting the scenario of LIS research in different states or universities but no comprehensive and exclusive work on research in Library Science in India was available. So the great need for such a source was always felt by the LIS professionals because it could have helped as a tool to know the research already done and also to avoid duplication in the topics /areas of research. With this in mind, the present study was taken up with three specific aims: firstly to fill up this gap of exclusive research data tool in LIS; secondly to identify the most popular areas of research, and thirdly to provide pervading trends and pattern of Library and Information Science research to assist the scholars in venturing the areas of research which can really help to expand the horizon of knowledge.

Initially when the idea of this study was conceived, I was of the opinion that Ph Ds being the most prestigious record of any department, such data would be easily available in all the LIS departments. But just with the start of work, I realised that large number of LIS departments were neither maintaining the Ph D data nor they were making any systematic efforts to do so. It was surprising to note that even with introduction of IT, which has made the job of record creation and compilation very easy; very few departments were making use of it. In such cases, many departments directed me to collect the information from the University's Examination Branch but it was beyond my imagination to approach such offices being huge set up of each university, particularly for asking such a data. Although today, majority of the universities are maintaining their own websites, but not many are providing information about LIS departments, and if they provide, the information about Ph D awarded is either not given or not up dated or complete. However in some universities, it was heartening to find that their websites were providing adequate information about LIS departments, including Ph Ds awarded and other research activities. It was a joy to go through such university websites.

Present book is an attempt to prepare a comprehensive list of Ph Ds awarded, starting from the first Ph D awarded in 1950 by other than Library Science department and by full-fledged Department of Library Science, University of Delhi in 1957 till 2012. For this purpose, a basic list of 83 LIS departments involved in conducting Ph D program on regular basis was compiled using *Universities Handbook*, published by Association of Indian Universities (Delhi) and some other sources. For collecting the data, a small questionnaire was designed and before starting the process, mail addresses of heads and faculty members of LIS departments were collected by scanning different sources. Questionnaire was sent to departments through e mails or by post. Repeated e mails and postal reminders were sent. Although it was a painful process but regular requests through e mails and phone calls bore the fruits and the data from could be collected. The process of data collection was started in the month of August 2012 and the same was completed by March 2013. Secondary sources were also consulted simultaneously for supplementing the data. Though all possible efforts were made to make the work most comprehensive, but there might be lapses due to non availability of complete or up to date information.

At the end, I earnestly feel that this work would be of great help to the library schools, faculty members, planners, administrators, library personnel and research scholars who are directly or indirectly involved in academic and research activities at planning, executing or practicing level. I hope this work will give a fairly good idea about the trends in Library & Information Science research in India.

Prof (Mrs) Shashi Prabha Singh

List of Tables

PART I

INTRODUCTION

Introduction

Library and Information Science (LIS) education in India completed its 100 years in 2011. Therefore, the time is ripe enough to introspect how LIS education has grown and developed over the period of time and achieved its present status. Foundation of LIS education in India dates back to 1911 when William Alanson Borden (1853-1931), an American disciple of Melvil Dewey started a short term training programme in Library Science at Baroda under the patronage of Maharaja Sayaji Rao Gaekwad II (1862-1939), the Ruler of erstwhile princely State of Baroda. This was the first formal training course in Library Science, started in India. Four years later in 1915, another American disciple of Melvil Dewey, Asa Don Dickinson (1876-1960), the then Librarian of Punjab University, Lahore (now in Pakistan) started a three-month's apprentice training programme for working librarians (Satija, 1993, p.37). In 1935, LIS education got a boost when Dr M O Thomas at Andhra University started a diploma course in Library Science which in 1961 was upgraded to post-graduate diploma. In 1938, first Post-Graduate Diploma in Library Science was started at University of Madras by Dr S R Ranganathan. Before independence only five universities namely- Andhra, Banaras, Bombay, Calcutta and Madras were offering the diploma course in Library Science (Singh, 2003, p.1).

After independence, with the emergence of many new universities, the number of Library Science schools also started increasing. In 1946, a first full-fledged Department of Library Science was established by Dr S R Ranganathan at University of Delhi which at that time was the only university level department in India at par with other departments of the University. In 1947, University of Delhi started a post-graduate diploma course and the first batch was awarded Diploma in Library Science in 1948. However in 1948, Delhi University instituted a two year degree course of B Lib Sc which at that time was the first Indian degree course in Library Science (a post graduate course). In 1949 the first batch completed its B Lib Sc degree of two years. Thereafter in 1949, a two year master's course, leading to the award of M Lib Sc degree was introduced to replace the existing programme of B Lib Sc. The first batch of M Lib Sc received its M Lib Sc degree in 1951. At that time, it was the first university in whole of the British Commonwealth to introduce this course at master's level (Krishan Kumar & Sharma, 2009, p. 297). Till 1957, Diploma in Library Science and two years M Lib Sc continued but later in 1958, Diploma in Library Science was converted into B Lib Sc (one year) and two year M Lib Sc into one year M Lib Sc.

During 1956 and 1959, six new LIS departments were established at Aligarh Muslim University; M S University of Baroda; Nagpur University; Osmania University; Pune University and Vikram University. Thereafter, the number of LIS schools has been continuously increasing (Singh, 2003, p.1). Today in India, around 181 universities and their affiliated colleges/institutions are offering Library & Information Science courses at different levels, of which, 93 (including 10 distance education universities) are offering Ph D programme.

PRESENT POSITION

Now LIS education has grown and developed into a full-fledged discipline. Different levels of courses are being offered by university departments, institutions, library associations and specialized institutions. Data collected from published and unpublished sources, including responses received through questionnaires reveal that the present position of LIS courses offered by various universities (including distance education universities) is as follows:

- 181 universities are offering library science courses,
- 131 are offering bachelor's degree,
- 136 are offering master's degree,
- 41 (out of 136) are offering two-year integrated course,
- 21 are presently offering M Phil degree (19 departments started and closed M Phil), and
- 93 universities (including 10 distance education universities) are offering Ph D degree).

BEGINNING OF LIS RESEARCH IN INDIA

Research is a process that ensures continuous growth and development of a subject, deep-and-wide and helps to establish sound theories. Ever since the establishment of Library Science as a discipline, Dr S R Ranganathan was able to realize the importance of research in this field. Therefore, he took steps of initiating the research programme in Library & Information Science in India. The process of introducing Ph D programme was started at University of Delhi and the proposal was moved to the authorities in 1948. Formulation of rules and regulations took nearly 4 years and the first candidate for Ph D in Library Science was registered in 1952. At that time, University of Delhi was the only university in the British Commonwealth to start the Ph D programme in Library Science. However later in 1978, M Phil, another research degree course was also started to bridge the gap between M Lib Sc course and Ph D programme. This was another first of Library Science in India that goes to the credit of Department of Library Science, University of Delhi.

With the inception of Ph D programme, LIS faculty at University of Delhi thought of inculcating the research aptitude among the students even at master's level. With this end, two papers were introduced at master's level to provide a basic exposure on how to step into the process of research. These papers were on *Literature Survey* (1st Semester) and *Project Report* (IInd Semester), resulting into *Project Report* and *Dissertation* respectively. Both these papers helped the master's level students to acquire the research skills, critical thinking and writing skills. Further, these also helped the students to develop new tools and techniques of research in librarianship. This initiative of University of Delhi was also adopted by many other universities with LIS departments.

For Ph D programme, Mr D B Krishna Rao was the first candidate who was registered in 1952 at University of Delhi. He worked under the guidance of Dr S R Ranganathan on a topic, *'Facet analysis and depth classification of Agriculture'* and was awarded Ph D in 1957. Then after a gap of twenty years, second Ph D in LIS was awarded in 1977 to Pandey S K Sharma from Panjab University on the topic, *'Expansion and modification of DDC.........Indian religion"*. Data reveals that 1 Ph D was awarded in 1950 before D B Krishna Rao and 6 after that (before Pandey S K Sharma) but those were not awarded from LIS departments. Initially, the process of research was quite slow as total 25 Ph Ds were awarded up to 1982 including the Ph Ds awarded from other than Library Science departments. After 1982, the situation improved as is evident from the fact that 98 Ph Ds were awarded in 7 years by the end of 1989. This number grew further to 340 in 1997 (Sharma, 1997), 633 in 2005 (Soma Raju, 2008, p.5) and 802 in 2008 (Chandrashekara and Ramasesh, 2009, p. 532). By the end of 2012, this number has grown to more than double (1754). These Ph Ds were awarded by 81 regular institutes/ departments from 22 states of India. However, this number does not include the Ph Ds awarded by distance education departments as they are not a part of this study.

NEED FOR BIBLIOGRAPHICAL CONTROL

Till 1970s, research activities in LIS were at low ebb as only few departments were offering Ph D programme and limited number of Ph Ds were awarded. Hence, the need for bibliographical control was not felt and a general bibliography namely, *Social Sciences: A Bibliography of Doctoral Dissertations accepted by Indian Universities, 1867-1970,* published by Inter University Board of India (now known as Association of Indian Universities) was available that covered only 4 Ph Ds in Library Science (Satija, p. BM6). After that, Association of Indian Universities started *Annual Bibliography of Doctoral Dissertations,* which covered Library Science under Social Sciences but this too was discontinued after 1993.

The first exclusive bibliography in LIS was compiled by Vijay Pathak in 1983 under the title, *Librarian's Diary* which included MLIS and Ph D dissertations of some Indian universities. This was revised and published in 1986 as *Bibliography of research in Library & Information Science in India,* covering 56 Ph Ds. Another work by Prof P S G Kumar, *Research in Library & Information Science in India, a bibliography of Ph D, M Phil and MLIS dissertations* superseded it by covering 72 Ph Ds awarded till 1985. However during 1980s, research activities got sudden momentum as in this single decade, 103 Ph Ds were awarded, bypassing the output of last 30 years (72 Ph Ds). With this increase in research activities, the number of Ph Ds was multiplying but no exclusive bibliographical tool in LIS was available after 1987 so need for such a document was realized and the study was taken up to bring out an up to date and comprehensive bibliography of Ph Ds starting from 1950 to 2012 .

SCOPE

Teaching indeed is an important activity of any university but research is the most important endeavor that enhances the growth of a subject in depth and breadth, contributing to the overall development of knowledge. In today's competitive knowledge-based era, no university can afford to remain static, rather it has to evolve continually and consciously by adding new ideas, inventions and discoveries in different fields of knowledge through consciously conducted research programmes. Therefore to help research scholars to know potential areas of research and avoid duplication in research, need for some such source was realized.

The present study aims to collate all possible data of Ph Ds awarded up to 2012 by various regular LIS Departments/ Schools of India. It covers a span period of 63 years, from 1950 to 2012. Presently there are 83 universities with LIS departments in India offering Ph D programme. Of these 83 departments, 6 departments (Appendix V, SN 13, 15, 30, 48, 53, and 66) had started Ph D programme during 2008-2012 and no Ph D had been awarded by any of these university department till date. Two departments (Appendix V, S N 21 & 72) did not respond in spite of repeated reminders. Data for this study has been collected from 81 university departments (including 6 such universities which facilitated award of Ph Ds from other departments). All possible efforts were made to be comprehensive in data collection but the same cannot be claimed due to various limitations faced during this study and stated under *Limitations and Problems Faced*. All relevant information required for the Ph Ds awarded has been collected from 81 universities/departments/ schools, located in 22 states of India. Around 10 universities conducting Ph D programmes through distance mode have not been included in this study.

OBJECTIVES

The basic objective of this study is to trace the overall growth and development of LIS research in India since the award of first Ph D in Library Science. The other objectives are:

a. to know chronological distribution of Ph Ds in LIS during the last 63 years;

b. to find out university-wise contributions, and the most productive universities of India in terms of LIS research;

c. to find out state-wise contributions and identify the most productive states of India;

d. to provide supervisor-wise contributions and to identify the top ranking supervisors;

e. to provide language-wise distribution of Ph Ds;

f. to provide subject-wise distribution and identify the most popular areas of research in LIS; and

g. to find out the emerging areas of research and identify the current trends of research.

METHODOLOGY

To begin with, *Universities Handbook, 2010, 32nd Ed* (latest edition) published by AIU, Delhi was consulted to identify the universities/departments/ schools/colleges conducting Ph D program on regular basis. Since the *Handbook* listed only 70 universities, other sources were also consulted to make the list comprehensive. Thus a list of 83 departments, conducting Ph D programme was prepared. A small and simple questionnaire was designed for collecting the requisite information, and the same was sent to all these 83 regular LIS departments through e mail and/or post. In addition to sending the questionnaire, simultaneous search of printed and online sources was also started to collect the relevant data. Among print sources, *PEARL: A Journal of Library & Information Science (V1, No.3, July-Sep 2007; 53-79 & V5, No.4, Oct-Dec 2011; 40-62); DESIDOC Bulletin of Information Technology (V 18, N0.1, Jan 1998);* proved to be very helpful as they formed the base for this study. In addition, regular scanning was done of the sources like, weekly issues of *University News;* monthly issues of *IASLIC Newsletter* (both print and online) and *CLIS Observer,* etc., for filling up the gaps and collecting the current data.

Two main online repositories on Ph D theses, namely *Vidyanidhi Shodhganga* and INFLIBNETwere also accessed. Access to *OPAC*, of NASSDOC; *Website* of *Universities* and *Departments* proved to be more helpful. Personal phone calls were also made to the heads and faculty members of LIS department, requesting them to send the Ph D data of their departments. Repeated personal requests proved to be very helpful as majority of them took pains of collecting the data and sending the same. Although, the process of reminding the professional colleagues through regular phone calls and e mails was a very painful task but it bore results. The process of data collection took six to seven months and finally data of about 81 departments could be collected. A database was created in Ms-Access, using 21 elements for analysing the data under different headings for presenting in various tables and appendices.

LIMITATIONS AND PROBLEMS FACED

All possible efforts were made to make the work comprehensive and up to date but many departments did not respond or provide information or complete information in spite of repeated reminders, mails and phone calls. So other sources as mentioned above were also used. During this process, it was surprising to find that large numbers of LIS departments were not maintaining the data of Ph Ds awarded by them. As regards the two main online repositories on Ph Ds namely, *Vidyanidhi* and *Shodhganga* are concerned, *Vidyanidhi* was found to be non-functional most of the times, and *Shodhganga* was not comprehensive in coverage as at that time, it was covering only 190 Ph Ds in LIS. While collecting data from departments, one of the main problems faced was that in many cases, the information provided was not complete in terms of titles, years of award or name of supervisors. Sometimes different dates/ supervisors were given in different sources or different spellings of same names were used which created a lot of confusion. In some cases, same candidate was found to be listed more than once under different spellings or even under different universities/supervisors/years with the same topic. In such cases, efforts were made to contact the supervisors for confirmation of correct information. Ph D titles are given as provided by departments or listed in secondary sources.

Nowadays, majority of the universities are maintaining their websites but surprisingly many of them are either not providing information about LIS departments or if they are, very limited information was available about the departments. In majority of the cases, no data for Ph Ds awarded was given. Many departments' websites could not be accessed despite repeated visits because either server was found to be down or the site was under construction. However in case of some universities, it was really heartening to find that not only up to date information was available about the LIS department but also the list of Ph Ds awarded. However, the number of such universities was very less.

DATA ANALYSIS AND INTERPRETATION

The data of total 1754 Ph Ds in LIS, awarded by 81 departments (up to 2012) was collected. The database was prepared in Ms-Access, containing the name of Ph D scholar, topic of research, name of supervisor, year of award, subject and the name of the university, state, etc. Subject headings were derived using *Sears List of Subject Headings, Ed 20* and other such sources, wherever needed. Quantitative analysis of the data has been presented under the following heads:

- ✓ Year-wise
- ✓ Decade-wise
- ✓ University-wise
- ✓ Top ranking universities
- ✓ State-wise
- ✓ Top ranking states
- ✓ Subject-wise
- ✓ Emerging areas of research

- ✓ Top ranking single & joint supervisors
- ✓ Language-wise
- ✓ Ph Ds from other departments

A. Year-wise Distribution

Year-wise distribution in Table 1 reveals that during the initial span of 33 years (1950-1982), research activities in LIS in India were at a snail pace, as only 25 Ph Ds were awarded. The first Ph D in LIS (registered and conducted under Library Science Department) was awarded in 1957 and second, after a gap of two decades in 1977. However, Ph Ds at S N. 1, 3-7 (Table 1) are also in library science areas but these were awarded from other departments as at that time, some universities were facilitating registration and award of Ph Ds in LIS from other departments also. Till 1995, approximately 17 such Ph Ds on different aspects of librarianship were awarded from other than LIS departments (Chatterjee, etc., 1995, p. 56). The reason for such a situation was that at that time very few LIS departments were having Ph D programme, moreover qualified guides and adequate infrastructure facilities were also not available in the departments. Later on with the increase of LIS departments and introduction of research programme, sudden rise was witnessed in the number of Ph Ds. As a result, during the next period of 31 years i.e. 1982-2012, 1730 Ph Ds were awarded at an average of 55.8 Ph Ds every year. This rise was there because the number of LIS departments was increasing, and the demand for qualified librarians was also emphasized by UGC, by giving preference to Ph D qualified candidates for selection of faculty in departments as well as for senior positions in libraries. Ministry of Human Resource Development, Govt of India is also paying adequate attention in its current Five Year Plans by increasing number of fellowships for M.Phil, Ph D and Post Doctoral Program to create potential faculty for universities and colleges (Department of Higher Education 2011, p.12). As a result, larger number of universities and institutions were also emphasizing upon the recruitment of Ph D qualified candidates for the senior positions in libraries. All these factors motivated the library professionals to acquire Ph D degree and played a very significant role in this continuous growth. In addition to all these factors, IT is another important factor which has not only facilitated the conduct of Ph D programme but affected the growth of Ph Ds. Today the situation is that just in three years during 2010-12, 432 Ph Ds have been awarded at an average of 144 Ph Ds per year.

Table 1: Year-wise Growth of Ph Ds

S N	*Years*	*No. of Ph Ds*	*%*	*Rank*
1.	1950	1	0.06	30
2.	1957	1	0.06	30
3.	1963	1	0.06	30
4.	1966	1	0.06	30
5.	1972	2	0.11	29
6.	1973	1	0.06	30
7.	1976	1	0.06	30
8.	1977	4	0.22	27
9.	1978	5	0.28	26
10.	1979	3	0.17	28
11.	1980	1	0.06	30
12.	1981	3	0.17	28
13.	1982	1	0.06	30
14.	1983	12	0.68	24
15.	1984	19	1.08	21
16.	1985	17	0.97	22
17.	1986	9	0.51	26
18.	1987	11	0.63	25
19.	1988	13	0.74	23
20.	1989	17	0.97	22
21.	1990	22	1.25	20
22.	1991	35	2.00	19
23.	1992	41	2.34	16
24.	1993	43	2.45	14
25.	1994	43	2.45	14
26.	1995	42	2.39	15
27.	1996	37	2.11	18
28.	1997	40	2.28	17
29.	1998	43	2.45	13
30.	1999	49	2.79	12
31.	2000	42	2.39	15

Table contd...

S N	Years	No. of Ph Ds	%	Rank
32.	2001	60	3.42	11
33.	2002	86	4.90	6
34.	2003	82	4.68	7
35.	2004	74	4.22	9
36.	2005	81	4.62	8
37.	2006	69	3.93	10
38.	2007	102	5.82	5
39.	2008	106	6.04	4
40.	2009	102	5.82	5
41.	2010	145	8.27	2
42.	2011	138	7.87	3
43.	2012	149	8.49	1
	Total	**1754**	**100%**	

B. Decade-wise Distribution

Decade-wise analysis in Table 2 reveals that during the first two decade of 1950-59 and 1960-69 just 2 Ph Ds were awarded in each decade but this number was increased eight times in the next decade of 1970-79. During the decades of 1980-89 and 1990-99, the growth of Ph Ds was increased 6.43 and 3.83 times as the number increased from 16 to 103 and 103 to 395 Ph Ds in these decades. The growth rate was much higher in next two decades of 2000-09 and 2010-12. However, last decade superseded the growth rate of all previous decades as 432 Ph Ds were awarded just within these 3 years at an average rate of 144 Ph Ds per year.

Table 2: Decade-wise Distribution of Ph Ds

S N	Years	No. of Ph Ds	%	Rank
1	1950-59	2	0.11	6
2	1960-69	2	0.11	6
3	1970-79	16	0.91	5
4	1980-89	103	5.87	4
5	1990-99	395	22.52	3
6	2000-09	804	45.84	2
7	2010-12*	432*	24.63*	1
	Total	**1754**	**100%**	

* Data is just for three years only

C. University-wise Distribution

Table 3 presents the listing of 81 universities in ascending order of number of Ph Ds awarded by them till 2012. Analysis reveals that out of 81 universities, 31 universities awarded 1-9 Ph Ds; 16 universities 10-19 Ph Ds; another 12 and 11 universities 20-29 Ph Ds and 30-44 Ph Ds respectively. There are 11 universities which have awarded more than 50 Ph Ds. All these 11 universities have been projected with rank order in Table 4.

Table 3: University-wise Number of Ph Ds in Ascending Order

S N	*Name of Universities*	*Ph Ds*	*%*	*Rank*
1.	Allahabad University	1	0.06	44
2.	Hemawati Nandan Bahuguna University	1	0.06	44
3.	Jamia Millia Islamia	1	0.06	44
4.	Jawaharlal Nehru University	1	0.06	44
5.	University of Patna	1	0.06	44
6.	Birla Institute of Technology	2	0.11	43
7.	Gujarat University, Ahmedabad	2	0.11	43
8.	Indian Institute of Technology, Delhi	2	0.11	43
9.	Kachchh University	2	0.11	43
10.	Lalith Narayan Mithila University	2	0.11	43
11.	Maharshi Dayanand University	2	0.11	43
12.	Saurashtra University	2	0.11	43
13.	Tilak Maharashtra Vidyapeeth	2	0.11	43
14.	Bhavnagar University	3	0.17	42
15.	Madurai Kamaraj University	3	0.17	42
16.	North Maharashtra University	3	0.17	42
17.	Ranchi University	3	0.17	42
18.	Anna University, Chennai	4	0.23	41
19.	Cochin University of Science & Technology	4	0.23	41
20.	Rabindra Bharati University	4	0.23	41
21.	Babasaheb Bhimrao Ambedkar University, Lucknow	5	0.28	40
22.	Mumbai University	5	0.28	40
23.	Mahatma Gandhi Chitrakoot Gramodaya Vishwavidyalaya, Satna	6	0.34	39
24.	Makhanlal Chaturvedi National University of Journalism and Mass Communication	6	0.34	39
25.	Tilka Manjhi Bhagalpur University	6	0.34	39
26.	M S University, Baroda	7	0.40	38
27.	Shivaji University, Kolhapur	7	0.40	38
28.	Swami Ramanand Teerth Marathwada University	7	0.40	38
29.	Mizoram University	8	0.46	37

Table contd...

S N	Name of Universities	Ph Ds	%	Rank
30.	Sardar Patel University	9	0.51	36
31.	SNDT Women's University	9	0.51	36
32.	Mohan Lal Sukhadia University	10	0.57	35
33.	Pt Ravishankar University	10	0.57	35
34.	University of Jammu	10	0.57	35
35.	Bharathidasan University	11	0.63	34
36.	University of Kashmir	12	0.68	33
37.	Kuvempu University	13	0.74	32
38.	Punjabi University	13	0.74	32
39.	University of Lucknow	14	0.80	31
40.	Sant Gadge Baba Amravati University	15	0.85	30
41.	University of Kerala	15	0.85	30
42.	Aligarh Muslim University	16	0.91	29
43.	Kurukshetra University	17	0.97	28
44.	Sri Krishnadevaraya University	18	1.02	27
45.	Awadhesh Pratap Singh University	19	1.08	26
46.	Hemchandracharya North Gujarat University	19	1.08	26
47.	Manipur University	19	1.08	26
48.	North East Hill University	20	1.38	26
49.	Vidyasagar University	21	1.19	25
50.	Bangalore University	22	1.25	24
51.	Guru Ghasidas University	22	1.25	24
52.	Berhampur University	23	1.31	23
53.	Mangalore University	24	1.37	22
54.	University of Burdwan	26	1.48	21
55.	Dr B R Ambedkar University, Agra	27	1.54	20
56.	Osmania University	27	1.54	20
57.	University of Calcutta	27	1.54	20
58.	Guru Nanak Dev University	29	1.65	19
59.	Vikram University	29	1.65	19
60.	University of Calicut	30	1.71	18
61.	Bundelkhand University	31	1.76	17
62.	Sambalpur University	32	1.82	16
63.	Banaras Hindu University	33	1.88	15
64.	Dr Babasaheb Ambedkar Marathwada University, Aurangabad	33	1.88	15
65.	Dr Hari Singh Gour Vishwavidyalaya	33	1.88	15
66.	Gulbarga University	33	1.88	15
67.	Utkal University	34	1.93	14
68.	Gauhati University	38	2.16	13
69.	Jadhavpur University	43	2.45	12
70.	Sri Venkateswara University	44	2.50	11
71.	University of Mysore	51	2.90	10
72.	Rashtrasant Tukadoji Maharaj Nagpur University	51	2.90	10
73.	University of Rajasthan	52	2.96	9
74.	Panjab University	54	3.07	8
75.	University of Delhi	58	3.30	7
76.	Andhra University	61	3.47	6
77.	University of Madras	63	3.58	5

Table contd...

S N	Name of Universities	Ph Ds	%	Rank
78.	University of Pune	67	3.81	4
79.	Karnataka University	84	4.78	3
80.	Annamalai University	88	5.01	2
81.	Jiwaji University	97	5.52	1
	Total	**1754**	**100%**	

D. High Performing Universities

The universities listed in Table 4 are the 11 high performing universities ranked according to the total number of Ph Ds awarded by each one of them. These 11 universities account for 41.33% of total research output (725/1754 Ph Ds). Till recently, Karnataka University was on top in terms of number of Ph Ds awarded but now Jiwaji University and Annamalai University have attained first and second rank by surpassing Karnataka University.

Table 4: Ranking of High Performing Universities

S N	Name of Universities	Ph Ds	%	Rank
1.	Jiwaji University	97	5.53	1
2.	Annamalai University	88	5.02	2
3.	Karnataka University	84	4.79	3
4.	University of Pune	67	3.82	4
5.	University of Madras	63	3.59	5
6.	Andhra University	61	3.48	6
7.	University of Delhi	58	3.31	7
8.	Panjab University	54	3.08	8
9.	University of Rajasthan	52	2.96	9
10.	Mysore University	51	2.91	10
11.	RTM Nagpur University	50	2.85	11
	Total	**725**	**41.33%**	

E. State-wise Distribution

Table 5 presents the state-wise distribution of Ph Ds in 22 states of India from where data was collected. Number of universities in these states ranges between 1-9, therefore, the number of Ph Ds awarded also vary between 1-224. Table 5 projects the collective position of Ph Ds awarded in each state.

Table 5: State-wise Distribution of Ph Ds

S N	Name of Universities	Ph Ds	%	Rank
1.	Andhra Pradesh	150	8.55	5
2.	Assam	38	2.17	13
3.	Bihar	14	0.80	18
4.	Chhattisgarh	32	1.82	14
5.	Delhi	62	3.53	10
6.	Gujarat	44	2.51	12
7.	Haryana	19	1.08	17
8.	Jammu and Kashmir	22	1.25	15
9.	Karnataka	224	12.77	1
10.	Kerala	49	2.79	11
11.	Madhya Pradesh	190	10.83	3
12.	Maharashtra	199	11.35	2
13.	Manipur	19	1.08	17
14.	Meghalaya	20	1.14	16
15.	Mizoram	8	0.46	19
16.	Orissa	89	5.07	9
17.	Punjab	96	5.47	8
18.	Rajasthan	62	3.53	10
19.	Tamil Nadu	169	9.64	4
20.	Uttar Pradesh	127	7.24	6
21.	Uttranchal	1	0.06	20
22.	West Bengal	120	6.84	7
	Total	**1754**	**100%**	

F. High Performing States

Table 6 reveals that 11 (50%) out of 22 states, account for 84.83% (1488/1754 Ph Ds) of total research output. On individual basis, Karnataka is on the top with highest contribution of 12.77% Ph Ds; followed by Maharashtra (11.35%); Madhya Pradesh (10.83%); Tamil Nadu (9.64%) and Andhra Pradesh (8.55%). Among these 11 states, the first 5 states have emerged as the still high performing states contributing to 53.14% (932 Ph Ds) of total research output of 22 states of India.

Table 6: Ranking of High Performing States

S N	Name of Universities	Ph Ds	%	Rank
1.	Karnataka	224	12.77	1
2.	Maharashtra	199	11.35	2
3.	Madhya Pradesh	190	10.83	3
4.	Tamil Nadu	169	9.64	4
5.	Andhra Pradesh	150	8.55	5
6.	Uttar Pradesh	127	7.24	6
7.	West Bengal	120	6.84	7

Table contd...

S N	Name of Universities	Ph Ds	%	Rank
8.	Punjab	96	5.47	8
9.	Orissa	89	5.07	9
10.	Delhi	62	3.53	10
11.	Rajasthan	62	3.53	10
	Total	**1488**	**84.83**	

G. Subject-wise Distribution

For subject analysis, all Ph Ds were grouped into 99 subject headings (Appendix II). Table 7 projects 13 top ranking subjects contributing to 53.24 % of the total research output on which maximum number of Ph Ds have been awarded. Bibliometrics/ Scientometrics/ Webometrics Studies (taken together) have been found to be the most popular area of research, contributing to 171 (9.75%) Ph Ds. Next most sought areas of research are Library Personnel with 114 (6.5%) Ph Ds; Information Seeking Behaviour with 94 (5.36%) Ph Ds; and Information Services with 73 (4.16%) Ph Ds. These four subject areas account for 25.77% of total research output.

Table 7: Top Ranking Subjects in LIS Research

S N	Subjects	Ph Ds	%	Rank
1.	Bibliometric + Scientometric + Webometric Studies	118+49+4	9.75	1
2.	Library Personnel	114	6.50	2
3.	Information Seeking Behaviour	94	5.36	3
4.	Information Services	73	4.16	4
5.	Information Needs	69	3.93	5
6.	Technical Processing, Tools and Techniques	65	3.71	6
7.	Library Studies	53	3.02	7
8.	E Resources	52	2.96	8
9.	IT Application in Libraries	52	2.96	8
10.	Library Services	51	2.91	9
11.	Library Administration and Management	50	2.85	10
12.	Networks and Consortia	49	2.79	11
13.	Information Systems	41	2.34	12
	Total	**934**	**53.24**	

H. Emerging Areas in Research

In present day environment, Information Technology plays very significant role for overall social development of a country because of its unimaginable speed and multitude of merits. IT has direct impact on the field of Library and Information Science, as a result, it is gaining significant attention in LIS literature, as well as in libraries for performing various library operations and providing cutomer-oriented wide range of services. It is also evident from the fact that during last one decade or so, there is a shift in thrust areas of LIS research from traditional librarianship to IT related areas. As a consequence, several Ph Ds have been awarded on IT related areas (Table 8). First three areas in Table 8 are of very generic and popular nature so maximum Ph Ds were awarded in these areas. Other 17 areas projected in Table 8 are some prominent areas listed in descending order which are slowly gaining attention in LIS research.

Table 8: Emerging Areas in LIS Research

S N	*Subject Headings*	*Ph Ds*	*%*	*Rank*
1.	IT Application in Libraries	52	2.96	1
2.	E Resources	52	2.96	1
3.	Networks and Consortia	49	2.79	2
4.	Library Automation	21	1.20	3
5.	Internet Resources	19	1.08	4
6.	Library Management Software	15	0.86	5
7.	Total Quality Management	14	0.80	6
8.	Digital Libraries	11	0.63	7
9.	Institutional Repositories	10	0.57	8
10.	Digitization	9	0.51	9
11.	Expert Systems	7	0.40	10
12.	Web Resources	6	0.34	11
13.	Open Access Resources	5	0.29	12
14.	Web Sites	5	0.29	12
15.	Web Portals	3	0.17	13
16.	Customer Relationship Management	3	0.17	13
17.	Web Search Engines	3	0.17	13
18.	E Learning and E Learning Resources	3	0.17	13
19.	Knowledge Audit	2	0.11	14
20.	RTI Act and Censorship Impact	1	0.06	15

I. Supervisor-wise Distribution

According to data analysis, total 1754 Ph Ds have been awarded under the guidance of 348 single supervisors (Appendix III) and 72 joint supervisors (Appendix IV). Table 9 provides the listing of 16 top ranking supervisors (guided up to 16 Ph Ds) who account for 329 (18.76%) Ph Ds. Table 9 reveals that Prof C R Karisiddappa and Prof P S G Kumar have guided highest number of Ph D scholars as single supervisor. However, 152 Ph Ds (Appendix IV) have been awarded under joint supervision also. In this list of 16 *High Performing Supervisors* (who guided up to 16 Ph Ds), 4 supervisors in Table 9 (at S N 3, 5, 6 & 9) were also found in the list of joint supervisors (Appendix IV). On adding their number of Ph Ds under joint guidance, the rank order has changed. Prof C R Karisiddappa maintained his first rank, even without having any Ph D under joint supervision. Prof Soma Raju has very aptly compared him with master blaster, Sachin Tendulkar, the epitome of cricket (2008, p.7).

Table 9: Ranking of High Performing Single Supervisors

S N	*Name of Supervisors*	*Ph Ds*	*Rank*
1.	C R Karisiddappa	36	1
2.	P S G Kumar	33	2
3.	N R Satyanarayana	24	3
4.	B Ramesh Babu	23	4
5.	S L Sangam	22	5
6.	J N Gautam	20	6
7.	K C Panda	20	6
8.	M Nagarajan	19	7
9.	Hemant Sharma	18	8
10.	M Suriya	17	9
11.	S R Gunjal	17	9
12.	M R Kumbhar	16	10
13.	M T M Khan	16	10
14.	Manorama Srinath	16	10
15.	S Ravi	16	10
16.	U C Sharma	16	10
	Total	**329**	**18.76%**

Table 10 reveals that on adding the number of Ph Ds under joint supervision, the rank of Prof J N Gautam has moved on to 2nd from 6th rank; Prof P S G Kumar has moved down to 3rd from 2nd rank; Prof Hemant Sharma moved to 4th from 9th rank; Prof S L Sangam moved to 6th rank and Prof N R Satyanarayana has gone down to 5th rank from 3rd rank. Prof S M Tripathi received 8th rank as a joint supervisor but could not find place in Table 9 because of guiding less than 16 Ph Ds (taken as a criteria) as single supervisor.

Table 10: Joint Ranking of High Performing Supervisors

S N	*Name of Supervisors*	*Ph Ds*	*Joint Rank*
1.	C R Karisiddappa	36	1
2.	J N Gautam	35	2
3.	P S G Kumar	33	3
4.	Hemant Sharma	28	4
5.	N R Satyanarayana	25	5
6.	S L Sangam	24	6
7.	B Ramesh Babu	23	7
8.	S M Tripathi	22	8
9.	K C Panda	20	9
10.	M Nagarajan	19	10

J. Language-wise Distribution

In Library Science, majority of the theses submitted and awarded by different universities are in English language. However, some departments allow submission of Ph Ds in local languages also such as Hindi, Marathi and Bengali languages. Data in Table 11 reveal that out of total 1754 Ph Ds awarded, 60 Ph Ds were submitted in these four languages. Of these 60 Ph Ds, maximum are in Hindi (44); followed by Marathi (7); Bengali (5); and Gujarati (4) language.

K. Ph Ds From Other Departments

Initially very limited number of departments were offering Ph D programme because adequate research facilities and research

Table 11: Distribution of Ph Ds Awarded in Regional Languages

S N	Period Range	Bengali	Gujarati	Hindi	Marathi	Total
1.	Up to 1985	Nil	Nil	Nil	Nil	Nil
2.	1986-1990	Nil	Nil	2	1	3
3.	1991-1995	1	1	8	Nil	10
4.	!996-2000	Nil	Nil	2	Nil	2
5.	2001-2005	2	Nil	9	Nil	11
6.	2006-2010	1	3	10	4	18
7.	2011-12	1	Nil	13	2	16
8.	**Total**	**5**	**4**	**44**	**7**	**60**

supervisors were not available. At that time, many universities provided an opportunity to library professionals who were willing to do Ph D in library science to register themselves in other departments of their university. First such Ph D was awarded to Manindranath Basu in 1950 from University of Calcutta on a topic *Museum methods and the process of cleaning and preservation*. Table 12 provides listing of 18 such departments which facilitated and helped to award 33 Ph Ds in Library Science related areas from their respective universities. Table 12 deveals that maximum number of PhDs (9) were awarded from History department.

Table 12: Distribution of Ph Ds Awarded by Other Departments

S N	Departments	Ph Ds	%
1.	Buddhist Studies	02	6.06
2.	Commerce	02	6.06
3.	Economics	02	6.06
4.	Education	02	6.06
5.	English	01	3.03
6.	Hindi	01	3.03
7.	History	09	27.27
8.	Management	02	6.06
9.	Marathi	01	3.03
10.	Political Science	01	3.03
11.	Psychology	01	3.03
12.	Public Administration	02	6.06
13.	Religion	01	3.03
14.	Sanskrit	01	3.03
15.	Social Science (IIT)	02	6.06
16.	Sociology	01	3.03
17.	Telugu	01	3.03
18.	Urdu	01	3.03
	Total	**33**	**100%**

CONCLUSION

Initially, research in Library and Information Science in India was at a slow pace as very limited number of departments were offering Ph D programme. Because LIS departments in India were not adequately equipped with infrastructure facilities and qualified supervisors in Library Science were also not available. As a result, during the initial span period of 32 years (1950-1982), only 25 Ph Ds (including the Ph Ds awarded from other than Library Science departments) were awarded. Later on, situation was improved as new departments in Library Science started emerging, moreover need and importance of research at wider level was recognized by the government and other national bodies. At this juncture, Library Science departments realized the importance of research and started equipping themselves with infrastructure facilities. Senior teachers started guiding the research scholars which is clearly visible from the data, as just within the span of eight years (1983-1990), 120 Ph Ds were awarded although these Ph Ds were on traditional areas of librarianship. Thereafter, this trend is continuously increasing, as the number of research scholars registering for doctoral research is increasing year by year. The most important reason for this growth is that majority of the universities are demanding doctoral degree for LIS faculties as well as for senior professional positions in universities, professional organizations and research libraries, etc. Another important trend witnessed is that with the introduction of information technology, there is a clear-cut shift in thrust areas of research as now a days, good number of Ph Ds are being awarded in IT related areas.

REFERENCES

Abdul Kalam, A P J. (2008). Knowledge into power. In *Beyond Degrees: Finding Success in Higher Education.* Ed. Ira Pande. India, Harper Collins. Pp.20 - 29.

Chandrashekara M and C. P Ramasesh. (2009). Library and Information Science Research in India. Proceedings of the Asia - Pacific Conference on Library and Information Education. Pp. 530-537.

Chatterjee, Amitabha, etc. (1995). Research trends in library and information science in India. *Annals of Library Science and Documentation. V 42, 2; 54-60.*

Dhiman, Anil Kumar. (2011). Research output in LIS: A bibliometric study of the Ph Ds awarded in India during 2006-2010. *PEARL: A Journal of Library & Information Science. V5, 4; Oct-Dec ; 40-62.*

http://www.aiuweb.org/Research/Theses.asp

http://www.iaslic1955.org.in/Default.aspx?PageId=87

http://www.inflibnet.ac.in

http://www.vidyanidhi.org

Krishna Kumar and Sharma, Jaideep. (2009). Library and information science education in India. New Delhi, Har-Anand.

Kumar, P S G. (1987). Research in library and information science in India, indexed by A Tejomurty and H R Chopra. New Delhi, Concept. Pp. 285-305.

Pathak, Vijay and Ramaiah, L S. (1986). Bibliography of research in library and information science in India. Gurgaon, Indian Documentation Service. Pp. 113-120.

PEARL: A Journal of Library & Information Science. V1, 3; July-Sep 2007; 53-79

Report of the Working Group on Higher Education for the XII Five Year Plan, MHRD, Department of Higher Education, 2011, p. 12

Satija, M.P. (1987). Garnering the fruits of research: Sources of Indian LIS dissertations. In ILA/IASLIC/GILA/IATLIS library education centenary celebration national seminar on hundred years of library education and its future. Nagpur, Department of Library & Information Science, 10-12 Oct. Pp. BM1-11.

Satija, M.P. (1993). Research in Librarianship before and after Ranganathan. *In*: Navalani, K and Satija, M.P, eds. Pettits petals: A tribute to S R Ranganathan. New Delhi, ABC Publishing House. Pp 27-45.

Sharma, Devraj. (1997). Doctoral research in library and information science in Indian universities. The Author, Palampur.

Singh, S P. (2003). LIS Education in India: Issues and Trends. *Malaysian Journal of Library & Information Science. V8, 2; Dec .; 1-17*

Soma Raju, P. (2008). Research in library and information science. *PEARL: A Journal of Library & Information Science. V2, 1; Jan-Mar; 3-9*

Verma, Prabha and Shailaja, N L. (1998). Bibliography of doctoral theses in Library & Information Science. *Desidoc Bulletin of Information Technology. Vol 18, 1; Jan.; 25-44.*

Universities Handbook, 2010. 32nd Ed. Association of Indian Universities, New Delhi, 2010.

University News. Association of Indian Universities, New Delhi. (consulted all available issues).

PART II

ALPHABETICAL SUBJECT LIST OF Ph Ds

Alphabetical Subject List of Ph Ds

Entry No.

ADMINISTRATIVE TRAINING LIBRARIES

Academic staff college libraries in India: Emergence, services and problems. Sai Ramesh, Thota. Andhra University, Andhra Pradesh, 2006. Guide- K Somasekhara Rao. 1

Colleges of education libraries in Maharashtra: A survey. Veer, Dharmraj Kalayanrao. Dr Babasaheb Ambedkar Marathwada University, Aurangabad, Maharashtra, 2002. Guide- Ashwini Anand Vaishnav. 2

Modernization of libraries attached to defense training and education institutes with reference to services and sources. Sudge, Suresh M. Tilak Maharashtra Vidyapeeth, Maharashtra, 2012. Guide- N B Dahibhate. 3

Shaskiy vibhagiy granthalayachya vikasache tulnatmak adhyayan. Panchal, Ghansham Namdevrao. Dr Babasaheb Ambedkar Marathwada University, Aurangabad, Maharashtra, 2007. Guide- S M Mohal. 4

Survey of libraries of state administrative training institutes (ATIs) in India with special reference to quality library services. Kulkarni, Manoj Krishnarao. University of Pune, Maharashtra, 2010. Guide- N J Deshpande. 5

Entry No.

Teacher education college libraries in West Bengal. Chatterjee, Barun Kumar. Jadhavpur University, West Bengal, 1995. Guide- A K Ohdedar. 6

Use of information technology in the state administrative training institute libraries in India: A study. Venkata Rao, Pokuri. Panjab University, Chandigarh, Punjab, 2008. Guide- H R Chopra. 7

ADULT EDUCATION

Pradh shukscha me pustakalaya ki bhumika: Madhya Pradesh ke vishesh sandarbh ek adhyayan. Shukla, Surya Prakash. Mahatma Gandhi Chitrakoot Gramodaya Vishwavidyalaya, Satna, Madhya Pradesh, 1998. Guide- H S Sengar. 8

Role of public libraries in the development of adult education of Arunachal Pradesh - with special view on Papumpare District: An analytical approach. Tiwari, Vijay Raghav. Gauhati University, Assam, 2011. Guide- N N Sharma. 9

The role of libraries in adult education in India. Sud, Neelam (Ms). Panjab University, Chandigarh, Punjab, 1985. Guide- U K Tikku. 10

The role of public libraries in adult education programme of Assam. Sharma, Narendra Nath. Gauhati University, Assam, 1989. Guide- Banikanta Sarma. 11

AREA STUDIES

Area studies libraries in Indian universities: Problems and prospects. Trikha, Sudha. University of Rajasthan, Jaipur, Rajasthan, 1991. Guide- Pushpa Dhyani. 12

Area study of Latin America and the Caribbean. Kakodkar, Archana. University of Pune, Maharashtra, 2000. Guide- M B Konnur. 13

Entry No.

Geographic library and information science in India: A critical study and development design. Promila (Ms). Panjab University, Chandigarh, Punjab, 1996. Guide- S S Pal. 14

AUTOMATED LIBRARY MANAGEMENT SYSTEM

Application of computer in library management with special reference to Marathwada University Library. Vaishnav, Ashwini Anand (Ms). Dr Babasaheb Ambedkar Marathwada University, Aurangabad, Maharashtra, 1994. Guide- N G Bapat. 15

Automated serial control at IIT libraries in India: An evaluative study. Ghosh, Tapas Kumar. Sambalpur University, Orissa, 2012. Guide- K C Panda. 16

Automation of library acquisition system. Durga Prasad, K. Andhra University, Andhra Pradesh, 2009. Guide- K Somasekhara Rao. 17

Computerized information system for library managers based on operation research techniques. Rajagopalan, N. Karnataka University, Karnataka, 1987. Guide- K S Deshpande. 18

Development of a computer based integrated information system: A case study with information requirement of users for international tendering with specific reference to Indian machine tools. Chandran, Ranjita. Karnataka University, Karnataka, 1988. Guide- C R Karisiddappa. 19

Development of a methodology for domain ontology - an application in the area of accelerated driven system in nuclear physics: A study. Deokattey, Sangeeta (Ms). University of Mumbai, Maharashtra, 2008. Guide- P A Gokhale. 20

Information output of research and development and its management: Case studies in the design of computer based 21

Entry No.

integrated information system. Bandi, M K. Karnataka University, Karnataka, 1993. Guide- C R Karisiddappa.

Integration of new technologies: A framework for decision making for automating library operations. Kundu, A K. Banaras Hindu University, Uttar Pradesh, 1995. Guide- Y P Dubey. 22

Some aspect of computer aided library and information management. Lomte, Shakuntala S (Ms). Dr Babasaheb Ambedkar Marathwada University, Aurangabad, Maharashtra, 2002. Guide- Shivshankar Mishra. 23

a. Bibliographic Database Design

Bibliographic database management system in India: Problems and prospects. Goriya, Sunil. Vikram University, Madhya Pradesh, 1999. Guide- S Kumar. 24

Design and development of bibliographic database for engineering science: An evaluation study. Prakash, T N. Bangalore University, Karnataka, 1998. Guide- M A Gopinath. 25

Design and development of digital database of homoeopathic information resources in India: A plan proposal. Verma, Om Prakash. University of Delhi, Delhi, 2010. Guide- P K Walia. 26

Design and development of national energy database: A case study. Gopalkrishnan, N K. Karnataka University, Karnataka, 1991. Guide- C R Karisiddappa. 27

Designing content based document recommender system for aerospace grey literature. Nageswara Rao, K. University of Mysore, Karnataka, 2008. Guide- V G Talwar. 28

Designing of bibliographical database management system: An object oriented approach. Majumdar, Kamalendu. Guru Ghasidas University, Chhattisgarh, 2009. Guide- U N Singh. 29

Entry No.

Development of legacy database management system compliant with the open archives initiative protocol for metadata harvesting. Jayakanth, Francis. Bangalore University, Karnataka, 2010. Guide- Lalitha Aswath. 30

Factors that need to be considered in creating a bibliographic dataset: A study with special reference in indexing of Indian environment. Sinnarkar, S N (Ms). Rashtrasant Tukadoji Maharaj Nagpur University, Nagpur, Maharashtra, 1997. Guide- P S G Kumar. 31

Indigenous databases in the field of science and technology: A survey of their present status and study of their utility for library and information services and future prospects. Kanaujia, Shiva (Ms). University of Lucknow, Uttar Pradesh, 2006. Guide- N R Satyanarayana. 32

Structural design of a bibliographic database on gas turbine using AACR 2, UNIMARC and CDS/ISIS. Aroti, Aruna (Mrs). Vidyasagar University, West Bengal, 1999. Guide- Ashok Basu. 33

b. Library Services

Awareness and utilization of information and communication technology based services by the users of self financing medical college libraries in Pondicherry: A study. Saravanan, K. Annamalai University, Tamil Nadu, 2012. Guide- S Ravi. 34

Impact of computer based library services on teaching and research in agricultural universities of Rajasthan. Rajpurohit, Chetan Prakash. Mohan Lal Sukhadia University, Udaipur, Rajasthan, 2011. Guide- L N Verma. 35

Impact of computerization on technical and users services of special libraries: Formation of norms in Indian context. Sharma, R K. Dr Hari Singh Gour Vishwavidyalaya, Sagar, Madhya Pradesh, 1995. Guide- R G Prasher. 36

Entry No.

Information users preference to computer based information services in research libraries of Bangalore City. Sami, Lalitha K. University of Mysore, Karnataka, 2004. Guide- N B Pangannaya. 37

Planning and implementation of automated circulation system for open university library system. Laxman Rao, N. Osmania University, Andhra Pradesh, 1993. Guide- A V Satyanarayana Rao. 38

BIBLIOGRAPHICAL CONTROL

Bibliographical control and services in Thailand: A survey and study with emphasis on the role of the Thai National Library. Bodhibukkana, Dhida (Ms). University of Delhi, Delhi, 1988. Guide- Krishan Kumar. 39

Development of systematic bibliography in India. Rath, Pravash Narayana. University of Calcutta, West Bengal, 2004. Guide- Tarun Kumar Mitra. 40

Granth Mitra N V Deshpande Yanchya Granthalaya chalvalitil sahbhag: Ek abhyas. Dhakne, Balaji Nivruti. Dr Babasaheb Ambedkar Marathwada University, Aurangabad, Maharashtra, 2005. Guide- Ashwini Anand Vaishnav. 41

Paperless documentation data control and its contribution towards massive industrialization. De, Partha. Dr B R Ambedkar University, Agra, Uttar Pradesh, 2000. Guide- U C Sharma. 42

Role of the national library of Bangladesh in bibliographic organization and control: A study. Akhter, Roshan (Ms). University of Burdwan, Rajbati, Bardhaman, West Bengal, 1994. Guide- Pulin Behari Barua. 43

Entry No.

a. Language and Literature

Bibliographical control in Malayalam literature: Problems and prospects. Kochukoshy, K K. University of Calcutta, West Bengal, 2007. Guide- Bhubaneswar Chakrabarti. 44

Bibliographical control of Kannada literature: Problems and prospects. Chandrashekharaiah, H. Utkal University, Orissa, 2001. Guide- Pitambar Padhi. 45

Critical study of the bibliographies and documentation lists of printed Hindi literature published during 1838 to 1978. Kamal, Kumud Kumar. Lalith Narayan Mithila University Darbangha, Bihar, 1983. Guide- Srinarayan Singh. 46

b. Sciences

Documentation in jute technology: Its origin and development. Mukhopadhyay, Chaitali (Ms). University of Calcutta, West Bengal, 1996. Guide- Tarun Kumar Mitra. 47

Geological documentation in India and development of an integrated geosciences information centre and services. Ghosh, Sibabrata. Jadhavpur University, West Bengal, 1995. Guide- M L Chakraborty. 48

Meteorological data in India: Its origin development and management in Indian libraries. Khanna, B M. University of Pune, Maharashtra, 1990. Guide- M R Riswadkar. 49

c. Social Sciences

Bibliographical control of social science literature in post independent India. Vyas, S D. University of Rajasthan, Jaipur, Rajasthan, 1988. Guide- S P Sood. 50

Labour information in Maharashtra: An information consolidated package. Deshmukh, Asmita (Ms). University of Mumbai, Maharashtra, 2010. Guide- V P Rajhans. 51

Entry No.

Serial literature in sociology and its document delivery capacity in India: Bibliographical study. Sudarshan Rao, S. Osmania University, Andhra Pradesh, 1995. Guide- A A N Raju. 52

BIBLIOMETRIC STUDIES

A model system for evaluating the resources of special library on the basis of users' satisfaction using bibliometric techniques: A case study at Regional Research Laboratory, Jorhat, Guwahati. Barooah, Pranab Kumar. Gauhati University, Assam, 2004. Guide- N N Sharma. 53

Bibliometric study of the literature in the field of Islamic Studies. Taher, Mohamed. University of Calicut, Calicut, Kerala, 1989. Guide- M Bavakutty. 54

Impact of citation peaking on impact factor. Ponnudurai, R. Annamalai University, Tamil Nadu, 1999. Guide- P Pichappan. 55

Indian contribution to American study: An investigation into the growth of literature using the bibliometrics, citation analysis. Behranuddin, Muhammad. Jiwaji University, Madhya Pradesh, 1991. Guide- S M Tripathi. 56

a. Children Literature

Children's literature in Malayalam: A bibliometric study. Ajit Kumari, T. University of Kerala, Kerala, 2009. Guide- G Devarajan. 57

Children's literature in Marathi: A bibliometric analysis 1901-2000. Urkudkar, Sunil. Rashtrasant Tukadoji Maharaj Nagpur University, Nagpur, Maharashtra, 2007. Guide- P S G Kumar. 58

Entry No.

b. Classificationists

Landmarks in library classification: A citation study of famous classificationists, classifiers and their writings from 1970-1978. Dung, Raghbir Singh. Panjab University, Chandigarh, Punjab, 1986. Guide- U K Tikku. 59

c. Diseases

A bibliometric study of the progress of research on asthma in India. Gomathi, P. Annamalai University, Tamil Nadu, 2012. Guide- R Ponnu Durai. 60

Collaborative research in oncology: An analytical study. Ambuja, R. University of Madras, Tamil Nadu, 1999. Guide- K S Raghavan. 61

Growth and collaboration trends in acquired immune deficiency syndrome (AIDS) research literature: A bibliometric analysis. Suresh, B. Annamalai University, Tamil Nadu, 2003. Guide- S Ravi. 62

Research productivity of cancer disease in the SAARC countries with special reference to India: A bibliometric analysis. Batcha, M Sadik. Annamalai University, Tamil Nadu, 2003. Guide- M Nagarajan. 63

Research productivity of ophthalmic diseases in India: A bibliometric study. Senthilkumar, R. Annamalai University, Tamil Nadu, 2010. Guide- R Ponnu Durai. 64

d. Eugene Garfield

Eugene Garfield: A biobibliometric study. Savanur, K P. Karnataka University, Karnataka, 2011. Guide- S L Sangam. 65

Entry No.

e. Language and Literature

Bibliographical and bibliometric study of scientific and humanistic literature in Hindi language produced in Hindi speaking states. Garg, Ram Gopal. Jiwaji University, Madhya Pradesh, 2002. Guide- R G Prasher & J N Gautam. 66

Contribution of parasis to Gujarati literature bibliography and bibliometrics study. Prajapati, Narendrakumar Prabhudas. Hemchandracharya North Gujarat University, Gujarat, 2012. Guide- M K Prajapati. 67

Literature from Vidharbha in Marathi (1975-1999): A survey and bibliometric study. Sable, S N. Rashtrasant Tukadoji Maharaj Nagpur University, Nagpur, Maharashtra, 2010. Guide- P S G Kumar. 68

Literature use pattern of scholars in Telugu language and literature: A study of the Ph D theses submitted in Andhra University during 1946-1992. Valasayya, G. Andhra University, Andhra Pradesh, 1999. Guide- B Vijayalakshmi. 69

f. LIS Literature

A comparative study of robustness of Zipf's Law across literature. Jauhari, Monika. Bundelkhand University, Jhansi, Uttar Pradesh, 2008. Guide- Pandey S K Sharma. 70

Bibliographic analysis of library and information science literature since 1980. Meera, B M (Ms). Bangalore University, Karnataka, 1998. Guide- M A Gopinath. 71

Co-word analysis of literature on information. Amudhavalli, A (Ms). University of Madras, Tamil Nadu, 1994. Guide- K S Raghavan. 72

Growth and development of Indian library and information science periodical literature, 1970-1985: A bibliometric study. Tripathi, Tridib. University of Burdwan, Rajbati, Bardhaman, West Bengal, 1992. Guide- Pulin Behari Barua. 73

Entry No.

NACLIN, IASLIC, and CALIBER proceedings: A bibliometric study. Kulkarni, Jagdish. Dr Babasaheb Ambedkar Marathwada University, Aurangabad, Maharashtra, 2011. Guide- Ashwini Anand Vaishnav. 74

g. LIS Periodicals

Bibliometric study of contributions made to documentation as reflected in the selected periodicals of library and information science publishes in India: A quantitative analysis (1969-88). Banwari Lal. Jiwaji University, Madhya Pradesh, 1992. Guide- S M Tripathi & Krishan Kumar. 75

Citation pattern among the Indian library and information science journals in English from 1975 to 1985. Mahapatra, Gayatri. Utkal University, Orissa, 1992. Guide- S R Gunjal. 76

Indian contribution to library and information science: A bibliometric study of micro literature from 1975 to 1995. Tiwari, Ashwini. University of Rajasthan, Jaipur, Rajasthan, 2003. Guide- S P Sood. 77

h. LIS Theses

Bibliometric study of doctoral theses in library and information science awarded by different universities. Surya Narayana, V V. Andhra University, Andhra Pradesh, 2008. Guide- C Sasikala. 78

Citation analysis of doctoral dissertations in library and information science accepted by the universities of Karnataka. Kannappanavar, B U. Karnataka University, Karnataka, 1991. Guide- S R Ijari. 79

Citation analysis of doctoral dissertations in library and information science accepted by the universities of Orissa and Manipur till 1993: A comparative study. Mishra, Rabi Narayan. Sambalpur University, Orissa, 1997. Guide- K C Panda. 80

Entry No.

Citation analysis of Ph D dissertations in library and information science submitted to university of M P and Punjab. Ghai, Daljeet. Jiwaji University, Madhya Pradesh, 2001. Guide- Hemant Sharma. 81

Granthalaya evam soochna vigyan ke shodh prabandhon ka granthmiti evam uddharan vishleshan, 2001-2008. Sharma, Ram Nivas. Maharani Laxmi Bai Govt. College of Excellence, Jiwaji University, Madhya Pradesh, 2012. Guide- Arvind Kumar Sharma. 82

i. Research Output

A database of research output of Berhampur University 1970-2006: An analytical study. Patro, K Damayanti. Berhampur University, Orissa, 2010. Guide- R K Mahapatra. 83

Bibliometric analysis of research output in Madurai Kamaraj University, Madurai. Padma, P. AVVM Sri Pushpam College, Bharathidasan University, Tamil Nadu, 2010. Guide- A Ganesan. 84

Research productivity of faculty members in the universities of Tamil Nadu: A bibliometric analysis. Sivaraman, P. Annamalai University, Tamil Nadu, 2006. Guide- M Nagarajan. 85

j. Science Literature

A bibliometric analysis of literature in the field of nuclear and particle science based on *Annual Review of Nuclear and Particle Science*, 1990-1998. Jena, Kamal Lochan,. Sambalpur University, Orissa, 2004. Guide- K C Sahoo. 86

A bibliometric analysis of phytopathology literature. Maheswarappa, B S. Karnataka University, Karnataka, 1993. Guide- S L Sangam. 87

Entry No.

A critical study of the growth of tea literature with special reference to India from 1970-2002. Baruah, Smiriti Rekha. Gauhati University, Assam, 2008. Guide- Alaka Buragohain. 88

A quantitative analysis of Indian research output on spices since 1970. Susmadevi, C K. Annamalai University, Tamil Nadu, 2002. Guide- M Nagarajan. 89

An investigation into the progress of research on marine fauna publications: A bibliometric analysis. Sundararajan, D. Annamalai University, Tamil Nadu, 2012. Guide- R Ponnu Durai. 90

An investigation of the growth pattern and formation of subjects in the field of agricultural sciences during twentieth century in India. Shive, Ganga. Banaras Hindu University, Uttar Pradesh, 1998. Guide- P N Kaula. 91

Application of subject analysis in the creation of knowledge base mapping the development and interrelationship of a subject field: A bibliometric analysis of superconductivity. Chudamani. K S. Bangalore University, Karnataka, 2002. Guide- A Y Asundi. 92

Assessment of research output: A bibliometric analysis of research output of Indian agricultural universities. Munshi, Usha Mujju. Jiwaji University, Madhya Pradesh, 1993. Guide- C P Vashishth & J N Gautam. 93

Bibliometric analysis and bibliographical control of literature in immunology. Arora, Jagdish. University of Rajasthan, Jaipur, Rajasthan, 1993. Guide- Usha Pawan. 94

Bibliometric analysis and evaluation of Indian research writing in physics. Paul, Mohan Roy. Madurai Kamaraj University, Tamil Nadu, 1988. Guide- D B Krishna Rao. 95

Entry No.

Bibliometric analysis of air pollution research using E-CD. Parameswaran, R. University of Madras, Tamil Nadu, 2002. Guide- B Ramesh Babu. 96

Bibliometric analysis of literature on wireless communication (1970-2009) based on bibliographic databases. Dhanakar, M Arul. Anna University, Chennai, Tamil Nadu, 2012. Guide- G Krishnamoorthy. 97

Bibliometric analysis of scientific speciality: A case study on theoretical population genetics. Gupta, B M. Karnataka University, Karnataka, 2000. Guide- C R Karisiddappa. 98

Bibliometric analysis of the impact of the growth of biochemical knowledge on other biological and medical sciences. Sengupta, I N. Karnataka University, Karnataka, 1984. Guide- K S Deshpande. 99

Bibliometric studies in physics. Mandal, A K. Gauhati University, Assam, 2010. Guide- R K Barman. 100

Computer science literature: A bibliometric study. Singh, Shuchita (Ms). Banaras Hindu University, Uttar Pradesh, 2005. Guide- H N Prasad. 101

Growth and collaboration trends in the field of biodiversity research: A bibliometric analysis. Revathi, R. Annamalai University, Tamil Nadu, 2011. Guide- S Ravi. 102

Growth and collaboration trends of research in the field of ecology: A bibliometric analysis. Maheswari, K. Annamalai University, Tamil Nadu, 2012. Guide- S Ravi. 103

Indian contribution to agronomy bibliometrics investigation in the growth of micro literature. Bhupendra Mall. Jiwaji University, Madhya Pradesh, 1995. Guide- H S Sengar. 104

Entry No.

Literature use pattern of researchers in chemistry: A bibliometric study. Srivastava, Ranjana (Ms). Banaras Hindu University, Uttar Pradesh, 1998. Guide- S N Singh. 105

Mapping the literature (1986-2000) on chernobyl nuclear reactor oxidant using bibliographic databases. Chandra, R. Annamalai University, Tamil Nadu, 2004. Guide- S Ravi. 106

Polymer science research in India (1992 - 2006): A bibliometric study. Gobbur, Devendra S. Gulbarga University, Karnataka, 2011. Guide- N Parvathamma. 107

Quantitative analysis of medical literature in India: A bibliographic study. Kundra, Ramesh. University of Pune, Maharashtra, 2003. Guide- I K Ravichandra Rao. 108

R & D output on spices amongst the Asian countries: A cross national analysis. Senthil Kumaran, P. University of Madras, Tamil Nadu, 2005. Guide- A Amudavalli. 109

Research productivity in astronomy science in G 7 countries with special reference to India: A bibliometric analysis. Saravanan, T. Annamalai University, Tamil Nadu, 2001. Guide- M Nagarajan. 110

Research productivity of science faculties in central universities of India: A bibliometric analysis. Sevukan, R. Annamalai University, Tamil Nadu, 2008. Guide- M Nagarajan. 111

Research publication trends in pharmacology: A bibliometric study. Ahila, M. Annamalai University, Tamil Nadu, 2012. Guide- M Nagarajan. 112

Research undertaken in Physical Research Laboratory (PRL): A bibliometric study. Anil Kumar, Nishtha (Ms). M S University, Baroda, Gujarat, 2012. Guide- Shyama Rajaram. 113

Entry No.

Trends in growth of Indian earth science literature 1978-1988: A bibliometric study. Parvathamma, N. Gulbarga University, Karnataka, 1990. Guide- S R Gunjal. 114

Trends of Indian oceanographic research publications (1963-92): A bibliometric study by development and use of CDS / ISIS based application software. Tapaswi, M P. Karnataka University, Karnataka, 2000. Guide- B S Maheswarappa. 115

World agricultural and allied science databases: A bibliometric study of literature with reference to Himachal Pradesh. Nabi Hasan. Guru Nanak Dev University, Amritsar, Punjab, 2004. Guide- Sewa Singh. 116

k. Science Periodicals

Bibliometric analysis of citations in journals in agricultural economics: A comparative study of the *Indian Journal of Agricultural Economics* and the *American Journal of Agricultural Economics*, 2000-2001. Pushpa, K (Ms). Andhra University, Andhra Pradesh, 2005. Guide- B Vijayalakshmi. 117

Bibliometric analysis of scientific productivity in biomedical and health science research journals in India. Sahoo, Banamber. Utkal University, Orissa, 2000. Guide- B B Shukla. 118

Bibliometric analysis of the science journals published from India. Jalaja, V (Ms). University of Calicut, Calicut, Kerala, 1995. Guide- M Bavakutty. 119

Identification of main stream journals of science specialty and the study of their relationships. Pichappan, P. Annamalai University, Tamil Nadu, 1993. Guide- M Suriya. 120

Literature on surgery: A bibliometric study of articles published in surgery journals during 2000-2005. Nageen, Zeba (Ms). University of Lucknow, Uttar Pradesh, 2012. Guide- N R Satyanarayana. 121

Entry No.

l. Science Theses

A citation analysis of doctoral dissertations of plant pathology in the agricultural universities of Bihar. Arjun Lal. Sambalpur University, Orissa, 2001. Guide- K C Panda. 122

An annotated bibliometric study of doctoral theses of chemistry in Jiwaji University Gwalior, 1981 to 1991. Verma, Naresh Narayan. Jiwaji University, Madhya Pradesh, 2008. Guide- J N Gautam. 123

An investigation into the characteristics of research literature used by medical scientists in India: A statistical analysis of bibliographic citations of M D theses. Gupta, Awadh Bihari. Banaras Hindu University, Uttar Pradesh, 1989. Guide- Y P Dubey. 124

Bibliometric study of citations in Ph D theses in biological sciences. Vimala, V (Ms). Sri Venkateswara University, Tirupati, Andhra Pradesh, 1997. Guide- V Pulla Reddy. 125

Bibliometric study of citations in Ph D theses in chemistry accepted by S V University, Tirupati. Aruna Prasada Reddy, C. Andhra University, Andhra Pradesh, 2000. Guide- B Vijayalakshmi. 126

Bibliometric study of citations in Ph D theses in geology accepted by Andhra University, Visakhapatnam, 1954-2001. Siva Prasad, G. Andhra University, Andhra Pradesh, 2007. Guide- B Vijayalakshmi. 127

Bibliometric study of M D dissertations submitted to medical colleges in U P during 1996-2005. Purvendra Kumar. Jiwaji University, Madhya Pradesh, 2007. Guide- B K Sharma & Hemant Sharma. 128

Bibliometric study of Ph D theses in physics awarded by Andhra University. Andhra Matha, K. Andhra University, Andhra Pradesh, 2006. Guide- C Sasikala. 129

Entry No.

Citation analysis of Ph D theses in chemistry submitted to Berhampur University. Panda, B P. Berhampur University, Orissa, 2000. Guide- P S G Kumar. 130

Citation analysis of Ph D theses of geography. Murthy, A Omkara. Sri Venkateswara University, Tirupati, Andhra Pradesh, 2007. Guide- V Pulla Reddy. 131

Citation analysis of the doctoral dissertations submitted to the Shivaji University, Kolhapur in pure science (1962-1992). Abbas Khan. Shivaji University, Kolhapur, Maharashtra, 1999. Guide- S R Gunjal. 132

Financial management and use of science journals: A bibliometric study of doctoral theses in chemistry in the university libraries of Madhya Pradesh since 1986-1996. Dongare, Sanjay. Pt Ravishankar University Raipur, Chhattisgarh, 2006. Guide- A K Varma. 133

Literature use pattern in biological sciences: A bibliometric study of doctoral theses submitted to Dr Babasaheb Ambedkar Marathwada University, Aurangabad. Khaparde, Vinita Sovind (Ms). Dr Babasaheb Ambedkar Marathwada University, Aurangabad, Maharashtra, 2008. Guide- S M Mohal. 134

Literature use pattern in biosciences (ecology, biochemistry, biophysics, physiology) at the universities of Sagar and Sambalpur: A bibliometric study based on Ph D theses, 1975-1990. Sahoo, K C. Dr Hari Singh Gour Vishwavidyalaya, Sagar, Madhya Pradesh, 1996. Guide- R G Prasher. 135

m. Scientists

Determination of performance measures of scientists in Council of Scientific and Industrial Research (India): A bibliometric study of research papers published in journals during 1988-1992. Narendra Kumar. University of Delhi, Delhi, 1999. Guide- P B Mangla. 136

Entry No.

Evaluation of research productivity of the marine scientists in India: A bibliometric analysis. Nagarajan, M. Annamalai University, Tamil Nadu, 1995. Guide- M Suriya. 137

Productivity patterns of scientists in Marathwada: A bibliometric study. Adhe, Govind Dalsing. Dr Babasaheb Ambedkar Marathwada University, Aurangabad, Maharashtra, 2009. Guide- Ashwini Anand Vaishnav. 138

Research productivity of the nuclear scientists In India: A bibliometric analysis. Ravi, S. Annamalai University, Tamil Nadu, 1996. Guide- M Suriya. 139

n. Social Science Literature

Bibliometric analysis of gender research based on *SCOPUS* database. Umadevi, L N. Annamalai University, Tamil Nadu, 2011. Guide- M Suriya. 140

Bibliometric analysis of the international conference proceedings on gender and ICT. Balakrishnan, S. Annamalai University, Tamil Nadu, 2010. Guide- M Suriya. 141

Citation analysis in the field of social sciences. Purnima Devi. Karnataka University, Karnataka, 1997. Guide- S L Sangam. 142

Gender differences in productivity psychology, 1987-1996. Goel, Kamlesh. Annamalai University, Tamil Nadu, 1999. Guide- P Pichappan. 143

Growth and development of literature in the field of strategic management from 2002-2006: A bibliometric study. Sahu, Sada Bihari. Sambalpur University, Orissa, 2010. Guide- B K Choudhury. 144

Indian management literature: Analysis and evaluation. Chandrappa, S. Bangalore University, Karnataka, 1997. Guide- P Sadashivmurthy. 145

Entry No.

Research productivity using *Econlit* database. Khatri, N K. Annamalai University, Tamil Nadu, 2001. Guide- P Pichappan. 146

Samajshastriya shodho mein prayukt pralekhon ki pravritti: Chhattisgarh ke samajshastra ke shodh prabandho ka ek granthmitiya adyayan. Awadhiya, Monika. Pt Ravishankar University Raipur, Chhattisgarh, 2012. Guide- A K Varma. 147

Use of social science literature in India: A bibliometric study. Singh, Shambhu Nath. Banaras Hindu University, Uttar Pradesh, 1982. Guide- P N Kaula. 148

Use pattern of literature by economics researchers: A bibliometric study. Verma, Maya. Pt Ravishankar University Raipur, Chhattisgarh, 1994. Guide- A K Varma. 149

o. Social Science Periodicals

Bibliometric analysis of citation patterns in Indian periodical literature on economics. Dheerendra, P T. Osmania University, Andhra Pradesh, 1999. Guide- A A N Raju. 150

India's contribution to world sociological literature: An analysis of *Sociological Abstracts* (1990-2002). Johari, Nutan. Vikram University, Madhya Pradesh, 2010. Guide- S S Chandel. 151

Research productivity analysis using *International Political Science Abstract* data base: A study. Tiwari, Rishi Kumar. Jiwaji University, Madhya Pradesh, 2008. Guide- J N Gautam. 152

p. Social Science Theses

A bibliomaniac analysis of doctoral dissertations of political science in universities of M P: A critical study. Nijam, Fazilat. Awadhesh Pratap Singh University, Madhya Pradesh, 2005. Guide- A K Verma. 153

Entry No.

A bibliometric analysis of citations of doctoral dissertations in economics: A comparative study of universities of Madhya Pradesh. Bopapurkar, Prashant. Pt Ravishankar University Raipur, Chhattisgarh, 2004. Guide- A K Varma. 154

An analysis of the citations of doctoral dissertations in social sciences accepted by the Bundelkhand University during the last twenty years: A study. Haridasan, Sudharma. Bundelkhand University, Jhansi, Uttar Pradesh, 2003. Guide- M T M Khan. 155

An annotated bibliographical study of doctoral theses in sociology. Sharma, Archana. Jiwaji University, Madhya Pradesh, 2008. Guide- J N Gautam. 156

Citation analysis of doctoral dissertations in economics accepted by Andhra University. Govinda Raju, N. Andhra University, Andhra Pradesh, 2007. Guide- C Sasikala. 157

Citation analysis of doctoral dissertations in social sciences accepted by the Karnataka University theses during 1964-1982. Sangam, S L. Gulbarga University, Karnataka, 1985. Guide- S R Gunjal. 158

Citation analysis of doctoral theses in economics accepted by Nagpur University, Nagpur during 1981-2000. Astunkar, S G. Rashtrasant Tukadoji Maharaj Nagpur University, Nagpur, Maharashtra, 2012. Guide- U P Nahle. 159

Citation analysis of Ph D theses in psychology. Zafrunnisha, N. Sri Venkateswara University, Tirupati, Andhra Pradesh, 2008. Guide- V Pulla Reddy. 160

Citation analysis of the Ph D theses in social sciences accepted by Gauhati University during 1970-1980. Devi, Thoidingjam Purnima (Ms). Manipur University, Manipur, 1996. Guide- R Lahiri & S L Sangam. 161

Entry No.

Effectiveness of library collection through citation analysis of doctoral dissertations in political science of Berhampur University. Panda, Biswanath. Berhampur University, Orissa, 1997. Guide- P S G Kumar. 162

Information use pattern of social scientists: A citation analysis study based on the Ph D theses in social sciences accepted by the Kurukshetra University. Narendar Kumar. Awadhesh Pratap Singh University, Madhya Pradesh, 2010. Guide- N R Satyanarayana. 163

Literature use pattern by researchers in social sciences: A bibliometrics analysis of doctoral theses submitted to Dr Babasaheb Ambedkar Marathwada University, Aurangabad. Dalve, Daya Baburao (Ms). Dr Babasaheb Ambedkar Marathwada University, Aurangabad, Maharashtra, 2004. Guide- S M Mohal. 164

Samaj vigyan sodh prabandhakan ka udharan vishleshan Jiwaji vishwavidyalaya Gwalior evam Vikaram vishwavidyalaya ke sodh prabandhakan ki Ph D mein prayukt granth suchiyon ka granthmitiya adhyayan. Dixit, Sanad Kumar. Jiwaji University, Madhya Pradesh, 1996. Guide- A K Varma. 165

q. Theses

Bibliometric analysis of doctoral dissertations of University of Burdwan: A study of information flow in some selective disciplines. Bandyopadhyay, Amit Kumar. Jadhavpur University, West Bengal, 2002. Guide- M L Chakraborty. 166

Bibliometric analysis of Ph D theses awarded to Amravati University, Amravati: A study of information flow in some selective disciplines. Khokale, Revati (Ms). Sant Gadge Baba Amravati University, Maharashtra, 2007. Guide- D Rajyalakshmi. 167

Entry No.

Citation analysis of Ph D theses submitted to P K U during 1990-1994. Deshmukh, P P. Sant Gadge Baba Amravati University, Maharashtra, 2001. Guide- P S G Kumar. 168

Literature use pattern in doctoral research at IIT Bombay: A bibliometric study during 1995-2000. Gawande, Nilesh. Sant Gadge Baba Amravati University, Maharashtra, 2007. Guide- D Rajyalakshmi. 169

Research productivity of Indian Institutes of Technology in India: A bibliometric analysis. Vijaya Kumar, K. Annamalai University, Tamil Nadu, 2007. Guide- M Nagarajan. 170

BIO BIBLIOGRAPHY

A study of Dr P S G Kumar's academic contributions in library and information science. Agashe, Ajay. Rashtrasant Tukadoji Maharaj Nagpur University, Nagpur, Maharashtra, 2008. Guide- D Rajyalakshmi. 171

Contribution of Rajsekhara to the development of subject classification. Mitra, Tarun Kumar. University of Calcutta, West Bengal, 1979. Guide- N A. 172

Kazi Nazrul Islam (1899-1976) ekti tathwanistha jiboni granther upadan samuher panjikaran evam visleson. Das, Biswajit. Jadhavpur University, West Bengal, 2005. Guide- Prabir Roy Choudhury. 173

Life and works of Dr S R Gunjal: A study. Patil, Shrishail. Gulbarga University, Karnataka, 2004. Guide- V T Kamble. 174

Study of biographies of Buddha: Based on Pali and Sanskrit sources. Seth, Ved (Ms). University of Delhi, Delhi, 1988. Guide- Sanghasen Singh. 175

Entry No.

CHILDREN LITERATURE

Children literature in school libraries in Punjab in the context of new educational policy: An evaluation. Amrik Singh. Guru Nanak Dev University, Amritsar, Punjab, 1995. Guide- Navjot Kaur. 176

Evaluation of children's literature in Telugu and the development of children libraries in Andhra Pradesh. Venkatappaiah, Velaga. Andhra University, Andhra Pradesh, 1981. Guide- N A. 177

COLLECTION

An analysis of obsolescence in library collection: A case study of academic libraries. Jagannath, Uma (Ms). Bangalore University, Karnataka, 2002. Guide- T D Kemparaju. 178

Collection evaluation of engineering and technology libraries: A study of Indian Institute of Technology, New Delhi; University of Roorkee, Roorkee and Thaper Institute of Engineering and Technology, Patiala. Sharma, Rama. Punjabi University, Patiala, Punjab, 2002. Guide- K Navalani. 179

Evaluation of biological science collection in Dr Babasaheb Ambedkar Marathwada University Library. Khaparde, Vaishali Sovind (Ms). Dr Babasaheb Ambedkar Marathwada University, Aurangabad, Maharashtra, 2002. Guide- Ashwini Anand Vaishnav. 180

Evaluation of social science collection in Dr Babasaheb Ambedkar Marathwada University Library. Takarwankar, Ganesh D. Dr Babasaheb Ambedkar Marathwada University, Aurangabad, Maharashtra, 2009. Guide- S M Mohal. 181

Evaluation of Urdu collection in Dr Babasaheb Ambedkar Marathwada University, Aurangabad with special reference to quantity, quality and use. Shahabuddin, Shaista Parvin (Ms). Dr Babasaheb Ambedkar Marathwada University, Aurangabad, Maharashtra, 2002. Guide- S M Mohal. 182

Entry No.

Gujarat rajya me sarvajanik granthalayo ki sangathit samagree sewa par smalochna. Bhatt, Kaushik Kumar. Hemchandracharya North Gujarat University, Gujarat, 2005. Guide- S M Charan. 183

Gujarat rajya vishwavidyalaya granthalaya me vibhinn bhasha me suvidha. Darbar, Maheshbhai R. Hemchandracharya North Gujarat University, Gujarat, 2005. Guide- S M Charan. 184

Measuring book availability performance of university libraries in Tamil Nadu: An evaluative study. Domenic. University of Mysore, Karnataka, 2002. Guide- Shalini R Urs. 185

Navodaya vidyalay granthalayao ke sankalan evam sevaon ka vivechnatmak adhyayan: Ek adhyayan. Duvedi, Pradeep. Bundelkhand University, Jhansi, Uttar Pradesh, 2003. Guide- M T M Khan. 186

Uttar Gujarat vishwavidyalaya pathan samagree grameen sewa mahavidlyao me granthalaya sabhi ke liye abhyas. Shukla, Kiritkumar Harsukhray. Hemchandracharya North Gujarat University, Gujarat, 2005. Guide- S M Charan. 187

Viswa varati granthagare prachin o dushprapya Bangla grantha: Bisoy bishleshan o gabeshanar upadan. Bhattacharya, Sanat. Jadhavpur University, West Bengal, 2011. Guide- Krishnapada Majumder. 188

a. Grey Literature

Grey literature in Indian agricultural research in relation to soil sciences. Cyraic, Jiji (Ms). Rashtrasant Tukadoji Maharaj Nagpur University, Nagpur, Maharashtra, 2004. Guide- P S G Kumar. 189

Entry No.

Grey literature, generation, access and dissemination: A study. Gokhale. Pratibha A (Ms). University of Mumbai, Maharashtra, 2001. Guide- S R Ganpule. 190

Organization and use patterns of grey literature by faculty and researchers in research centers affiliated to Visvesvaraya Technological University: A study. Chowdappa, N. University of Mysore, Karnataka, 2010. Guide- C P Ramasesh. 191

Use pattern of grey literature by social scientists in India: With special reference to Hyderabad. Devi, V Rama (Ms). Osmania University, Andhra Pradesh, 2003. Guide- N Laxman Rao. 192

COLLECTION DEVELOPMENT

Collection building in university libraries. Rawtani, M R. University of Rajasthan, Jaipur, Rajasthan, 1994. Guide- S C Verma. 193

Collection development and evaluation in university libraries in Punjab, Haryana and Himachal Pradesh. Nirmaljeet Kaur (Ms). Guru Nanak Dev University, Amritsar, Punjab, 1997. Guide- Sewa Singh. 194

Collection development and services in the engineering college libraries of Orissa: An evaluative study. Das, Prangya. Dr B R Ambedkar University, Agra, Uttar Pradesh, 2007. Guide- U C Sharma. 195

Collection development in agricultural university libraries: Case study of Maharashtra. Munde, Baliram Tukaram. Swami Ramanand Teerth Marathwada University, Maharashtra, 2004. Guide- S P Satarkar. 196

Collection development in agriculture university libraries in Gujarat. Solanki, B M. Hemchandracharya North Gujarat University, Gujarat, 2012. Guide- U A Thaker. 197

Entry No.

Collection development in CBSE affiliated senior secondary school libraries of Orissa. Das, Debabrata. Berhampur University, Orissa, 2006. Guide- K C Panda. 198

Collection development in degree college libraries in Andhra Pradesh: With special reference to S V University area. Narayana Redddy, N. Sri Venkateswara University, Tirupati, Andhra Pradesh, 2009. Guide- K Padmini. 199

Collection development in university libraries of Orissa: A study. Mohanta, Rabindra Nath. Sambalpur University, Orissa, 2010. Guide- B K Choudhury. 200

Collection development of Pali language and literature in academic libraries of West Bengal during 20th century. Barui, Subalkumar. University of Calcutta, West Bengal, 2012. Guide- Biplab Chakrabarti. 201

Gujarat rajyanon ke vishwavidyalaya granthalayao mein sangrah vikas: Mulyanakanatamak avam tulnatmak abhyas. Gohel, Batukbhai Mathurdas. Bhavnagar University, Gujarat, 2006. Guide- Kirit M Vyas. 202

Madhya Pardesh evam Chattisgarh ke vishwavidyalaya granthalayao me sangrah vikas ki samsyaen a pustkiya evam e documents ke sandarbh mein. Shukla, Supriya. Awadhesh Pratap Singh University, Madhya Pradesh, 2010. Guide- N R Satyanarayana. 203

Resource development in engineering colleges library of U P: A study. Nagpal, Neetu. Jiwaji University, Madhya Pradesh, 2009. Guide- Hemant Sharma. 204

a. IT Environment

Impact of information technology on collection development, organization and services in university and special libraries of Karnataka State. Vatnal, R M. Karnataka University, Karnataka, 2003. Guide- S L Sangam. 205

Entry No.

Library collection development in the era of IT in the state university libraries with particular reference to Allahabad, Agra, Indore and Sagar. Jain, Sanjay Kumar. Jiwaji University, Madhya Pradesh, 2002. Guide- Hemant Sharma & B K Sharma. 206

b. Periodicals

Acquisition of foreign periodicals in Indian universities: A system approach. Hukmani, Padma. University of Rajasthan, Jaipur, Rajasthan, 1991. Guide- S C Verma. 207

Collection development of periodicals in select special libraries of Hyderabad. Muralidhar, G. Osmania University, Andhra Pradesh, 2010. Guide- J Yadagiri Reddy. 208

Earth science periodicals collection in the three university libraries of Assam - their impact on research activities during 1988-98: A critical study. Lahkar, Bina Medhi. Gauhati University, Assam, 2004. Guide- Alaka Buragohain. 209

Growth and development of journals in economics with special reference to e journals: A study of the libraries of central universities in Delhi. Topan Dass. University of Delhi, Delhi, 2011. Guide- R K Bhatt. 210

Indian historical periodicals as source of research. Dasgupta, Arjun. Jadhavpur University, West Bengal, 1992. Guide- Prabir Roy Choudhury. 211

c. Policy

A study of acquisition policy and procedure of reading material of university libraries in India with special reference to M P with a view to formulate a model. Trivedi, Pradeep Kumar. Dr Hari Singh Gour Vishwavidyalaya, Sagar, Madhya Pradesh, 2004. Guide- B P Shrivastava. 212

Entry No.

Collection development in Calcutta University Library System - policies and utilization: A critical study. Basak, Anita (Ms). University of Calcutta, West Bengal, 2010. Guide- Ratna Bandyopadhyay. 213

Collection development in university libraries, policy and procedures: A study of university libraries in the state of Orissa. Misra, Prafulla Kumar. Berhampur University, Orissa, 1997. Guide- P Soma Raju. 214

Collection development policy and procedure in Madhya Pradesh university libraries. Baghel, Shaligram. Guru Ghasidas University, Chhattisgarh, 2005. Guide- Brajesh Tiwari. 215

Collection development policy of agriculture university libraries of Uttar Pradesh and Madhya Pradesh: A comparative study. Singh, Dinesh Pratap. Dr B R Ambedkar University, Agra, Uttar Pradesh, 2002. Guide- U C Sharma. 216

Collection development policy of science college libraries affiliated to Hemchandracharya North Gujarat University. Patel, Bipinchandra Amrutlal. Hemchandracharya North Gujarat University, Gujarat, 2010. Guide- C N Rawal. 217

Policies and procedures of collection development and management in university libraries of U P: A comparative study. Verma, Rekha (Ms). University of Lucknow, Uttar Pradesh, 2008. Guide- N R Satyanarayana. 218

d. Problems

A study of problems and prospects of libraries and publishers with special reference to collection development in university libraries of Karnataka. Gandhi, R T D Ramesh. University of Mysore, Karnataka, 2002. Guide- V G Talwar. 219

Acquisition of documents in special libraries in India and publishing trade: A study of problems and linkages. Tariq, Ashraf. University of Delhi, Delhi, 2002. Guide- Shashi Prabha Singh. 220

Entry No.

COLLECTION MANAGEMENT

Collection development, organization and management among academic libraries in Karnataka State. Tadasad, P G. Karnataka University, Karnataka, 2000. Guide- B S Maheswarappa & B V Rajashekhar. 221

Information resource management of engineering college libraries in West Bengal. Chattopadhyay, Tridib. University of Calcutta, West Bengal, 2011. Guide- Biplab Chakrabarti. 222

Information resource management of three major health science libraries of Orissa. Satapathy, Santosh Kumar. Berhampur University, Orissa, 2009. Guide- K C Das. 223

Information resources management and utilization in transport corporations of Tamil Nadu. Daniel Thomas Sigamani, M. University of Madras, Tamil Nadu, 2004. Guide- A Amudavalli. 224

Library collection development and management practices with reference to Annamalai University distance education libraries: A study. Subramainan, R M. Annamalai University, Tamil Nadu, 2011. Guide- S Ravi. 225

Management of library collections of professional colleges in India. Gupta, S R. Banaras Hindu University, Uttar Pradesh, 1988. Guide- P N Kaula. 226

Public library provision and document problems in developing countries: A study in Kenya and Indian context. Wanderi, M O. Rashtrasant Tukadoji Maharaj Nagpur University, Nagpur, Maharashtra, 1994. Guide- P S G Kumar. 227

a. Non Book Materials

Acquisition and organization of non book materials in agriculture university libraries of Uttar Pradesh and Madhya Pradesh: A comparative study. Umesh Chandra. Jiwaji University, Madhya Pradesh, 1998. Guide- H S Sengar. 228

Entry No.

Collection, organization and determination of non print media in libraries: A comparative survey and investigation into problems and prospects with reference to special libraries in Kerala. Nair, Gopalakrishnan. Cochin University of Science & Technology, Kerala, 1991. Guide- C V Rajan Pillai. 229

Non book materials and their use in Indian libraries: A fact finding study with special reference to Karnataka State. Patil, S B. Gulbarga University, Karnataka, 1994. Guide- S L Sangam. 230

Non print media as a source of information: A study of selected university libraries of Andhra Pradesh. Vijaya Kumar, B. Sri Venkateswara University, Tirupati, Andhra Pradesh, 2003. Guide- K Padmini. 231

Organization and use of multimedia resources in Indira Gandhi National Centre for Arts and Desidoc, Delhi: A comparative study. Bakshi, Samar Iqbal. Aligarh Muslim University, Uttar Pradesh, 2011. Guide- P M Naushad Ali. 232

Organization of non book materials: Survey of Calcutta metropolis libraries and computerized model for different types of NBM. Upadhyay, J L. Tilka Manjhi Bhagalpur University, Bihar, 1996. Guide- S Sahay. 233

Origin and development of publications related to motion pictures in Bengali language, 1898-1998. Thakur, Biswajit Das. Rabindra Bharati University, West Bengal, 2006. Guide- Pinaki Nath Mukhopadhyay. 234

The organization and management of map collection in Indian libraries: A study. Patnaik, Satyavathi (Ms). Andhra University, Andhra Pradesh, 2003. Guide- K Somasekhara Rao. 235

Entry No.

b. Periodicals

Periodical collection in IIT Delhi, Kanpur and Delhi universities libraries: Acquisition and use. Faizul, Nisha (Ms). Aligarh Muslim University, Uttar Pradesh, 2010. Guide- P M Naushad Ali. 236

Serial control systems of the university libraries in the north eastern region: A case study. Lahiri, Ramansu. Manipur University, Manipur, 1990. Guide- M R Kumbhar. 237

c. Preservation and Digitization

A study of conservation and preservation techniques followed in the libraries of U P. Misra, Jyoti (Ms). University of Lucknow, Uttar Pradesh, 2002. Guide- N R Satyanarayana. 238

Care and preservation of library documents in universities, archives and colleges of Punjab, Haryana and Chandigarh. Narang, Asha (Ms). Guru Nanak Dev University, Amritsar, Punjab, 2005. Guide- H S Chopra. 239

Conservation and digitization of manuscripts in university libraries in India. Sharma, Arti (Ms). Panjab University, Chandigarh, Punjab, 2011. Guide- Ranjana Vohra. 240

Conservation and preservation of library material with special reference to digitization rare materials. Pange, Babasaheb Murlidhar. University of Pune, Maharashtra, 2004. Guide- N J Deshpande. 241

Conservation in archives and libraries: A study. Rajendran, M. University of Madras, Tamil Nadu, 2007. Guide- R Vengan. 242

Contribution of IFLA and UNESCO to the preservation and conservation of world's documentary heritage: A critical study. Rajiv. Punjabi University, Patiala, Punjab, 2007. Guide- Jagtar Singh. 243

Entry No.

Contribution of Jain librarians in preserving books in Hindi literature. Mishra, Bhavanath. Lalith Narayan Mithila University Darbangha, Bihar, 1986. Guide- Srinarayan Singh. 244

Museum methods and the process of cleaning and preservation. Basu, Manindra Nath. University of Calcutta, West Bengal, 1950. Guide- V Venkata Rao. 245

Preservation and digitization of manuscripts in India, with special reference to Madhya Pradesh. Jain, Anil Kumar. Vikram University, Madhya Pradesh, 2005. Guide- S Kumar & B K Sharma. 246

Preservation of historical records in libraries. Mehta, S P. Jiwaji University, Madhya Pradesh, 1984. Guide- S M Tripathi. 247

Preservation system of college and university libraries of West Bengal in relation to climatic condition. Chattopadhyay, Abira. University of Calcutta, West Bengal, 2007. Guide- Biplab Chakrabarti. 248

Security care and maintenance of books in university libraries in India: A critical study. Kale, Kishore B. Rashtrasant Tukadoji Maharaj Nagpur University, Nagpur, Maharashtra, 2004. Guide- P S G Kumar. 249

COMMUNITY INFORMATION CENTRES

Community information and the libraries in the developing society: A state-of-the-art and prognostic study with particular reference to rural Andhra Pradesh. Vishwa Mohan, V. Osmania University, Andhra Pradesh, 1995. Guide- A A N Raju. 250

Health care information to rural people in Andhra Pradesh with special reference to Chittoor District. Babu, K Surendra. Sri Venkateswara University, Tirupati, Andhra Pradesh, 2000. Guide- V Pulla Reddy. 251

Entry No.

Impact of information communication technology on rural development in Uttar Pradesh and Haryana. Shukla, Sourabh. Jiwaji University, Madhya Pradesh, 2010. Guide- J N Gautam. 252

Role of information and communication technology in village knowledge centre in Puducherry: A study. Prabakaran, T. Annamalai University, Tamil Nadu, 2012. Guide- P Ravichandran. 253

Rural information centre for government schemes. Thirumagal, A. University of Madras, Tamil Nadu, 2004. Guide- Manorama Srinath. 254

Rural libraries and community resource centres (RLs, RCs) in India with special reference to study having library legislation problem and prospects. Sunil Kumar. Jiwaji University, Madhya Pradesh, 2003. Guide- J N Gautam & C P Vashishth. 255

CONTENT ANALYSIS

Press and its social responsibility in Northeast India: A content analysis. Plathottam, George. North East Hill University, Shillong, Meghalaya, 2011. Guide- P Hangsing. 256

Reviewing of library science books: A content analysis approach. Savanur, S K. Karnataka University, Karnataka, 1990. Guide- S R Ijari. 257

COST BENEFIT ANALYSIS

Cost analysis of university libraries in India: With special reference to P U Library, Chandigarh; Kurukshetra University and H P University Library, Shimla. Gupta, Kamini (Ms). Panjab University, Chandigarh, Punjab, 2002. Guide- Preeti Mahajan. 258

Entry No.

Cost benefit analysis study of university libraries in India with special reference to central universities. Sharma, Umesh Chandra. University of Rajasthan, Jaipur, Rajasthan, 1994. Guide- S C Verma. 259

Costing and cost benefit analysis of academic libraries. Bidarkar, Shubhangi (Ms). Dr Babasaheb Ambedkar Marathwada University, Aurangabad, Maharashtra, 2011. Guide- Ashwini Anand Vaishnav. 260

Library economics in Manipur. Chanambam, Tanuja Devi. Manipur University, Manipur, 2011. Guide- Madhuri Devi. 261

a. Library Services

Cost benefit analysis of reprographic and microfilming techniques in university libraries and information centres of Haryana, Punjab, U P and Delhi. Joshi, Shyam Sunder. Kurukshetra University, Haryana, 1996. Guide- N K Sharma. 262

Cost effectiveness of library services of Bhopal, Gwalior, Agra and Allahabad university libraries. Jitendra Kumar. Jiwaji University, Madhya Pradesh, 2000. Guide- Shalini Rewadikar. 263

b. Technical Services

Time and cost analysis of technical service in Indian libraries. Saikia, Mukesh. North East Hill University, Shillong, Meghalaya, 2006. Guide- A S Chandel. 264

Workflow and decision making in processing of documents in four university libraries of Orissa: A comparative study. Jena, Pushpanjali. Utkal University, Orissa, 1999. Guide- Manoranjan Mahapatra. 265

Entry No.

CUSTOMER RELATIONSHIP MANAGEMENT

Customer relationship management in special libraries in Tamil Nadu: A study. Magudeeswaran. Bishop Heber College, Bharathidasan University, Tamil Nadu, 2011. Guide- S Ally Sornam. 266

Data mining application in customer relationship management of Yazd Electric Supply Company: A case study. Sehati, Mohamad Ali. University of Mysore, Karnataka, 2010. Guide- V G Talwar. 267

Study of customer satisfaction management in libraries and information centers of regional engineering colleges in India. Deshpande, R M. Rashtrasant Tukadoji Maharaj Nagpur University, Nagpur, Maharashtra, 2004. Guide- P S G Kumar. 268

DEVELOPMENT STUDIES – LIBRARIES

Growth and development of libraries in India from earliest period to 1707 A D. Munshi, Minoti (Ms). Banaras Hindu University, Uttar Pradesh, 1993. Guide- P C Pant. 269

Growth and development of libraries in Manipur: A critical study. Veenapani, Salem Chanu. Manipur University, Manipur, 2012. Guide- Khomdon Singh. 270

Origin and development of libraries in the East and West Africa (1960-1981). Gupta, Rashmi (Ms). Panjab University, Chandigarh, Punjab, 1985. Guide- J S Sharma. 271

The study of emergence and development of libraries, information centre and information professionalism in Nepal. Karki, Madhusudan. Dr B R Ambedkar University, Agra, Uttar Pradesh, 2002. Guide- S M Tripathi. 272

Entry No.

a. Academic Libraries

Changing higher educational scenario vis-à-vis college library development in West Bengal: A case study. Bhattachary, Mitali. Jadhavpur University, West Bengal, 2009. Guide- Amitabha Chatterjee. 273

Development and growth of university libraries and their services in Punjab. Trishanjit Kaur. Punjabi University, Patiala, Punjab, 1994. Guide- K Navalani. 274

Development of university libraries in Gujarat State. Purohit , Dhavalben. Dr Hari Singh Gour Vishwavidyalaya, Sagar, Madhya Pradesh, 2007. Guide- B P Shrivastava. 275

Development of university libraries in Madhya Pradesh. Singhai, Manjulata (Ms). Dr Hari Singh Gour Vishwavidyalaya, Sagar, Madhya Pradesh, 2002. Guide- B P Shrivastava. 276

Development of university libraries in Uttar Pradesh after independence. Singh, Sonal. Vikram University, Madhya Pradesh, 1992. Guide- S S Agarwal. 277

Growth and development of college libraries in the electronic environment: A case study of impact of quality awareness and competence building measures. Horakeri, M D. Karnataka University, Karnataka, 2011. Guide- R R Naik. 278

Gujarat rajayanon ke vividh vishwavidyalaya granthalayaona me vikasatmak abhays. Vyas, Himjaben Jyotindra. Hemchandracharya North Gujarat University, Gujarat, 2006. Guide- S M Charan. 279

Pattern and development of university libraries in Andhra Pradesh. Venkata Ramana, V. Andhra University, Andhra Pradesh, 1992. Guide- K Siva Reddy. 280

Entry No.

Perspective plan for the development of Mahatma Gandhi International Hindi University Library. Thanekar, A G. Rashtrasant Tukadoji Maharaj Nagpur University, Nagpur, Maharashtra, 2011. Guide- D R Deshpande. 281

Structure and development of non-agricultural university libraries in Maharashtra: A critical study. Paradkar, Ashwini Abhay. Rashtrasant Tukadoji Maharaj Nagpur University, Nagpur, Maharashtra, 2003. Guide- P S G Kumar. 282

b. National Libraries

Growth and development of NUL in the changing scenario of IT. Sambare, A P (Ms). Rashtrasant Tukadoji Maharaj Nagpur University, Nagpur, Maharashtra, 2004. Guide- P S G Kumar. 283

Growth, development and services of National Agriculture Library, New Delhi; National Medical Library, New Delhi and National Science Library, New Delhi: A comparative study. Nishat Fatima (Ms). Aligarh Muslim University, Uttar Pradesh, 2010. Guide- Self Adjudication. 284

c. Public Libraries

An analytical study of the growth and development of public libraries in Bengal since the inception of Calcutta Public Library in 1836. Sarkar, Soumitra (Ms). University of Calcutta, West Bengal, 1995. Guide- A Dasgupta. 285

Bharat ke rajyon ke pustakalaya adhiniyam ke anubhav ke adhar per Madhya Pradesh ke liye ek adarsh sarvajanik pustakalaya adhiniyamon ka nirman. Kapse, Santosh. Makhanlal Chaturvedi National University of Journalism and Mass Communication, Madhya Pradesh, 2009. Guide- B S Nigam. 286

Entry No.

Chattisgarh mein sarvajanik pustkalayon ka vikas, itihas, unka darshan evam sahitya mein yogdan. Yadav, Shyama. Guru Ghasidas University, Chhattisgarh, 2002. Guide- J L Saini. 287

Development of public libraries in Punjab from 1947 to 1987. Uppal, Om Prakash. Utkal University, Orissa, 1991. Guide- B B Shukla. 288

Madhya Pardesh evam chhatisgarh rajya mei sarvajanik pustkalaya ka udbhav evam vikas: Ek adhyayan. Shrivastav, Nagendar Kumar. Awadhesh Pratap Singh University, Madhya Pradesh, 2009. Guide- R K Sharma. 289

d. Research Libraries

CSIR laboratories libraries in Delhi and Lucknow: Development and use. Gupta, Vibha. Aligarh Muslim University, Uttar Pradesh, 2012. Guide- Mehtab Alam Ansari. 290

Growth and development of research libraries in economics in union territory of Delhi and their role or research in the discipline. Sher-ul-Din. Jiwaji University, Madhya Pradesh, 1999. Guide- J N Gautam. 291

Growth and development of the ICSSR research institutes libraries and their services. Dharam Kumar. University of Delhi, Delhi, 2010. Guide- R K Bhatt. 292

e. Special Libraries

A study of the industrial development pattern of Kerala in the context of information technology revolution and the emerging cyber society. Rajan, A C. University of Calicut, Calicut, Kerala, 2007. Guide- Raju M Mathew. 293

Entry No.

Development of ayurveda college libraries in India with special reference to Vidharbha Region. Dakhole, Pramod S. Rashtrasant Tukadoji Maharaj Nagpur University, Nagpur, Maharashtra, 2004. Guide- P S G Kumar. 294

Growth and development of mosque libraries in Iran from Safavid era to Pahlavi era: A critical study. Barader, Roya (Ms). University of Delhi, Delhi, 2002. Guide- S R Gupta. 295

Health science research libraries of India: A study of their growth, development and services with particular reference to North India. Shafi, S M. University of Kashmir, Jammu and Kashmir, 1994. Guide- Self Adjudication. 296

Vishesh granthalayao ka vikas: Chhattisgarh ke sandarbh mein ek adhyayan. Mukherjee, Sapna. Guru Ghasidas University, Chhattisgarh, 2005. Guide- Brajesh Tiwari. 297

DIGITAL LIBRARIES

An analysis of web ontology tools and techniques for the development of a conceptual frame work for digital library perspectives. Suman, Aparajita (Ms). Vidyasagar University, West Bengal, 2008. Guide- Devika P Madalli & J K Sarkhel. 298

Cybercafés in Chennai: Their use and implication. Manivannan, S. University of Madras, Tamil Nadu, 2002. Guide- Manorama Srinath. 299

Digital library initiative in higher education institutions in India: A case study of Indira Gandhi Memorial Library, University of Hyderabad. Varatharajan, N. University of Mysore, Karnataka, 2010. Guide- M Chandrashekara. 300

Digital library initiatives in engineering educational institutions in Rayalaseema Region of Andhra Pradesh: A study. Kumar, K. Sri Venkateswara University, Tirupati, Andhra Pradesh, 2012. Guide- D Chandran. 301

Entry No.

Digital library initiatives in engineering educational institutions of Tamil Nadu: An analytical study. Vinayagamoorthy, P. University of Madras, Tamil Nadu, 2007. Guide- B Ramesh Babu. 302

Electronic/digital library: Its concept, impact, application and user behaviour, global trend with special reference to India. Siddiqui, Abdul Moyeed. University of Lucknow, Uttar Pradesh, 2003. Guide- N R Satyanarayana. 303

Evaluation of digital library projects: A cross country analysis. Manimekalai, S. Annamalai University, Tamil Nadu, 2006. Guide- M Suriya. 304

Exploring Internet based digital libraries for academic institutions: A comprehensive study of libraries in the M P and Chhattisgarh States. Saxena, Narsingh Narayan. Guru Ghasidas University, Chhattisgarh, 2009. Guide- Brajesh Tiwari. 305

Importance of Ph D theses in furthering research: A model digital library. Kumar, J K Vijaya. Bundelkhand University, Jhansi, Uttar Pradesh, 2005. Guide- T A V Murthy. 306

Status of digital libraries in India: An analytical study. Amzad Ali. Sambalpur University, Orissa, 2012. Guide- K C Panda. 307

Trends and development of digital libraries. Kar, Debal Chandra. University of Delhi, Delhi, 2010. Guide- R K Bhatt. 308

DIGITIZATION

An evaluative study of some selected libraries in India undergoing the process of digitization. Das, Anup Kumar. Jadhavpur University, West Bengal, 2009. Guide- Chaitali Dutta & B K Sen. 309

Entry No.

Application of digital technology for the development of manuscript information systems with special reference to ancient Indian manuscripts. Chaubey, Opendra Nath. Dr B R Ambedkar University, Agra, Uttar Pradesh, 2002. Guide- B K Sharma. 310

Automation and digitization of university libraries: A study of university libraries of North West India. Sharma, Neelam (Ms). Panjab University, Chandigarh, Punjab, 2010. Guide- Ranjana Vohra. 311

Digitization and open access initiatives: A study of special libraries in National Capital Region, Delhi. Paul, Shampa (Ms). University of Delhi, Delhi, 2011. Guide- Shashi Prabha Singh. 312

Digitization of heritage documents. Ramadasi, Nagnath R. University of Pune, Maharashtra, 2005. Guide- S K Patil. 313

Digitization of Indian cultural heritage material with special reference to photographs: A study. Polrau, Lalitha. Bundelkhand University, Jhansi, Uttar Pradesh, 2007. Guide- T A V Murthy & M T M Khan. 314

Digitization of rare materials: A study of rare collections of Dr V S K Library, rare collections Andhra University. Srilatha, G (Ms). Andhra University, Andhra Pradesh, 2012. Guide- R S R Varalakshmi. 315

Impact of digital technology on information users of higher education in Mysore City. Chetana, M. University of Mysore, Karnataka, 2005. Guide- C P Ramasesh. 316

Problems and prospects of digitization in agricultural university libraries of India: A critical study. Balwan Singh. Guru Ghasidas University, Chhattisgarh, 2011. Guide- Brajesh Tiwari. 317

Entry No.

DRDO LIBRARIES

Information management in DRDO libraries/technical information centres. Rathore, R S. University of Rajasthan, Jaipur, Rajasthan, 1996. Guide- S P Sood. 318

Organisation, administration and utilization of DRDO libraries. Santha Kumari, M. University of Calicut, Calicut, Kerala, 2004. Guide- Rosamma Joseph. 319

Role of technical information centres of DRDO in support of Defense research in India: A study. Rao, B Naga Mohan. Guru Nanak Dev University, Amritsar, Punjab, 2009. Guide- Sewa Singh. 320

E RESOURCES

A study of the growth and development of electronic information in the libraries of academic and research institutes of Uttaranchal. Pandey, Sujit Kumar. Bundelkhand University, Jhansi, Uttar Pradesh, 2011. Guide- M T M Khan. 321

Adhibition of electronic resources in libraries of business schools in Orissa: A study. Swain, Dillip Kumar. Sambalpur University, Orissa, 2010. Guide- K C Panda. 322

Collection building through e resources in university libraries of India: A study of U P State university libraries in digital environment. Mal, Vidyut Kumar. Mahatma Gandhi Chitrakoot Gramodaya Vishwavidyalaya, Satna, Madhya Pradesh, 2009. Guide- R P Bajpai. 323

Development of web resources in select fields of social sciences with a view to design a model subject gateway. Gul, Sumeer. University of Kashmir, Jammu and Kashmir, 2009. Guide- S M Shafi. 324

Electronic information resources in home science with special reference to food and nutrition: A study. Vaidya, Sachin. University of Mumbai, Maharashtra, 2010. Guide- P A Gokhale. 325

Entry No.

Electronic information sources in engineering - identification, evaluation and utilization in special libraries of Andhra Pradesh: A study. Srikanth Reddy, C. Osmania University, Andhra Pradesh, 2012. Guide- V Chandrasekhara Rao. 326

The collection of electronic information sources and services in Karnataka State university libraries and their awareness and use by the academic staff: A study. Walmiki, Ramappa Hanumanthappa. Kuvempu University, Shimoga, Karnataka, 2009. Guide- K C Ramakrishne Gowda. 327

The emergence of electronic publication with special reference to electronic serials: A case study in the context of academic and research libraries in India. Kushwaha, Shivpal Singh. Jiwaji University, Madhya Pradesh, 2004. Guide- J N Gautam. 328

a. Evaluation

Evaluation of electronic information sources in botany. Juttiyavar, Mahesh N. Kuvempu University, Shimoga, Karnataka, 2011. Guide- B S Biradar. 329

Evaluation of electronic sources of information in physics: Analytical study with particular reference to web based sources. Sampath Kumar, B T. Kuvempu University, Shimoga, Karnataka, 2003. Guide- B S Biradar. 330

b. Impact

Impact of e resources and user perception in professional education: A study on Puducherry Region. Vasanthi, J. Annamalai University, Tamil Nadu, 2011. Guide- S Ravi. 331

Impact of electronic information resources on users in university libraries of Karnataka State: An analytical study. Hadagli, G S. Karnataka University, Karnataka, 2008. Guide- B D Kumbhar. 332

Entry No.

Impact of electronic media on library and information centres with specific reference to India. Moorthy, A L. Karnataka University, Karnataka, 2000. Guide- C R Karisiddappa. 333

Impact of electronic media on special libraries. Gaikawad, D T. University of Pune, Maharashtra, 2008. Guide- Shivani Sengupta. 334

c. Journals

Trends in use of electronic journals: A study of the universities in Punjab. Dhingra, Navjoti (Ms). Panjab University, Chandigarh, Punjab, 2009. Guide- Preeti Mahajan. 335

Usage of e journals in university libraries in A P. Anil Kumar, M. Sri Venkateswara University, Tirupati, Andhra Pradesh, 2012. Guide- V Pulla Reddy. 336

Use of e journals among self-financing engineering institutions in Tamil Nadu: A study. Sasireka, G. Anna University, Chennai, Tamil Nadu, 2012. Guide- S Gopalakrishnan. 337

Use of electronic journals in astronomy and astrophysics libraries in India. Pathak, Sandeep Kumar. University of Pune, Maharashtra, 2007. Guide- N J Deshpande. 338

Use pattern of electronic journals by the research scholars at the university libraries in Iran: A study. Dastforoush, Masoumeh Tajafari. University of Mysore, Karnataka, 2012. Guide- Y Venkatesha. 339

User awareness and use of online journals in central university libraries of U P and Delhi: An evaluative study. Singh, Pankaj Kumar. Banaras Hindu University, Uttar Pradesh, 2012. Guide- H N Prasad. 340

Entry No.

d. Learning Resources

Assessment and usability of web based open source e learning courseware and their use by the educators and students in engineering colleges. Ghalib, Mohamed Abdulla M. University of Mysore, Karnataka, 2010. Guide- M Chandrashekara. 341

Designing e learning resource model in library and information science in India. Anas, K. University of Delhi, Delhi, 2009. Guide- Shailendra Kumar. 342

E learning and its resources and their application in the development of academic libraries, with special reference to university libraries of Delhi. Sharma, Amit Kumar. Jiwaji University, Madhya Pradesh, 2008. Guide- Hemant Sharma. 343

e. Management

A study of electronic collection management and services in the libraries of institutes of engineering and technology in North India. Sarbinder Kaur (Ms). Guru Nanak Dev University, Amritsar, Punjab, 2008. Guide- M P Satija. 344

A study of the management of electronic information resources in the libraries of engineering colleges in Tamil Nadu. Bala Subramani, R. Annamalai University, Tamil Nadu, 2007. Guide- P Ravichandran. 345

Information management in medical libraries of Rajasthan with special reference to electronic resources: An analysis. Sharma, Arvind. Mohan Lal Sukhadia University, Udaipur, Rajasthan, 2012. Guide- T D Tilwani. 346

Information management in science and technology libraries of Delhi with special reference to electronic resources. Naushad Ali, P M. University of Lucknow, Uttar Pradesh, 2003. Guide- N R Satyanarayana. 347

Entry No.

Management and utility of electronic resources in Indian Institutes of Management (IIMs) libraries in India: A survey. Sonkar, Sharad Kumar. Babasaheb Bhimrao Ambedkar University, Lucknow, Uttar Pradesh, 2011. Guide- K L Mahawar. 348

Management of digital information material: A comparative study of special libraries in Uttaranchal. Arya, Sukriti. Mohan Lal Sukhadia University, Udaipur, Rajasthan, 2011. Guide- U K Aggarwal. 349

Organization of e resources and their use in Indira Gandhi Memorial Library, University of Hyderabad: A study. Srinivasulu, P. Sri Venkateswara University, Tirupati, Andhra Pradesh, 2011. Guide- K Padmini. 350

f. Use and User Studies

A study of information communication technology infrastructures and the usage of e resources in special libraries in Tamil Nadu. Latha, J K. Annamalai University, Tamil Nadu, 2011. Guide- M Nagarajan. 351

A study of users' attitude to electronic information resources with reference to engineering college libraries in Puducherry. Ramesh, R. Annamalai University, Tamil Nadu, 2011. Guide- M Nagarajan. 352

Access and use of e resources in science and technology libraries in N C R: A study of current status and future strategies of library consortia. Ratnakar, K V. Jiwaji University, Madhya Pradesh, 2009. Guide- Hemant Sharma. 353

An investigation into the awareness, attitude and use of electronic resources in post graduate colleges in Kerala. Sunil Kumar. University of Kerala, Kerala, 2009. Guide- G Devarajan. 354

Entry No.

Diffusion and utilization of electronic information in university libraries in Andhra Pradesh, India: A case study. Ramachandraiah, V. Sri Krishnadevaraya University, Andhra Pradesh, 2007. Guide- P Kamaiah. 355

E resource usage among university teachers and research scholars in universities of Tamil Nadu. Praveena, K. Annamalai University, Tamil Nadu, 2010. Guide- M Nagarajan. 356

Electronic information resources and services in national institutes of technology libraries in South India: A study. Leelavathi, N (Ms). Sri Venkateswara University, Tirupati, Andhra Pradesh, 2010. Guide- I Chandraiah. 357

Electronic resources: A study of their usage in central universities of NCR Delhi. Nayar, Kiran. Jiwaji University, Madhya Pradesh, 2012. Guide- Hemant Sharma. 358

The use of electronic information sources in fisheries sciences in South India. Sujatha, H R (Ms). Mangalore University, Karnataka, 2009. Guide- M V Mudhol. 359

Use and user perception of ICT based resources and services in selected affiliated colleges of Thiruvalluvar University, Vellore: A study. Magesh, R. Annamalai University, Tamil Nadu, 2011. Guide- S Mohamed Esmail. 360

Use of e resources by the scholars and the faculty members in central universities in the field of management sciences. Tribhuvan Kumar. Maharani Laxmi Bai Govt. College of Excellence, Jiwaji University, Madhya Pradesh, 2011. Guide- Arvind Kumar Sharma. 361

Use of e resources in university libraries of Madhya Pradesh. Paliwal, Sangeeta. Vikram University, Madhya Pradesh, 2011. Guide- Sonal Singh. 362

Entry No.

Use of electronic information sources by medical professionals. Kumar, C Shijith. University of Mysore, Karnataka, 2005. Guide- N B Pangannaya. 363

Use of electronic information sources by the users of Karnataka State universities: An evaluative study. Sarmast, Syed Shah Ahmed. Makhanlal Chaturvedi National University of Journalism and Mass Communication, Madhya Pradesh, 2007. Guide- B S Nigam. 364

Use of electronic resources and services by marine scientists in South India. Maranna, O. Kuvempu University, Shimoga, Karnataka, 2011. Guide- B S Biradar. 365

Use of electronic resources in the libraries of agricultural universities and institutes of Rajasthan. Sharma, Kanhaya Lal. Mohan Lal Sukhadia University, Udaipur, Rajasthan, 2012. Guide- L N Verma. 366

Use pattern of e resources by health science professionals in Christian mission hospitals in Tamil Nadu. Joyson Soundrarajan, D. University of Madras, Tamil Nadu, 2011. Guide- B Ramesh Babu. 367

Use pattern of electronic information resources in the college libraries in Kerala: An analytical study. Vijayakumar, A. University of Calicut, Calicut, Kerala, 2008. Guide- V Jalaja. 368

Use patterns of electronic information resources by aerospace scientists and engineers in Bangalore. Guruprasad, Ramachandran. University of Mysore, Karnataka, 2010. Guide- Khaiser Nikam. 369

Utilization of e resources by the faculty members of constituent colleges of Tamil Nadu agricultural universities: A study. Sankaranarayanan, D. Annamalai University, Tamil Nadu, 2011. Guide- M Nagarajan. 370

Entry No.

Utilization of e resources by the users of Annamalai University in Tamil Nadu: An evaluative study. Natarajan, K. Annamalai University, Tamil Nadu, 2010. Guide- M Nagarajan. 371

Utilization of electronic resources in special libraries in Chennai City: A study. Ashok kumar, N. Annamalai University, Tamil Nadu, 2010. Guide- T Saravanan. 372

EXPERT SYSTEMS

Design and development of a rule based expert system for Anglo American Cataloguing Rules. Jose, Anthony. University of Pune, Maharashtra, 2007. Guide- A R D Prasad. 373

Design of an expert system for siddha medicine. Gnana Sekari, G. University of Madras, Tamil Nadu, 2003. Guide- Manorama Srinath. 374

Diagnostic expert system for bovine diseases. Mohana Sundari, T (Ms). University of Madras, Tamil Nadu, 2007. Guide- Manorama Srinath. 375

Evaluation for knowledge management systems used in IT companies in Pune. Raool, Aditi. University of Pune, Maharashtra, 2011. Guide- N J Deshpande. 376

Expert system for Indian medicinal pharmaceutical drugs. Palani, S. University of Madras, Tamil Nadu, 2003. Guide- Manorama Srinath. 377

Expert system for Indian medicinal plants. Thiruvengada Mani, T K. University of Madras, Tamil Nadu, 2005. Guide- Manorama Srinath. 378

Knowledge based system design for document selection in university libraries with special reference to central universities in India. Rama Reddy, E. Karnataka University, Karnataka, 2002. Guide- C R Karisiddappa. 379

Entry No.

FARRADANE'S LAW

Nature and applicability of Farradane's relation analysis with particular reference to the preservation of linear index entries. Chowdhury, Gobinda Gopal. Jadhavpur University, West Bengal, 1991. Guide- Mangala Prasad Singha. 380

FINANCIAL MANAGEMENT

A study of financial management of research libraries with special reference to agriculture and allied subjects in Madhya Pradesh. Pandey, Madhav. Dr Hari Singh Gour Vishwavidyalaya, Sagar, Madhya Pradesh, 2001. Guide- B P Shrivastava. 381

A study of financial management of university libraries in Western India with special reference to University of Pune Library. Gangurde, Lalita Hiraman. University of Pune, Maharashtra, 2012. Guide- S K Patil. 382

A study of university library finances in Andhra Pradesh. Narayanamoorthy, J. Sri Venkateswara University, Tirupati, Andhra Pradesh, 2010. Guide- T Rajagopal. 383

Allocation of resources in recently started university libraries of developing countries with special reference to some Indian university libraries. Mathew, Raju M. University of Kerala, Kerala, 1992. Guide- N Vedamani Manuel. 384

An investigation into the financing of the Kerala, Calicut and Cochin university libraries during the plan periods. Devarajan, G. University of Kerala, Kerala, 1992. Guide- K A Isaac. 385

Chhattisgarh evam Madhya Pradesh ke vishwavidyalaya granthalayao ka vittiya prabandh: Ek alochnatmak adhyayan. Soni, Sunil Kumar. Pt Ravishankar University Raipur, Chhattisgarh, 2012. Guide- A K Varma. 386

Entry No.

College library finance: A critical study of college libraries under jurisdiction of Amravati University. Mandgaokar, K O. Sant Gadge Baba Amravati University, Maharashtra, 2004. Guide- P S G Kumar. 387

Dr Babasaheb Ambedkar Marathwada University Granthalyachavittiy vyavstapanacha abhyas: Samajshastre vidhyshakhechya granthalaya shastra vishyat. Chavan, Subhash P. Dr Babasaheb Ambedkar Marathwada University, Aurangabad, Maharashtra, 2005. Guide- S A Vadikar. 388

Financial constraints in selected university libraries of H P, Punjab, Haryana, and Delhi: A comparative study. Saxena, Archna (Ms). Kurukshetra University, Haryana, 2001. Guide- N K Sharma. 389

Financial management in academic libraries in Karnataka with special reference to the first grade colleges. Mathad, R. Bangalore University, Karnataka, 1999. Guide- P Sadashivmurthy. 390

Financial management in central university libraries in India. Jawahar Lal. Banaras Hindu University, Uttar Pradesh, 1992. Guide- H N Prasad. 391

Financial management of public libraries in Marathwada. Dnyanoba, Mundhe Pallavi (Ms). Dr Babasaheb Ambedkar Marathwada University, Aurangabad, Maharashtra, 2011. Guide- Ashwini Anand Vaishnav. 392

Financial management of university libraries in India. Prem Chand. Punjabi University, Patiala, Punjab, 1999. Guide- K Navalani. 393

Financing of public libraries in Karnataka: A critical evaluation. Kumbar, B D. Karnataka University, Karnataka, 1994. Guide- C R Karisiddappa. 394

Entry No.

Inflation and its impact on collection development in university libraries of Orissa. Biswal, M K. Utkal University, Orissa, 2011. Guide- Pushpanjali Jena. 395

Public library finance: An analytical study. Chandrasekhara Rao, Valavala. Utkal University, Orissa, 1992. Guide- C R Karisiddappa. 396

Public library finance: An analytical study of Orissa Public Library System since independence. Rath, Pravakar. Utkal University, Orissa, 1992. Guide- C R Karisiddappa. 397

University library finance in Maharashtra. Deshpande, D R. Rashtrasant Tukadoji Maharaj Nagpur University, Nagpur, Maharashtra, 1998. Guide- P S G Kumar. 398

Working and finance of aided public libraries in Maharashtra with special reference to Nagpur Division. Nahale, U P. Rashtrasant Tukadoji Maharaj Nagpur University, Nagpur, Maharashtra, 2002. Guide- P S G Kumar. 399

a. Periodicals

Escalating periodical price and its impact on library subscription: An economic analysis. Nagi Reddy, Y. Andhra University, Andhra Pradesh, 1994. Guide- P Soma Raju. 400

Financial management of acquisition of serials in Delhi University and Jawaharlal Nehru University libraries. Jindal, Suresh Chand. University of Delhi, Delhi, 1999. Guide- J L Sardana. 401

Status of periodicals management in the university libraries in West Bengal, with special reference to subscription of some periodicals and its impact on economy. Jas, Nikhil Kumar. Jadhavpur University, West Bengal, 2006. Guide- Chaitali Dutta. 402

Entry No.

b. UGC Assistance

Critical study of UGC assistance to college libraries under SRTMU, Nanded. Basole, M G. Swami Ramanand Teerth Marathwada University, Maharashtra, 2007. Guide- S P Satarkar. 403

Evaluation of the role of UGC on development of college libraries. Taksande, Pratibha (Ms). Rashtrasant Tukadoji Maharaj Nagpur University, Nagpur, Maharashtra, 2006. Guide- P S G Kumar. 404

GOVERNMENT DOCUMENTS

a. Use and User Studies

Evaluating usage of Indian government publication: Proposals for improved access. Chadha, R K. University of Rajasthan, Jaipur, Rajasthan, 1996. Guide- Usha Pawan. 405

Public access to government information: A study with special reference to Rayalaseema District of Andhra Pradesh (India). Durga Devi, K (Ms). Sri Venkateswara University, Tirupati, Andhra Pradesh, 1999. Guide- T Rajagopal. 406

Use and non use of Government of India publications by social scientists in the University of Delhi (Delhi); Jawaharlal Nehru University (New Delhi); Punjab University (Chandigarh) and Punjabi University (Patiala): A comparative study. Walia, Paramjeet Kaur (Ms). University of Delhi, Delhi, 1997. Guide- J L Sardana. 407

GOVERNMENT LIBRARIES

A study of growth, development and services of Government of India libraries located in Delhi. Gupta, Anuradha (Ms). University of Delhi, Delhi, 1991. Guide- P B Mangla. 408

Entry No.

Legislature libraries in India: Problems and prospects. Gupta, Dinesh Kumar. University of Rajasthan, Jaipur, Rajasthan, 1995. Guide- Pushpa Dhyani. 409

Substantial role of governmental libraries of M P: A critical analysis of growth and its services. Quazi, Sultan Jahan. Awadhesh Pratap Singh University, Madhya Pradesh, 2001. Guide- N R Satyanarayana. 410

INFORMATION AND KNOWLEDGE SOCIETY

A comparative study of the treatment of information, knowledge and wisdom in the Bible and the Quran within the context of the emerging cyber society. Arifa, K (Ms). University of Calicut, Calicut, Kerala, 2005. Guide- Raju M Mathew. 411

Changing roles and responsibilities of library and information professionals in the knowledge society: A study of selected library and information centres in India. Kshema Prakash. Dayalbagh Educational Institute, Dr B R Ambedkar University, Agra, Uttar Pradesh, 2010. Guide- K Santi Sawrup. 412

India as an emerging information society with special reference to its politics, administration, cyber laws and the new role of librarians there of: An exploratory study. Babita (Ms). Guru Nanak Dev University, Amritsar, Punjab, 2007. Guide- M P Satija. 413

INFORMATION COMMUNICATION

A comparative study of the communication channel in different libraries with special reference to university libraries. Nandi, Subodh Gopal. University of Burdwan, Rajbati, Bardhaman, West Bengal, 1992. Guide- Pulin Behari Barua & Pranab Kumar Chakraborty. 414

Entry No.

A study of data communication system in military libraries in Madhya Pradesh. Malik, Mamata. Vikram University, Madhya Pradesh, 2004. Guide- Sonal Singh. 415

A study of scientific communication and information exchange pattern among fisheries scientists of India. Stanley, M K. Karnataka University, Karnataka, 1996. Guide- C R Karisiddappa. 416

A system approach to the study of commercial information organizations in India: Analysis of generation, collection, storage and dissemination functions. Kotresh, N. Bangalore University, Karnataka, 1998. Guide- A Y Asundi. 417

Communication and librarianship. Trivedi, Nand Kishore. Vikram University, Madhya Pradesh, 1992. Guide- T A V Murthy. 418

Environment and the law: A study of socioeconomic education, communication and information function. Reddy, Kengal Gopal. Kuvempu University, Shimoga, Karnataka, 2008. Guide- B S Biradar. 419

Information revolution and universal accessibility to information: Role of national and subject libraries in India. Sharma, Prabha. University of Rajasthan, Jaipur, Rajasthan, 1996. Guide- Pushpa Dhyani. 420

Information use and transfer among the Indian farmers: A study of role of communication media with special reference to Karnataka. Biradar, B S. Karnataka University, Karnataka, 1993. Guide- S L Sangam. 421

Kokana aadivasinchya ek pidhikadun dusary pidhikade moukhik dhyanacha hastatarn prakrriyecha abhyas. Narayan, Shirsat Ramesh. North Maharashtra University, Jalgaon, Maharashtra, 2012. Guide- Shamkant J Deshmukh. 422

Entry No.

Mass communication and public libraries: A critical study of Delhi Public Library System. Nigam, Bir Singh. Sambalpur University, Orissa, 1993. Guide- R K Rout. 423

Pattern of communication among scientists in Lucknow. Jaiswal, Babita (Ms). University of Lucknow, Uttar Pradesh, 2000. Guide- N R Satyanarayana. 424

Relevance in information communication: An inquiry into the factors affecting relevance assessment by users. Urs, Shalini R. University of Mysore, Karnataka, 1992. Guide- H A Khan. 425

Role of the state government in production and dissemination of information: A study of Rajasthan State. Sharma, Pramod. University of Rajasthan, Jaipur, Rajasthan, 1997. Guide- Usha Pawan. 426

Science communication: Problems and prospects with special reference to scientific and technical libraries in India. Malhan, Inder Vir. Panjab University, Chandigarh, Punjab, 1984. Guide- V A Kamath. 427

Television as media of information for social change: A study of Meghalaya. Mary, A F. North East Hill University, Shillong, Meghalaya, 2008. Guide- P Hangsing & A S Chandel. 428

INFORMATION GENERATION

Contribution of faculty members to the flow of information: A study at selected universities in Andhra Pradesh. Murali Prasad, M R. Sri Venkateswara University, Tirupati, Andhra Pradesh, 2003. Guide- K Padmini. 429

a. Use and User Studies

Agricultural information generation and its utilization in Khandesh (Mahaharashtra). Borse, T R. Dr Hari Singh Gour Vishwavidyalaya, Sagar, Madhya Pradesh, 2000. Guide- R G Prasher. 430

Entry No.

Information generation and its use by the scientists working in agricultural institutes in Uttar Pradesh, India. Sharma, Rakeshmani. Utkal University, Orissa, 2005. Guide- G Mahapatra. 431

Information generation and library use by university teachers: A case study of S V University, Tirupati. Durvasa Babu, A. Andhra University, Andhra Pradesh, 1992. Guide- G V S L Narasimha Raju. 432

Information generation, communication and use of library by teaching faculty of engineering colleges of Karnataka: A study. Manjunath, K V. Kuvempu University, Shimoga, Karnataka, 2009. Guide- B U Kannappanavar. 433

INFORMATION LITERACY

ICT literacy among the information professionals of university libraries in North East India: Current state of affairs and future potentials. Jena, Sudhir Kumar. Berhampur University, Orissa, 2012. Guide- K C Das. 434

Information literacy and seeking behaviour of faculty members of management institutions of Orissa with regards to use of electronic resources. Patra, Partha Sarathi. Berhampur University, Orissa, 2010. Guide- K C Das. 435

Information literacy in India, Nepal and Bangladesh: Plan and prospects. Choudhary, Shubhajit. Vikram University, Madhya Pradesh, 2008. Guide- S Kumar. 436

a. Academic Libraries

A study of teaching of library use and information literacy courses in the universities in Thailand. Pawinun, Prapat. Bangalore University, Karnataka, 2004. Guide- A Y Asundi. 437

Entry No.

Information literacy among research scholars of Madras University. Shaktirekha. Bishop Heber College, Bharathidasan University, Tamil Nadu, 2011. Guide- B S Swaroop Rani. 438

Role of school librarians in promoting information literacy among the school students. Dutta, Juin. M S University, Baroda, Gujarat, 2012. Guide- Shyama Rajaram. 439

User education in college and university libraries. Saikia, Gyandeep. Gauhati University, Assam, 2009. Guide- R K Barman. 440

b. Agriculture Libraries

Information management programmes for users in Indian agricultural universities. Gaddagimath, R B. Karnataka University, Karnataka, 1996. Guide- S L Sangam. 441

c. IT Environment

Curriculum design and strategy formulation for user education in the electronic environment with special reference to academic libraries in Mumbai. Hanchinal, Veeresh Basappa. Shivaji University, Kolhapur, Maharashtra, 2011. Guide- C R Karisiddappa. 442

E information literacy: A case study. Golwal, Madanshing. Dr Babasaheb Ambedkar Marathwada University, Aurangabad, Maharashtra, 2011. Guide- Ashwini Anand Vaishnav. 443

Educating users in context of computerization and networking of libraries and information centers in India. John, Kishor. University of Lucknow, Uttar Pradesh, 2003. Guide- N R Satyanarayana. 444

Entry No.

d. Module Design

Designing of library use education for teachers and researchers of management institutes. Bhadkamkar, Swati Sanjay. University of Pune, Maharashtra, 2012. Guide- N J Deshpande. 445

Developing an information literacy module for under graduate students in academic institutions affiliated to University of Pune in Pune District. Shelar, Vandana. University of Pune, Maharashtra, 2012. Guide- N J Deshpande. 446

Development of secondary school literacy system in Bangladesh: Problems and prospects. Rahaman, Mizanur. Vidyasagar University, West Bengal, 2010. Guide- P K Jana. 447

Need of effective model of user education for the P G colleges library in Western U P. Singh, Satya Prakash. Jiwaji University, Madhya Pradesh, 2008. Guide- Hemant Sharma. 448

e. Use and User Studies

An assessment of the attitude of the university library users towards information literacy: A comparative study between Iran and India. Hassan, Moghaddaszadah. University of Mysore, Karnataka, 2012. Guide- Khaiser Nikam. 449

Role of information literacy in maximizing the use of information for productivity and development: A case study of selected library and information centres of higher learning and research in Bangalore City. Rajagoli, I U. Karnataka University, Karnataka, 2008. Guide- C R Karisiddappa. 450

INFORMATION MANAGEMENT

Application of information technology vis-à-vis Ranganathan's Five Laws of library science with reference to information management in university libraries of Rajasthan. Sharma, Devendra Kumar. University of Rajasthan, Jaipur, Rajasthan, 2011. Guide- Dabir Singh. 451

Entry No.

Information management in health science libraries in India with special reference to Delhi. Dixit, R P. University of Rajasthan, Jaipur, Rajasthan, 1990. Guide- Pushpa Dhyani. 452

Information management in public libraries of Tehran: A study in the changing environment. Momeni, Esmat (Ms). University of Delhi, Delhi, 2010. Guide- P K Walia. 453

Information management in the advertising industries in India. Yagnik, Shailesh R. Sardar Patel University, Gujarat, 2009. Guide- C N Rawal. 454

Information management of Church archives in India: An analytical study. Vijay Kiran, A (Ms). University of Madras, Tamil Nadu, 2001. Guide- B Ramesh Babu. 455

Madhya Pradesh ke vishvidhyalin pustakalyo mei suchna ka parbandh: Networking ke vishesh sandarbh mein. Gupta, Aarti. Awadhesh Pratap Singh University, Madhya Pradesh, 2012. Guide- R K Sharma. 456

INFORMATION NEEDS

A study of information needs and information seeking behaviour of social scientists of Delhi and Haryana universities. Sharma, Sanjay Kumar. Kurukshetra University, Haryana, 2001. Guide- Ashu Shokeen. 457

An investigation into the information needs, use pattern and information seeking behaviour of post graduate dental students in the IT environment: A case study of South Kanara and Udupi Districts. Pooja, R (Ms). Mangalore University, Karnataka, 2012. Guide- K M Khan. 458

Business information needs of the Indian corporate sector. Anil Kumar. M S University, Baroda, Gujarat, 2010. Guide- Kautilya Shukla. 459

Entry No.

Information needs and information seeking behaviour of educated unemployed youth in Nagaland. Ao, Titilemsu. North East Hill University, Shillong, Meghalaya, 2004. Guide- Veena Saraf & N M Panda. 460

Information needs and use behaviour of members of state legislature: A case study of Karnataka. Mallikarjun, Vadankeri. Gulbarga University, Karnataka, 2009. Guide- B S Maheswarappa. 461

Information needs and use pattern of users in Anna University Library: An analytical study. Pandian, R. Anna University, Chennai, Tamil Nadu, 2012. Guide- G Krishnamoorthy. 462

Information needs of agricultural farmers in the rural areas of Chittoor District. Naidu, P Giri. Sri Venkateswara University, Tirupati, Andhra Pradesh, 2007. Guide- V Pulla Reddy. 463

Information needs of members of Indian Parliament and the role of Parliament Library. Yadav, Ved Raj. University of Delhi, Delhi, 2001. Guide- P B Mangla. 464

Information needs of SC/ST students, faculties and researchers of colleges and universities of Orissa. Seth, M K. Utkal University, Orissa, 2005. Guide- Baman Parida. 465

Restructuring the college library system towards serving the information needs of learners in distance education mode: A study based on colleges in the Burdwan Division of West Bengal. Nayak, Gurudas. University of Burdwan, Rajbati, Bardhaman, West Bengal, 2008. Guide- Tridib Tripathi. 466

Some aspects of information needs of pre employment of public sector banks of greater Gwalior. Verma, Neeraja. Jiwaji University, Madhya Pradesh, 1997. Guide- Shalini Rewadikar. 467

Entry No.

Special libraries in M P: A critical study in the light of users need. Sharma, Hemant. Jiwaji University, Madhya Pradesh, 1991. Guide- S M Tripathi. 468

Study of the information requirements and information use pattern of the members of grama panchayats in Kerala. Dinesan, K. University of Calicut, Calicut, Kerala, 2008. Guide- M Bavakutty. 469

University engineering college libraries in Andhra Pradesh: A survey with special reference to user information needs. Seshagiri Rao, V A. Sri Venkateswara University, Tirupati, Andhra Pradesh, 2001. Guide- N Guruswamy Naidu. 470

a. Communities

Community information needs in rural Manipur. Meitei, Lairenlakpam Shanta. Manipur University, Manipur, 2008. Guide- Purnima Devi. 471

Community information needs in tribal areas of Orissa. Das, Ranjit Kumar. Dr B R Ambedkar University, Agra, Uttar Pradesh, 2007. Guide- V K Sharma. 472

Community information needs: A study of Rourkela civil township of Orissa. Padhee, Birendra Kumar. Utkal University, Orissa, 2000. Guide- Manoranjan Mahapatra. 473

Community information services: A study on information needs of rural community. Dharani Kumar, P. Kuvempu University, Shimoga, Karnataka, 2011. Guide- B S Biradar. 474

Information needs and patterns of information seeking behaviour of the santal community of Jamboni Block in West Midnapore District, West Bengal. Kamila, Kanchan. University of Burdwan, Rajbati, Bardhaman, West Bengal, 2007. Guide- Subal Chandra Biswas. 475

Entry No.

Information needs of different communities: A survey of the Puri District of Orissa. Baliarsingh, R K. Utkal University, Orissa, 1990. Guide- Manoranjan Mahapatra. 476

Information needs of pilgrims visiting Tirumala Tirupati in Andhra Pradesh: A study. Ramana, B. Sri Venkateswara University, Tirupati, Andhra Pradesh, 2010. Guide- V Pulla Reddy. 477

Information needs, awareness, perception and source use behaviour of rural population: A study with special reference to social development information. Takalkar, Anil. Gulbarga University, Karnataka, 2005. Guide- B S Maheswarappa. 478

Social and economic information needs of community of Chhattisgarh: A study. Vaishnav, Girish Shankar. Guru Ghasidas University, Chhattisgarh, 2003. Guide- U N Singh & R K Rout. 479

b. Faculty

Analytical study of information needs and use pattern of faculty members and research scholars of Amravati University. Choukhande, Vaishali (Ms). Sant Gadge Baba Amravati University, Maharashtra, 2003. Guide- P S G Kumar. 480

Information needs and aspirations of faculty and students in affiliated colleges of University of Mysore: A study. Kuntgal, Arjun. Gulbarga University, Karnataka, 2011. Guide- V T Kamble. 481

Information needs and information seeking behaviour of chemistry and physics teachers of Gwalior and Chambal Region. Guatam, J N. Jiwaji University, Madhya Pradesh, 1992. Guide- H S Sengar. 482

Entry No.

Information needs and information seeking behaviour of faculty of engineering institutions in Tamil Nadu. Subramanian, N. University of Madras, Tamil Nadu, 2003. Guide- B Ramesh Babu. 483

Information needs and pursuits of the faculty of management in digital era: A case study of Orissa. Swain, C K. Sambalpur University, Orissa, 2010. Guide- K C Panda. 484

Information needs and seeking behaviour of management teachers: An evaluative study in the context of Madhya Pradesh. Tomar, Bhanu Pratap Singh. Jiwaji University, Madhya Pradesh, 2002. Guide- J N Gautam. 485

Information needs and seeking behaviour of the teachers of Allahabad University: A study. Gupta, Ranjana. Bundelkhand University, Jhansi, Uttar Pradesh, 2004. Guide- M T M Khan. 486

Information needs of faculty in government training institutions of Orissa. Behera, Sangeeta. Utkal University, Orissa, 2012. Guide- Pushpanjali Jena. 487

Rewa sambhag ke mahavidhyalayin Hindi pradhyapako ki suchna aavashyakta evam suchna khojne ki pravartiyon ka adhyayan. Jyotsana Singh. Awadhesh Pratap Singh University, Madhya Pradesh, 2011. Guide- R K Sharma. 488

Vishwavidyalayin bhotik avam ganit ke pradhyapkon ki suchna aavashyakta evam suchna khojne ki pravarti ka adhyayan: Uttrakhand Rajya ke sandarbh mein. Sati, Prem Parkash. Awadhesh Pratap Singh University, Madhya Pradesh, 2012. Guide- R K Sharma. 489

c. Industries

A study of information needs in industries in Delhi. Dhami, Sawita (Ms). University of Delhi, Delhi, 2002. Guide- P B Mangla. 490

Entry No.

Information needs in jute and allied fibre industries in India. Niyogi, Bratati. Jadhavpur University, West Bengal, 1993. Guide- M L Chakraborty & A K Ohdedar. 491

Information needs of cottage industries and the role of libraries in their development with special reference to Ganjam District of Orissa. Pati, S M. Berhampur University, Orissa, 1990. Guide- Manoranjan Mahapatra. 492

Information needs of cottage industries in Barrackpore and Barasat sub divisions of north 24 parganas district, West Bengal. Kundu, Dipak Kumar. University of Calcutta, West Bengal, 2009. Guide- Biplab Chakrabarti. 493

Information needs of craft Industries: Special reference to applique craft in Puri District of Orissa. Dalai, B K. Berhampur University, Orissa, 2008. Guide- K C Das. 494

Information needs of small scale industries: A case study in the state of Orissa. Mahapatra, Rabindra Kumar. Berhampur University, Orissa, 2003. Guide- P Soma Raju. 495

Information requirements of industries in Dakshina Kannada District: A case study. Divakara. Mangalore University, Karnataka, 2007. Guide- A K Baradol. 496

d. Journalists

Information needs and patterns of information seeking by journalists in Delhi. Gurdev Singh. University of Delhi, Delhi, 1998. Guide- Krishan Kumar. 497

Information needs and seeking behaviour of working journalists in Orissa: An analytical study. Mahallick, Rabibdra Kumar. Utkal University, Orissa, 1998. Guide- K C Panda. 498

Information needs of journalists of Sagar City M P: A study. Mishra, Shiromani. Dr Hari Singh Gour Vishwavidyalaya, Sagar, Madhya Pradesh, 2011. Guide- B P Shrivastava. 499

Entry No.

e. Lawyers

A critical study of information needs of the legal profession and legal information systems with particular reference to Andhra Pradesh (India). Saroja, G (Ms). Sri Venkateswara University, Tirupati, Andhra Pradesh, 1993. Guide- N Guruswamy Naidu. 500

A critical study of legal information needs of lawyers in Kerala High Court (India). Amminni, V K. Sri Venkateswara University, Tirupati, Andhra Pradesh, 2011. Guide- T Rajagopal. 501

f. Medical Sciences

Health science information needs and services in Bangladesh: Present status and suggestion for future development. Rejaul Islam, Mirza Mohamad. Jadhavpur University, West Bengal, 1998. Guide- Subal Chandra Biswas. 502

Information needs and reading habits of medical practioners of Sagar City: A study. Verma, Nilimesh. Dr Hari Singh Gour Vishwavidyalaya, Sagar, Madhya Pradesh, 2007. Guide- B P Shrivastava. 503

Integration of information needs and technology with reference to Healthnet Nepal. Pradhan, Mohan Raj. University of Delhi, Delhi, 2004. Guide- Shailendra Kumar. 504

g. Research Scholars

A survey of user needs and use patterns of the English scholars at Central Institute of English and Foreign Languages (CIEFL), Hyderabad. Nagar, Neeru (Ms). University of Lucknow, Uttar Pradesh, 2007. Guide- N R Satyanarayana. 505

Entry No.

Information needs and information gathering behaviour of research scholars in pure science departments of the University of Kerala. Geetha, P. University of Kerala, Kerala, 2003. Guide- G Devarajan. 506

Information needs and information seeking behaviour of chemistry students and research scholars in the Rayalaseema Region: A study. Suresh, P. Sri Krishnadevaraya University, Andhra Pradesh, 2012. Guide- D Ravinder. 507

Information needs and information seeking behaviour of research workers in the field of fishery and fish farmers in West Bengal. Basak, Rina. Jadhavpur University, West Bengal, 2010. Guide- Amitabha Chatterjee. 508

Information needs and seeking behaviour of researchers in the field of tibetan studies. Singh, Shyam Narayan. Guru Ghasidas University, Chhattisgarh, 2004. Guide- U N Singh. 509

h. Schools

Madhya Pradesh ke Gwalior evam Chambal ke sambagh kendriya madhiyamik vidhalayon mein adhyayan evam saman gyan bradhi hetu suchna ki aavashyakta. Suryawanshi, Neelima. Jiwaji University, Madhya Pradesh, 1993. Guide- H S Sengar & J N Gautam. 510

Needs and information gathering habits of secondary school teachers in Delhi and Gwalior: An evaluation study. Sathe, Sanjay. Jiwaji University, Madhya Pradesh, 2005. Guide- J N Gautam. 511

i. Scientists

Information needs and information seeking behaviour of users in major science and technology libraries of NE region with special reference to Assam. Choudhury, Bibhuti. Gauhati University, Assam, 2007. Guide- R K Barman. 512

Entry No.

Information needs and sources of information of subject matter specialists in the training and visit system of agricultural extension: A study. Sugunavathy, C. Osmania University, Andhra Pradesh, 1998. Guide- D B Eshwara Reddy. 513

Information needs of engineering scientists with special reference to engineering research group of laboratories of Council of Scientific and Industrial Research. Ramesh, D B. Utkal University, Orissa, 2000. Guide- C R Karisiddappa. 514

Information needs of Indian agricultural scientists: A study of Chhattisgarh Region. Sengupta, Suparna. Guru Ghasidas University, Chhattisgarh, 2002. Guide- Brajesh Tiwari. 515

Information needs of scientists and technologists of Oil and Natural Gas Corporation, India: A study. Das, Bhagwan. Utkal University, Orissa, 2005. Guide- G Mahapatra. 516

Information needs of sericulture scientists of India: A study towards planning and development of sericulture information system. Manjunath, K K. Bangalore University, Karnataka, 2000. Guide- A Y Asundi. 517

Information needs of the users of agricultural college libraries of Andhra Pradesh: A study. Ramalakshmi, (Ms). Sri Venkateswara University, Tirupati, Andhra Pradesh, 2010. Guide- D Chandran. 518

Information needs, awareness, habits and problems of defense scientists in India: A study. Vij, Rajiv. Panjab University, Chandigarh, Punjab, 1991. Guide- H R Chopra. 519

Information requirements and use pattern of agricultural scientists in some selected universities and institutions of U P: An evaluative study. Chakraborty, Hirakanti. Bundelkhand University, Jhansi, Uttar Pradesh, 2003. Guide- Y P Dubey. 520

Entry No.

i. Scientists - Medical

Information needs and information seeking behaviour of persons in medical education in Tamil Nadu. Balasubramanium, S. Vidyasagar University, West Bengal, 1999. Guide- Ashok Basu. 521

Information needs and information seeking behaviour of professionals in medical field: A case study of Jammu and Kashmir State. Ashraf, Mudasir. University of Kashmir, Jammu and Kashmir, 2011. Guide- S M Shafi. 522

Information needs and seeking behaviour of medical scientists of Lucknow and New Delhi based medical colleges: A comparative study. Singh, Asha. Sambalpur University, Orissa, 2004. Guide- K C Panda. 523

ii. Scientists - Veterinary

A study of information needs and information seeking behaviour of veterinary scientists in universities and research institutes of Haryana, Uttar Pradesh and Uttaranchal. Sharma, Superna (Ms). Kurukshetra University, Haryana, 2007. Guide- Ashu Shokeen. 524

Information needs and use pattern of veterinarians in the information technology environment. Gokul, Adarsh N. University of Kerala, Kerala, 2003. Guide- G Devarajan. 525

INFORMATION RETRIEVAL TOOLS, TECHNIQUES AND SYSTEM

A study of data retrieval techniques of online databases available in libraries of central universities in India. Roy, Projesh. University of Delhi, Delhi, 2010. Guide- Shailendra Kumar. 526

Entry No.

A study of the information retrieval systems in social sciences and the design of a model system for India. Pangannaya, N Balakrishna. University of Mysore, Karnataka, 1993. Guide- V G Talwar. 527

Automatic extraction and validation of keywords from HTML documents: A case study. Velumani, G. University of Madras, Tamil Nadu, 2006. Guide- K S Raghavan. 528

Design and development of a heuristics based expert system for automatic identification of bibliographic data elements from the title pages of documents. Rath, Durgashankar. Vidyasagar University, West Bengal, 2001. Guide- A R D Prasad. 529

Designing of online information retrieval system for education (EDULINE) in India with special reference to NCERT as a national resource centre: A critical appraisal. Jha, Balendu Kumar. University of Rajasthan, Jaipur, Rajasthan, 2012. Guide- M R Rawtani. 530

Development of algorithms for indexing and searching with special reference to Telugu documents in UNICODE. Patel, Dimple (Ms). Vidyasagar University, West Bengal, 2006. Guide- Devika P Madalli. 531

Framing of a model information retrieval system on government documents in India. Ghosh, Gopa. University of Calcutta, West Bengal, 2012. Guide- Biplab Chakrabarti. 532

Fuzzy information retrieval. Bhaskar, Karn. Birla Institute of Technology, Mesra, Ranchi, Bihar, 2003. Guide- C R Karisiddappa. 533

General theory of information analysis (GT-IA) for secondary information work and services. Sarkhel, Juran Krishna. Jadhavpur University, West Bengal, 1998. Guide- Prabir Roy Choudhury. 534

Entry No.

Identification and effectiveness of factors in designing a newspaper information retrieval system. Maity, Goutam. Vidyasagar University, West Bengal, 2006. Guide- Subal Chandra Biswas. 535

Knowledge retrieval methods of the libraries: A study of Manipur. Singh, Arambam Birajit. Manipur University, Manipur, 2008. Guide- Madhuri Devi. 536

Linguistic analysis and its application in information retrieval tools. Pandey, R C. North East Hill University, Shillong, Meghalaya, 1996. Guide- J C Binwal. 537

Sociological concepts and their representation in information retrieval tools: A comparative study of terminology. Pathak, Lalit P. North East Hill University, Shillong, Meghalaya, 1994. Guide- J C Binwal. 538

Study of pre-coordinate indexing systems for thesaurus construction. Rajendran, S. University of Calicut, Calicut, Kerala, 1993. Guide- M Bavakutty. 539

a. Indexing Standards

A study of the characteristics of indexes in philosophical books with reference to the standards on indexing. Ramesh Babu, B. University of Madras, Tamil Nadu, 1989. Guide- P Gangadhara Rao. 540

b. POPSI and PRECIS

Postulate based permuted subject indexing: A study of its effectiveness. Raghavan, K S. University of Mysore, Karnataka, 1984. Guide- A Neelameghan. 541

Studies of POPSI (postulate based permuted subject indexing) in terms of its retrieval efficiency and economic efficiency. Chandran, D. Madurai Kamaraj University, Tamil Nadu, 1986. Guide- D B Krishna Rao & G Bhattacharya. 542

Entry No.

Syntactical relationships and expressions in PRECIS and POPSI: A study in journal literature of social sciences. Patnayak, Binayak. Utkal University, Orissa, 1995. Guide- Manoranjan Mahapatra. 543

c. Sciences

Design of an online information retrieval system for meeting research requirements of health scientists. Kumar, Satyendra. Jiwaji University, Madhya Pradesh, 1994. Guide- N R Satyanarayana. 544

Designing of an information retrieval system for veterinary science. Sujatha, P L (Ms). University of Madras, Tamil Nadu, 2007. Guide- Manorama Srinath. 545

Development of a model information storage and retrieval system for laser technology. Singh, Jai Prakash. University of Delhi, Delhi, 1993. Guide- M M Kashyap. 546

d. Subject Indexing

An optimum algorithm for subject indexing systems. Awad, Atef Kamel. University of Delhi, Delhi, 1984. Guide- N C Khandekar. 547

Application of citation and subject analysis in information retrieval system design: A study with special reference to agricultural entomology and plant pathology. Veerabasavaia, M. Bangalore University, Karnataka, 2003. Guide- A Y Asundi. 548

Comparative effectiveness of indexing systems to information needs: A study of four indexing systems. Nath, P. Banaras Hindu University, Uttar Pradesh, 1989. Guide- S N Singh. 549

Entry No.

Computer based system for generating different types of subject indexes and alphabetical classaurus based on deep structure of subject indexing languages. Devadason, F J. Karnataka University, Karnataka, 1983. Guide- M R Kumbhar. 550

Representations of cross disciplinary subjects in information retrieval tools. Lalhmachhuana. North East Hill University, Shillong, Meghalaya, 2004. Guide- J C Binwal. 551

e. Subject Indexing Languages

Application of computer based natural language processing tools and techniques in developing subject indexing languages. Prasad, A R D. Karnataka University, Karnataka, 1994. Guide- C R Karisiddappa. 552

General theory of subject indexing language. Bhattacharya, G. Karnataka University, Karnataka, 1980. Guide- M R Kumbhar. 553

Role of subject indexing languages on the design and development of online bibliographic information storage and retrieval system. Chattopadhyay, Amit Kumar. Jadhavpur University, West Bengal, 1993. Guide- Mangala Prasad Singha. 554

Structure of indexing languages and retrieval effectiveness. Iyer, Hemalatha. University of Mysore, Karnataka, 1984. Guide- P K Patil. 555

INFORMATION SCIENCE

A study of the theoretical foundations of the information science/information technology based on the vedic approach towards information, knowledge and wisdom. Muraleedharan, P. University of Calicut, Calicut, Kerala, 2006. Guide- Raju M Mathew. 556

Entry No.

Information as a commodity: An inquiry into the characteristics of knowledge. Narayana, G J. University of Pune, Maharashtra, 1991. Guide- B Anderson. 557

INFORMATION SEEKING BEHAVIOUR

A study of information seeking behaviour of users of the select sectoral information centers in Southern India. Nikam, Khaiser. University of Mysore, Karnataka, 2001. Guide- V G Talwar. 558

Impact of information technology (IT) on the information seeking behaviour of corporate library users in Chennai. Shanmugam, V. University of Madras, Tamil Nadu, 2005. Guide- R Vengan. 559

Information seeking behaviour and the perceptions of information channels by journalists of selected national news papers of India. Ojha, Ram Awatar. Banaras Hindu University, Uttar Pradesh, 1993. Guide- Y P Dubey. 560

Information seeking behaviour and use of information sources in physical sciences and social sciences: A comparative study. Tripathi, Manorama (Ms). Banaras Hindu University, Uttar Pradesh, 1999. Guide- H N Prasad. 561

Information seeking behaviour of managers working in financial institutions in India: A study. Parvez, Akhtar. University of Delhi, Delhi, 2011. Guide- Shashi Prabha Singh. 562

Information seeking behaviour of members of legislative assembly of U P and Rajasthan: A comparative study. Zaffar, Md Safay. Aligarh Muslim University, Uttar Pradesh, 2011. Guide- S M K Q Zaidi. 563

Information seeking behaviour of tribal communities: A case study of toto community of Jalpaiguri District. Chakrabarti, Biplab. Vidyasagar University, West Bengal, 1996. Guide- Ashok Basu. 564

Entry No.

Information seeking behaviour of users in medical college libraries of M P: A study. Verma, Shail. Jiwaji University, Madhya Pradesh, 2009. Guide- Rochana Shrivastava. 565

Information seeking behaviour of users in university libraries in West Bengal: A case study of three university libraries. Biswas, Bidhan Chandra. Jadhavpur University, West Bengal, 2007. Guide- Chaitali Dutta. 566

Information seeking behaviour of visual artists in North Western India: A study. Gupta, Manisha. Panjab University, Chandigarh, Punjab, 2012. Guide- Promila. 567

Information seeking strategies: A study of North East India. Bharali, Bijoy. North East Hill University, Shillong, Meghalaya, 2001. Guide- Veena Saraf. 568

Micro modeling of individual level information seeking behaviour: A heterogeneity specific study. Chakrabarty, Mahua. Jadhavpur University, West Bengal, 2011. Guide-Chaitali Dutta. 569

Role of personality of information seeking behaviour: A survey of facilities in A P. Tholagappian. Sri Venkateswara University, Tirupati, Andhra Pradesh, 2012. Guide- D Chandran. 570

a. Faculty

A study on digital resources use behaviour among the faculty members of premier educational institutions in Tamil Nadu. Senthilkumar, V. Annamalai University, Tamil Nadu, 2011. Guide- P Ravichandran. 571

A study on information seeking and utilization behaviour among the university teachers in Tamil Nadu. Elavazhagan, K. Annamalai University, Tamil Nadu, 2011. Guide- P Ravichandran. 572

Entry No.

Communication pattern and information seeking behaviour among degree college lecturers in Nellore District. Prabhakar, N. Sri Venkateswara University, Tirupati, Andhra Pradesh, 2010. Guide- K Padmini. 573

Dr Hari Singh Gour Viswavidyalaya evam sambaddhit mahavidyalayo ke Hindi Vibhag ke shishako ki soochna prapti, pravrutti evam Hindi sahitya mein unka yogdan: Ek adhyayan. Awasthi, Sadhna(Ms). Dr Hari Singh Gour Vishwavidyalaya, Sagar, Madhya Pradesh, 2009. Guide- B P Shrivastava. 574

Information seeking behaviour of degree college faculty in Andhra Pradesh with special reference to Rayalaseema Region. Rajasekhar, R. Sri Krishnadevaraya University, Andhra Pradesh, 2010. Guide- P Rajarathnam Chetty. 575

Information seeking behaviour of faculty members and research scholars with reference to Punjabi literature: An analytical study. Gurmeet Singh. University of Delhi, Delhi, 2012. Guide- P K Walia. 576

Information seeking behaviour of faculty members of universities of Andhra Pradesh: A study. Dorasamy, M. Annamalai University, Tamil Nadu, 2000. Guide- M Nagarajan. 577

Information seeking behaviour of faculty members using Internet at various universities of Jammu and Kashmir. Sharma, Bindu (Ms). University of Jammu, Jammu and Kashmir, 2010. Guide- Sangita Gupta. 578

Information seeking behaviour of the teachers of Bundelkhand University, Jhansi: An evaluative study. Parmar, Arvind Singh. Bundelkhand University, Jhansi, Uttar Pradesh, 2002. Guide- M T M Khan. 579

Entry No.

i. Faculty - Sciences

An analysis of information seeking behaviour of the faculty members of medical colleges in Tamil Nadu: A critical study. Seethai, R M. Annamalai University, Tamil Nadu, 2009. Guide- M Nagarajan. 580

Communication pattern and information seeking behaviour among the teaching faculty of regional engineering colleges in India. Koganurmath, M M. Karnataka University, Karnataka, 1995. Guide- C R Karisiddappa. 581

Impact of IT and information seeking behaviour of teachers in medical college libraries with special reference to M P and Chhattisgarh. Jain, Yogesh Kumar. Jiwaji University, Madhya Pradesh, 2003. Guide- B K Sharma & Hemant Sharma. 582

Information seeking behaviour of faculty, research scholars and students of Indian Statistical Institute learning centres. Krishnamurthy, M. Bangalore University, Karnataka, 2002. Guide- Lalitha Aswath. 583

Information seeking behaviour of pharmaceutical faculty and researchers in academic institutions in Punjab and Chandigarh. Shrivastava, Vishwesh Dayal. Panjab University, Chandigarh, Punjab, 2007. Guide- H R Chopra. 584

Information seeking behaviour of teachers and researchers of Cochin University of Science and Technology and University of Kerala in the changed library environment. Shibu, Ray S. Cochin University of Science & Technology, Kerala, 2010. Guide- M D Baby. 585

Information seeking behaviour of teachers and researchers of engineering colleges in NCR. Rajput, Mamta. Jiwaji University, Madhya Pradesh, 2011. Guide- B K Sharma & Hemant Sharma. 586

Entry No.

ii. Faculty - Social Sciences

A critical study of information seeking pattern of social science teachers in the universities of Rajasthan. Tilwani, Thanwar Das. University of Rajasthan, Jaipur, Rajasthan, 2004. Guide- S P Sood. 587

A study of information seeking behaviour of faculty members of management colleges in Gujarat State. Lalwani, Suresh Lakhmichand. Kachchh University, Gujarat, 2012. Guide- M K Prajapati. 588

Attitude towards information: A study of post graduate teachers and researchers in social sciences. Satish, N G. University of Mysore, Karnataka, 1987. Guide- H A Khan. 589

Information seeking behaviour of social science faculty in universities in Iran and India. Vasantha Raju, N. University of Mysore, Karnataka, 2010. Guide- N S Harinarayana. 590

iii. Faculty and Students - Social Sciences

Information seeking behaviour of faculty and students in the changing environment: A study of commerce college libraries in Mumbai. Kadli, J H. Karnataka University, Karnataka, 2011. Guide- B D Kumbhar. 591

Information seeking behaviour of the students and faculty members in IIMs of Calcutta, Lucknow and Ahmedabad: A survey. Naved Ahmad. Aligarh Muslim University, Uttar Pradesh, 2011. Guide- Nishat Fatima. 592

Information seeking behaviour of the teachers and the students in Rajabhat University in Bangkok. Kingkaew, Patitungkho. University of Pune, Maharashtra, 2006. Guide- N J Deshpande. 593

Entry No.

Information use behaviour of students and faculty in management institutes of Bangalore. Ramanna, Shamrao. Gulbarga University, Karnataka, 2012. Guide- V T Kamble. 594

b. Farmers

Agricultural information access pattern of paddy growers in Nagapattinam District, Tamil Nadu: An analytical study. Anandhi, C. Annamalai University, Tamil Nadu, 2012. Guide- M Sadik Batcha. 595

Information seeking behaviour of groundnut growers in Cuddalore District. Ravichandran, P. Annamalai University, Tamil Nadu, 2003. Guide- S Ravi. 596

c. Industries

Information seeking behaviour and information needs of decision makers in silk industry: A case study of jute industry. Singh, D K. Banaras Hindu University, Uttar Pradesh, 1998. Guide- H N Prasad. 597

Information seeking behaviour of users of industrial libraries of Hyderabad, Karnataka Region: A study. Saibanna, Machendranath. Gulbarga University, Karnataka, 2011. Guide- V T Kamble. 598

Information use pattern among small scale industries with special reference to Dindigul District (Tamil Nadu). Abraham, J. University of Madras, Tamil Nadu, 2005. Guide- B Ramesh Babu. 599

d. Lawyers

An evaluative study of erudite and legal consultation behaviour of the bar judicature of Allahabad High Court. Tripathi, Veda Nand. Dr B R Ambedkar University, Agra, Uttar Pradesh, 2001. Guide- U C Sharma. 600

Entry No.

Information seeking behaviour and reading habits of high court lawyers of M P: An analytical study. Kesarwani, Krishna Kumar. Dr Hari Singh Gour Vishwavidyalaya, Sagar, Madhya Pradesh, 2008. Guide- K C Sahoo. 601

e. Linguists

Human factors in information seeking: A study of relationship between situational and psychological factors and information seeking behaviour of linguists. Suman, Kumari R. University of Mysore, Karnataka, 1999. Guide- Shalini R Urs. 602

f. Research Scholars

A survey of the pattern of literature search by the science researchers in Kerala, Calicut and Cochin universities. Alexander, Abraham. University of Calicut, Calicut, Kerala, 1993. Guide- A B George. 603

Information access pattern among the students of professional and non professional courses in Annamalai University: A study. Natarajan, R. Annamalai University, Tamil Nadu, 2010. Guide- M Aravinthan. 604

Information seeking behaviour (ISB) of researchers in three Karnataka State universities. Mudhol, V Mahesh. Sambalpur University, Orissa, 2001. Guide- R K Rout. 605

Information seeking behaviour of degree students of general colleges of Barak Valley. Bhattacharya, Sarita. Gauhati University, Assam, 2010. Guide- Narendra Lahkar. 606

Information seeking behaviour of research scholars in the field of chemistry. Raju, Ch Varada. Osmania University, Andhra Pradesh, 2003. Guide- V Vishwa Mohan. 607

Entry No.

Information seeking behaviour of researchers in biosciences of the universities of Chhattisgarh: An analytical study. Devagan, Leelam Kumar. Guru Ghasidas University, Chhattisgarh, 2008. Guide- Brajesh Tiwari. 608

Information seeking behaviour of social science researchers in the universities of Orissa: An analytical study. Rout, Benudhar. Sambalpur University, Orissa, 2002. Guide- R K Rout. 609

The information search pattern of doctoral students in the electronic environment. Verghese, Rekha Rani (Ms). University of Calicut, Calicut, Kerala, 2006. Guide- M Bavakutty. 610

g. School Children

Information seeking behaviour among school children at Tirupati: A survey. Maddaiah, N. Sri Venkateswara University, Tirupati, Andhra Pradesh, 2010. Guide- K Padmini. 611

Information seeking behaviour and reading habits of secondary school students in changing academic environment: A case study of Sahranpur District (U P). Gupta, Rakesh Kumar. Dr Hari Singh Gour Vishwavidyalaya, Sagar, Madhya Pradesh, 2009. Guide- K C Sahoo. 612

Information seeking behaviour of the users of the libraries in kendriya vidyalayas of Bhubaneswar Region covering Orissa, parts of Bihar and West Bengal. Dash, Prafulla Chandra. Berhampur University, Orissa, 2000. Guide- Biswanath Panda. 613

Information seeking patterns of users, services and resources of CBSE public school libraries in Rajasthan: A multivariate analysis. Gupta, Kamal Kant. University of Rajasthan, Jaipur, Rajasthan, 2012. Guide- M R Rawtani. 614

Entry No.

h. Scientists

Information seeking behaviour of scientists in research institutions of Tamil Nadu: A critical study. Avvai, R. Annamalai University, Tamil Nadu, 2003. Guide- S Ravi. 615

Information seeking behaviour of users in astronomy information centers and libraries in India: The impact of new information technology. Sahu, Hemant Kumar. University of Pune, Maharashtra, 2010. Guide- S N Singh. 616

i. Scientists - Agriculture

Impact of ICT on information seeking behaviour of teachers in agriculture universities of Haryana, H P, Punjab and U P. Kiran Lata. Bundelkhand University, Jhansi, Uttar Pradesh, 2012. Guide- Ashu Shokeen & M T M Khan. 617

Impact of information technology on the information seeking behaviour of scientists in agricultural institutes of Rajasthan. Dave, Rakesh Kumar. Mohan Lal Sukhadia University, Udaipur, Rajasthan, 2011. Guide- U K Aggarwal. 618

Information seeking behaviour of agriculture scientists working in selected ICAR institutions in Delhi and Punjab Agricultural University, Ludhiana: A study. Singh, K P. Guru Nanak Dev University, Amritsar, Punjab, 2007. Guide- M P Satija. 619

The impact of electronic information sources on information seeking behaviour of agricultural scientists. Maya Devi (Ms). Banaras Hindu University, Uttar Pradesh, 2012. Guide- H N Prasad. 620

ii. Scientists - DRDO

Information seeking behaviour of defense scientists and provision of library and information resources in defense research and development laboratories /establishments in India: An analytical study. Mohinder Singh. University of Rajasthan, Jaipur, Rajasthan, 1990. Guide- C D Sharma. 621

Entry No.

Studies of information seeking behaviour of DRDO scientists in India: A Study. Satish Kumar. Jiwaji University, Madhya Pradesh, 2010. Guide- J N Gautam. 622

iii. Scientists - Engineering

Information search pattern of engineering scientists in digital era with special reference to Anna University and IIT, Chennai. Kumaresan, A. Annamalai University, Tamil Nadu, 2011. Guide- P Sivaraman. 623

Information seeking behaviour of engineering and scientific personnel in graphite industries in India. Kittur, S B. Karnataka University, Karnataka, 1997. Guide- S R Ijari. 624

Information seeking behaviour of engineering scientists in JNTU. Ravinder, D. Sri Krishnadevaraya University, Andhra Pradesh, 2007. Guide- P Rajarathnam Chetty. 625

iv. Scientists - Medical

A critical study of information seeking behaviour of medical specialists in Madras City (INDIA). Rajagopal, T. Sri Venkateswara University, Tirupati, Andhra Pradesh, 1990. Guide- G V S L Narasimha Raju. 626

Communication patterns and information seeking behaviour of health science researchers/ scientists: A study of ICMR institutes. Solomon Raju, B. Andhra University, Andhra Pradesh, 2002. Guide- R S R Varalakshmi. 627

Impact of IT on information seeking behaviour of medical professionals in Chandigarh. Raj Kumar. Panjab University, Chandigarh, Punjab, 2007. Guide- H R Chopra. 628

Information gathering habits of health scientists and suggestions for national health information centre for India. Ramesh Kumar. University of Delhi, Delhi, 1995. Guide- Krishan Kumar. 629

Entry No.

Information seeking and information utilization pattern of psychiatrists in West Bengal: A survey. Chakraborty, Susmita. Jadhavpur University, West Bengal, 2008. Guide- Chaitali Dutta & B K Sen. 630

Information seeking behaviour of allopathic medical practioners in Coimbatore District. Sathivelmurugan. Bishop Heber College, Bharathidasan University, Tamil Nadu, 2012. Guide- S Ally Sornam. 631

Information seeking behaviour of medical practicing doctors. Prabhakara Rao, D. Sri Krishnadevaraya University, Andhra Pradesh, 2008. Guide- P Rajarathnam Chetty. 632

Information seeking behaviour of medical professionals working in three major hospitals of Delhi: An analytical study. Samantray, Indumati (Ms). Dr Hari Singh Gour Vishwavidyalaya, Sagar, Madhya Pradesh, 2012. Guide- K C Sahoo. 633

Information seeking behaviour of researchers and practitioners of homeopathy system of medicine: with special reference to North India. Aggarwal, Sunil Kumar. Jiwaji University, Madhya Pradesh, 2008. Guide- J N Gautam & Rochana Shrivastava. 634

Information seeking behaviour of the medical scientists and doctors of PGIMER, Chandigarh; AIIMS and Apollo Hospitals, New Delhi: A case study. Sengar, Keshvendra Pratabh. Jiwaji University, Madhya Pradesh, 2005. Guide- J N Gautam & H S Sengar. 635

Medline on CDROM: An analysis of user search behaviour. Joshi, Medha V (Ms). SNDT Women's University, Mumbai, Maharashtra, 2002. Guide- Harsha Parekh. 636

Entry No.

Resources and services, information gathering and use habits of users of health science libraries in Karnataka State. Mahesh, P S. Karnataka University, Karnataka, 2003. Guide- B S Maheswarappa & B V Rajashekhar. 637

v. Scientists - Space

A study of information seeking behaviour of space technologists with emphasis on correlating user characteristics with search behaviour. Sridhar, M S. University of Mysore, Karnataka, 1987. Guide- H A Khan. 638

Information resource management in space research libraries and information use behaviour of space scientists and engineers in India: An analytical study. Vijay Pandya, Manish Kumar. University of Rajasthan, Jaipur, Rajasthan, 2000. Guide- Pushpa Dhyani. 639

i. Social Scientists

Information gathering habits of economists and political scientists in the University of Delhi; JNU; Jamia Millia Islamia; AMU, Aligarh and BHU: A comparative study. Dhaka, Satendra Singh. University of Delhi, Delhi, 2002. Guide- Shashi Prabha Singh. 640

Information seeking behaviour in digital environment: A study of social scientists of Manipur. Bembem, Sarangthem. Manipur University, Manipur, 2012. Guide- Ch Ibohal Singh. 641

Information seeking behaviour of researchers in history and political science in Delhi. Talwar, Neena Kanungo (Ms). University of Delhi, Delhi, 1997. Guide- Krishan Kumar. 642

Information seeking behaviour of social scientists in Marathwada. Kamble, Veena M (Ms). Dr Babasaheb Ambedkar Marathwada University, Aurangabad, Maharashtra, 2005. Guide- S M Mohal. 643

Entry No.

Information seeking behaviour of the economists: A selective study of teachers and research scholars of University of Punjab, Haryana and U T (Chandigarh). Mittal, Savita (Ms). Kurukshetra University, Haryana, 1993. Guide- J K Khanna. 644

Information seeking behaviour of the political leaders in Manipur. Naorem, Vidyavati Devi. Manipur University, Manipur, 2012. Guide- Madhuri Devi. 645

Information seeking in Internet era: A case study of Indian economists. Pujar, S M. Karnataka University, Karnataka, 2008. Guide- S L Sangam. 646

Use of information sources vis-à-vis searching habits of social scientists: A case study of universities in Karnataka State. Shindhe, Ganapathi Z. Gulbarga University, Karnataka, 2009. Guide- B S Maheswarappa. 647

j. Use and User Studies

A case study of the utility pattern of information in the faculties of science and technology in Annamalai University. Raja, M. Annamalai University, Tamil Nadu, 2010. Guide- P Ravichandran. 648

Behaviour pattern of users in academic and research libraries with special reference to Central Library of IIT, Bombay. Waydande, Hindurao. University of Pune, Maharashtra, 2001. Guide- S P Ganpule. 649

Impact of information seeking behaviour of users in the libraries of engineering colleges: An analytical study with special reference to Madhya Pradesh. Dixit, Pramod. Jiwaji University, Madhya Pradesh, 2009. Guide- Hemant Sharma. 650

Information seeking pattern of users and provision of library and information sources in engineering colleges / institutes in Rajasthan. Sharma, Narendra. University of Rajasthan, Jaipur, Rajasthan, 2001. Guide- B S Garg. 651

Entry No.

INFORMATION SERVICES

A study of information services given in college libraries of Aurangabad District (M S). Sathe, V. Dr Babasaheb Ambedkar Marathwada University, Aurangabad, Maharashtra, 2006. Guide- Shakuntala S Lomte. 652

A study of reference and information services in university libraries in West Bengal: A qualitative and quantitative approach. Ghosh, Bhabani Kumar. Vidyasagar University, West Bengal, 2001. Guide- J K Sarkhel. 653

An evaluative study of reference and information services in university libraries of Bangladesh. Rahaman, Kazi Mokleswar. Vidyasagar University, West Bengal, 2011. Guide- P K Jana & J N Satpathi. 654

An investigation into the factors that influence the information services of a university library with special reference to Kerala University. Parameswaran, N. Cochin University of Science & Technology, Kerala, 1991. Guide- C V Rajan Pillai. 655

Development of reference service in the university libraries in India after 1947. Sewa Singh. Panjab University, Chandigarh, Punjab, 1985. Guide- J S Sharma. 656

Evolution of information services in university libraries: A study in Tirupati. Kalpalatha, N. Sri Venkateswara University, Tirupati, Andhra Pradesh, 2009. Guide- K Padmini. 657

Government information initiatives of India, since 1995: A study. Chikate, Anil. Rashtrasant Tukadoji Maharaj Nagpur University, Nagpur, Maharashtra, 2008. Guide- P S G Kumar. 658

Information access and management in the B School libraries of Orissa. Patro, Manaswini. Berhampur University, Orissa, 2011. Guide- K C Das. 659

Entry No.

Information services and their efficacy of science libraries in Pune metropolitan area: A critical study. Kulkarni, S N. University of Pune, Maharashtra, 2009. Guide- S K Patil. 660

Information services of universities: A study of UK and India. Kattimani, M T. Gulbarga University, Karnataka, 2008. Guide- Lalitha K Sami. 661

Infotech-based information services among scientific and research institutions in Karnataka State: A survey. Dakulge, Mehatab I. Gulbarga University, Karnataka, 2006. Guide- V T Kamble. 662

Library and information facilities in support of legal education: A study of academic law libraries in Andhra Pradesh. Manikya Rao, B. Andhra University, Andhra Pradesh, 2011. Guide- C Sasikala. 663

Library and information services in Gujarat: A perspective on their re-engineering. Udani, Niharika T (Ms). Guru Nanak Dev University, Amritsar, Punjab, 2005. Guide- Sewa Singh. 664

Library and information services in senior secondary schools: Problems and prospects. Jain, Shudarshan k. Bundelkhand University, Jhansi, Uttar Pradesh, 2001. Guide- Pandey S K Sharma. 665

Medical informatics and rural services: A study of maternal and child health information in the field practice area of Kasturba Medical College. Dayananda Pai, T. Bangalore University, Karnataka, 1997. Guide- P Sadashivmurthy. 666

Network ke peripeksha mein Madhya Pradesh vishwavidyalaya granthalayaona mein suchna sevaon ki gatividhyho ka alochnatmak adhyayan kendra. Jain, Manish Kumar. Jiwaji University, Madhya Pradesh, 2001. Guide- Hemant Sharma. 667

Entry No.

Provision and pattern of rural library and information services in U P with special reference to Jhansi District: A study. Devi, J Shri. Bundelkhand University, Jhansi, Uttar Pradesh, 2004. Guide- N R Satyanarayana. 668

Provision of library and information services for the visually impaired in India: A study. Pillai, Priya. University of Pune, Maharashtra, 2012. Guide- N J Deshpande. 669

Re-engineering library and information services: A study of management libraries in India with special references to Delhi, Gurgaon, Faridabad, Noida and Ghaziabad. Gour, R C. Dr B R Ambedkar University, Agra, Uttar Pradesh, 2001. Guide- B K Sharma. 670

Role of UNESCO in the development of library and information services in the third world countries with special reference to India: A study. Bhatt, Rakesh Kumar. Dr B R Ambedkar University, Agra, Uttar Pradesh, 2002. Guide- U C Sharma. 671

Scientific and technological information services for industrial innovations: A critical study of Indian situation. Sinha, Arun Kumar. University of Rajasthan, Jaipur, Rajasthan, 1988. Guide- C D Sharma. 672

Soochana sevaon ke pripekshya main M P ke swashashi mahavidhyalon granthalayon ka tulanatmak adhyan. Rathore, Shivendra Singh. Jiwaji University, Madhya Pradesh, 2009. Guide- J N Gautam & B K Sharma. 673

Strengthening of information services through CD ROM in biotechnology with a special reference to Delhi based central universities: A study. Chatopadhyay, Anjana. Bundelkhand University, Jhansi, Uttar Pradesh, 1998. Guide- N R Satyanarayana. 674

Entry No.

Vidhansabha pustkalaya ki suchna sevaon ke badalte paridrashyo ka gunatmak adhdhyayan evam mulyankan Uttari Bharat kei sandarbh mei. Harivasi, Vandana. Awadhesh Pratap Singh University, Madhya Pradesh, 2008. Guide- R K Sharma. 675

a. Agriculture Sciences

Agricultural information services in a developing society: A study on information support services to agricultural extension officers in Andhra Pradesh. Charyulu, A Srinivasa. Osmania University, Andhra Pradesh, 2005. Guide- V Vishwa Mohan. 676

Agricultural information to the farmers in Madhya Pradesh with special reference to Sagar District: A study. Sharma, Ashish Kumar. Dr Hari Singh Gour Vishwavidyalaya, Sagar, Madhya Pradesh, 2005. Guide- K C Sahoo. 677

Agriculture information communication and adoption of innovative practices in Nagaland: A case study of Dimapur. Longcher, Alem W. North East Hill University, Shillong, Meghalaya, 2007. Guide- Moses M Naga. 678

Evaluation of agricultural information facility in Andhra Pradesh for agricultural education, research and extension: A study. Renuka, P (Ms). Andhra University, Andhra Pradesh, 2003. Guide- C Sasikala. 679

Influence and documentation service in agriculture science in India: An evaluative study. Shrivastav, Mahendra Narayan. Jiwaji University, Madhya Pradesh, 2000. Guide- J N Gautam & C P Vashishth. 680

Information services for Jute research institutes in Bangladesh: A critical study of the present scenario and a plan for the future development. Banik, Manjusree. Jadhavpur University, West Bengal, 2001. Guide- M L Chakraborty. 681

Entry No.

Information services in agricultural university library, Indian council of agricultural library and research institutes library in Maharashtra. Rokade, S M. Sant Gadge Baba Amravati University, Maharashtra, 2007. Guide- D Rajyalakshmi. 682

Information services in libraries of agricultural universities and research institutes in the states of Punjab, Haryana and H P: A study. Amrit Pal Kaur (Ms). Guru Nanak Dev University, Amritsar, Punjab, 1995. Guide- Navjot Kaur. 683

Library and information services for agricultural research in India. Naidu, H S. Gulbarga University, Karnataka, 1989. Guide- S R Gunjal. 684

Library and information services in agricultural universities in India: An evaluative study with special reference to South India. Chidananda Swamy, H M. Kuvempu University, Shimoga, Karnataka, 2008. Guide- B U Kannappanavar. 685

Role of libraries in knowledge transfer from lab to land: A study of Punjab Agricultural University (PAU), Ludhiana and Sher-e-Kashmir, University of Agricultural Science and technology (SKUAST), Jammu. Shivarama Rao, K. University of Jammu, Jammu and Kashmir, 2008. Guide- I V Malhan. 686

b. Career Choice and Guidance

Information requirements of career seekers in Kerala in relation to information resources and services in libraries. Koovakkai. University of Calicut, Calicut, Kerala, 2004. Guide- V Jalaja. 687

Role of college libraries in career guidance: A study of government and autonomous college affiliated to Andhra Pradesh. Moly, T M. Andhra University, Andhra Pradesh, 2007. Guide- R S R Varalakshmi. 688

Entry No.

Sashatkar ke prakar me sarvajanik pustakalaya ki bhoomika: Rajasthan ke vishesh sandarva mei. Jiwaji University, Madhya Pradesh, 1996. Guide- H S Sengar & J N Gautam. 689

Study on the services extended to students preparing for competitive examinations: A comparative analysis of government and private college libraries in Chennai. Dilly, K T. University of Madras, Tamil Nadu, 2012. Guide- Manorama Srinath. 690

c. Communities

A village levels analysis of the flow and access to information: A study of Meghalaya and Nagaland. Naga, Moses Mao. North East Hill University, Shillong, Meghalaya, 2002. Guide- J C Binwal & Veena Saraf. 691

Community information services in Karnataka: A case study of Bellary District. Gadgin, B R. Gulbarga University, Karnataka, 2010. Guide- V T Kamble. 692

Development information support to rural end users. Upadhya, Padma V. University of Mysore, Karnataka, 1998. Guide- I K Ravichandra Rao. 693

d. Current Awareness Services

A study of CAS services in CSIR, ICAR and ICMR libraries in India. Kapade, Deepak Ganeshrao. Rashtrasant Tukadoji Maharaj Nagpur University, Nagpur, Maharashtra, 2008. Guide- D Rajyalakshmi. 694

Content personalization in a technical institute library: A model for Indian Institutes of Technology with special reference to IIT, Kharagpur. Jeevan, V K J. Utkal University, Orissa, 2006. Guide- Pitambar Padhi. 695

Entry No.

Current awareness services in science libraries in India. Bardol, A K. Karnataka University, Karnataka, 1989. Guide- S R Ijari. 696

Evaluation of abstracting services in the field of biomass: A study of coverage overlap, time lag, indexing and Indian contribution. Shukla, M D. University of Pune, Maharashtra, 1995. Guide- M R Riswadkar. 697

Indexing and abstracting services in Iran: A study. Bagheri, Masoumeh(Ms). Panjab University, Chandigarh, Punjab, 2002. Guide- G C Bansal. 698

Selective dissemination of information services in Karnataka. Radhakrishna, K A. Mangalore University, Karnataka, 1997. Guide- A K Baradol. 699

e. Distance Education

An evaluative study of library and information service to distance learners of open universities of Northern India. Goswami, Subhash Giri. Makhanlal Chaturvedi National University of Journalism and Mass Communication, Madhya Pradesh, 2010. Guide- N K Sharma. 700

Information availability and access to the teachers, counsellors and research scholars of the distance education: A study. Venkateshwar Rao, P. Osmania University, Andhra Pradesh, 2008. Guide- J Yadagiri Reddy. 701

Library and information services for students of distance learning in the universities in Kerala. Gopakumar. Mangalore University, Karnataka, 2008. Guide- A K Baradol. 702

f. Documentation Services

Development and activities of documentation and information centres in UK and India during 1970-1985: A comparative study. Mustafa Khan, Muhammad Tariq. Jiwaji University, Madhya Pradesh, 1994. Guide- S M Tripathi & Noorul Hasan khan. 703

Entry No.

Documentation and information activities in Bangladesh. Islam, Md Sirajul. Banaras Hindu University, Uttar Pradesh, 1983. Guide- P N Kaula. 704

Documentation works and services of forestry literature in Indian Council of Forestry Research and Education (ICFRE): A study. Hazarika, Tilak. Gauhati University, Assam, 2004. Guide- Narendra Lahkar. 705

Role of documentation centres in communication and dissemination of scientific and technological ideas in Bangladesh. Rahman, Md Mostafizur. North East Hill University, Shillong, Meghalaya, 1999. Guide- J C Binwal. 706

g. IT Impact

Application of information technology in library and information services and its impact on library management in the university libraries of Gujarat State: An analytical study. Dash, Ranjita Niladri. Sambalpur University, Orissa, 2012. Guide- B K Choudhury. 707

Electronic databases and their impact on library services with special reference to Canada: A survey. Randhawa, Sarwan Singh. Guru Nanak Dev University, Amritsar, Punjab, 2010. Guide- Amritpal Kaur. 708

Impact of Internet on library and information services of engineering institutes: A case study of IITs. Verma, Manoj Kumar. Guru Ghasidas University, Chhattisgarh, 2009. Guide- U N Singh. 709

Importance of information technology in library and information services: Its prospects for future development. Sinha, Manoj Kumar. Tilka Manjhi Bhagalpur University, Bihar, 2005. Guide- S Sahay. 710

Entry No.

Technological innovations in horticultural sciences diffusion problems. Bankapur, M B. Karnataka University, Karnataka, 1985. Guide- M R Kumbhar. 711

Uttrakhand kei mahavidyalayon ke granthalayao ki karya padhati evam sevaon ka adhyayan: Suchna prodhoygiki kei sandarbh mei. Sharma, Mamta. Awadhesh Pratap Singh University, Madhya Pradesh, 2010. Guide- N R Satyanarayana. 712

h. Medical Sciences

Comparative study of library and information services in the field of medical sciences in India and a proposal and design of its networking. Rawat, P P. Utkal University, Orissa, 1995. Guide- B B Shukla. 713

Evaluation of information services for medical education with special reference to the information services rendered by medical college libraries in Western Maharashtra. Shinde, Manohar Ganpati. Shivaji University, Kolhapur, Maharashtra, 2010. Guide- P V Konnur. 714

Health information services in the medical college libraries of West Bengal: A critical study. Maitra, Pubalika (Ms). University of Calcutta, West Bengal, 2009. Guide- Biplab Chakrabarti. 715

Role of medical librarians in information therapy (IT): A study of the problems and prospects in India and Iran. Zareagavgani, Vahideh. Osmania University, Andhra Pradesh, 2009. Guide- V Vishwa Mohan. 716

The design of integrated consumer health information services. Siddamallaiah, H S. Bangalore University, Karnataka, 1996. Guide- A Y Asundi. 717

Entry No.

i. Use and User Studies

Effectiveness and use of library and information services of the laboratories of Council of Scientific and Industrial Research in India. Thakur, Devendra Singh. Jiwaji University, Madhya Pradesh, 1997. Guide- K G Tyagi. 718

Information services and use pattern in humanities: Survey and proposal for setting up a national documentation center. Kanakachari, M. Andhra University, Andhra Pradesh, 1994. Guide- B Vijayalakshmi. 719

Information use pattern in private engineering college libraries in Andhra Pradesh. Satyanarayana, K. Andhra University, Andhra Pradesh, 1999. Guide- R S R Varalakshmi. 720

Study of user services in the libraries of ICSSR institutes. Singh, Sunil. Vikram University, Madhya Pradesh, 2000. Guide- Sonal Singh. 721

j. Web-based Services

Analysis of web based library services in university libraries in India. Nagabhushanam, V. University of Delhi, Delhi, 2010. Guide- M Madhusudhan. 722

Generating web based information services using semantic web technology. Dutta, Biswanath. University of Pune, Maharashtra, 2010. Guide- A R D Prasad. 723

Online information searching and services in select science and technology libraries and information centres in India: An evaluative study. Tyagi, Anil Kumar. University of Delhi, Delhi, 1996. Guide- M M Kashyap. 724

Entry No.

INFORMATION SOURCES

A historical and critical description of the reference sources in Gurmukhi script, Punjabi language and literature with a view to identify gaps in such sources. Lakhbir Singh. Guru Nanak Dev University, Amritsar, Punjab, 2008. Guide- M P Satija. 725

Application of hyper text methodology for animal encyclopedia for children. Bagavathi, A. University of Madras, Tamil Nadu, 1998. Guide- Manorama Srinath. 726

Development of reference tools in Oriya from 19th century AD: A technical study. Padhi, Pitambar. Utkal University, Orissa, 1992. Guide- K Siva Reddy. 727

Development, diffusion and utilization of information sources in drugs and pharmaceutical laboratories and their linkages with industries in Karnataka: Designing an information system. Arabagonda, N N. Karnataka University, Karnataka, 2008. Guide- M B Bankapur & S L Sangam. 728

Indian reference sources on science and technology: An evaluation. Gawali, S N. Rashtrasant Tukadoji Maharaj Nagpur University, Nagpur, Maharashtra, 2004. Guide- P S G Kumar. 729

Information and reference sources in physical education: A critical and comparative evaluation with special reference to users needs. Sharma, Anil Kumar. Jiwaji University, Madhya Pradesh, 1991. Guide- S M Tripathi. 730

Origin and development of reference sources in Sanskrit: A critical study with special reference to 19th and 20th century. Sharma, Arvind Kumar. Jiwaji University, Madhya Pradesh, 2001. Guide- Hemant Sharma. 731

Entry No.

Paschim bange banglay prakashito jibonimulak tathyo utsyo (1947-2002): Ponjikaran o bishleshanatyak samiksha. Das, Binod Behari. Jadhavpur University, West Bengal, 2009. Guide- Krishnapada Majumder. 732

Paschim banger sundarban anchal: Tathya sutra samikshao ka vislesan. Das, Subarna Kumar. Jadhavpur University, West Bengal, 2005. Guide- Prabir Roy Choudhury. 733

Reference books in Oriya. Das, Radha Gobinda. Sambalpur University, Orissa, 1985. Guide- N A. 734

Reference sources in Telugu since 1800 A D: A critical study. Shankar Reddy, M. Gulbarga University, Karnataka, 1993. Guide- S R Gunjal. 735

Reference sources published in Gujarati: A technical evaluation. Vyas, Kirit Manharlal. Bhavnagar University, Gujarat, 2000. Guide- C R Karisiddappa. 736

Reference tools in Kannada published since 1800 A D: A technical study. Karisiddappa, C R. Gulbarga University, Karnataka, 1983. Guide- S R Gunjal. 737

Shodh Vigyan Kosh: Sadhan ani sandharbh granth. Sant, D K. Shivaji University, Kolhapur, Maharashtra, 1987. Guide- N A. 738

Vigyan evam prodhyogiki ke shaiter me tritiyak suchana shroto ka alochnatmak evam samikchatmak adhyayan: Ek adhyayan. Tomar, G S. Bundelkhand University, Jhansi, Uttar Pradesh, 2002. Guide- J N Gautam. 739

a. Newspapers

Newspaper as a source of information: A survey of Tirupati. Padmini, K (Ms). Sri Venkateswara University, Tirupati, Andhra Pradesh, 1995. Guide- N Guruswamy Naidu. 740

Entry No.

Reflection of rural information in newspapers of Assam: A critical study. Haricharan Das. Gauhati University, Assam, 2007. Guide- N N Sharma. 741

Role of local dailies of Manipuri in dissemination of information: A case study. Devi, Keisham Sangeeta (Ms). Manipur University, Manipur, 2004. Guide- R Lahiri. 742

b. Use and User Studies

A study of the use of information sources in science and social science by the faculty and research scholars in women's university libraries in India. Rajeswari, P. Sri Krishnadevaraya University, Andhra Pradesh, 1997. Guide- P Kamaiah. 743

An investigation into the use of information sources by the scientists and engineers in petroleum R & D organizations. Singh, B K. Banaras Hindu University, Uttar Pradesh, 1998. Guide- S N Singh. 744

Use of information sources by social scientists: A comparative study of Banaras Hindu University and Mizoram University. Ajay Kumar. Mizoram University, Mizoram, 2010. Guide- S N Singh. 745

INFORMATION SYSTEMS

A comparative study of the manual and computerized systems in North Gujarat University. Pandya, Vaidehi Chandrakant. Hemchandracharya North Gujarat University, Gujarat, 2003. Guide- S M Charan. 746

A study of information systems and networks in India with special reference to Maharashtra. Lihitkar, Shalini R (Ms). Rashtrasant Tukadoji Maharaj Nagpur University, Nagpur, Maharashtra, 2010. Guide- D Rajyalakshmi. 747

Entry No.

Design of a nutrition information system in the City of Madras. Usha Kumari, N (Ms). University of Madras, Tamil Nadu, 1992. Guide- K S Raghavan. 748

Ecological model of growth, development and knowledge: A conceptual framework within system research perspectives. Shrivastav, R K. Jiwaji University, Madhya Pradesh, 2002. Guide- J N Gautam. 749

Growth development and structure of biotechnology information system in India: A critical study. Mitra, Rukmini. Jadhavpur University, West Bengal, 2001. Guide- Prabir Roy Choudhury. 750

Information system and services of fashion design technology: A study with special reference to India. Bandi, A N. Karnataka University, Karnataka, 2005. Guide- C R Karisiddappa. 751

Information system design for psychometrics social welfare in Calcutta. Mandal, Satyananda. Jiwaji University, Madhya Pradesh, 1996. Guide- S M Tripathi & Y P Dubey. 752

Library and information system for Yemen Arab Republic: Present problems and model for future. Al-Haddad, Abdulla Ali. University of Delhi, Delhi, 1991. Guide- J L Sardana. 753

Management information system in libraries: With special reference to university libraries of Chhattisgarh. Imtiaz Ahamad. Pt Ravishankar University Raipur, Chhattisgarh, 2011. Guide- A K Varma. 754

Modeling the information system for legal practitioners of high courts. Sharma, Sanjeev. Kurukshetra University, Haryana, 2003. Guide- Ashu Shokeen. 755

Railway library system for India: A model for northern railways. Bansal, Gian Chand. Panjab University, Chandigarh, Punjab, 1992. Guide- H R Chopra. 756

Entry No.

Sports information system of Manipur: A critical analysis. Laishram, Nandkumar Singh. Manipur University, Manipur, 2011. Guide- Khomdon Singh. 757

Study of design and development of an integrated university library and information system in India with reference to recent advances in IT. Cholin, V R. Karnataka University, Karnataka, 2003. Guide- C R Karisiddappa. 758

Trade and commerce information system for India: A proposed model. Majumdar, S. Jiwaji University, Madhya Pradesh, 2000. Guide- J N Gautam & J L Sardana. 759

Use of geographical information system (GIS) in libraries. Phadke, D N. University of Pune, Maharashtra, 1999. Guide- S P Ganpule. 760

a. Agriculture Sciences

A study of agricultural information systems in Andhra Pradesh (India). Veeranjaneyulu, K (Ms). Sri Venkateswara University, Tirupati, Andhra Pradesh, 1999. Guide- T Rajagopal. 761

Agricultural information system in Manipur: A study. Devi, Akoijam Swarnalata (Ms). Manipur University, Manipur, 1996. Guide- R Lahiri. 762

Information support system for sugarcane growers in Cuddalore District in Tamil Nadu. Esmail, S Mohamed. Annamalai University, Tamil Nadu, 1999. Guide- M Suriya. 763

b. Environmental Sciences

Design and development of an information system for environmental sciences. Chakraborty, Arun. Vidyasagar University, West Bengal, 1998. Guide- Ashok Basu. 764

Entry No.

Design and development of Himalayan studies information system: A model. Anil Singh. Jiwaji University, Madhya Pradesh, 2003. Guide- J N Gautam. 765

Role of environmental information system centres in dissemination of information to scientific and local communities. Sanjeevi, K. Annamalai University, Tamil Nadu, 2009. Guide- S Ravi. 766

c. Industries

Characteristics and problems of information system and services required in small scale industries in Southern Karnataka. Ramasesh, C P. University of Mysore, Karnataka, 1988. Guide- P K Patil. 767

Cotton industries information system with particular reference to hand loom silk weaving industries in Tamil Nadu. Aravindan. Annamalai University, Tamil Nadu, 1998. Guide- M Suriya. 768

Design and development of an information system for small scale industry. Murthy, T A V. Karnataka University, Karnataka, 1983. Guide- M R Kumbhar. 769

Information system on pharmaceutical industries: A case study on its design and development in Chennai, Tamil Nadu. Thandavamoorthy. University of Madras, Tamil Nadu, 1987. Guide- R Vengan. 770

d. Medical Care

Health information system. Sangeeta Devi. Mahatma Gandhi Chitrakoot Gramodaya Vishwavidyalaya, Satna, Madhya Pradesh, 2012. Guide- B P Shrivastava & R P Bajpai. 771

Health information system in Manipur: A study. Singh, Charoibam Ibohal. Manipur University, Manipur, 1999. Guide- R Lahiri. 772

Entry No.

e. Museums

A study and assessment of selected museum information systems in India. Raja Gopal, B. Sri Venkateswara University, Tirupati, Andhra Pradesh, 1998. Guide- T Rajagopal. 773

Information management system in museums in West Bengal: A critical study. Bhattacharyya, Swapna (Ms). University of Calcutta, West Bengal, 2004. Guide- Bhubaneswar Chakrabarti. 774

f. Rural Development

Design and development of an information system for rural development: A national plan. Upadhyay, Mangla Prasad. Mahatma Gandhi Chitrakoot Gramodaya Vishwavidyalaya, Satna, Madhya Pradesh, 2008. Guide- R P Bajpai. 775

Rural information system: Design and development. Harish Chandra. Jiwaji University, Madhya Pradesh, 1993. Guide- S M Tripathi. 776

g. Sciences

Design and development of an information system for soil survey and land use planning. Patil, Y M. Rashtrasant Tukadoji Maharaj Nagpur University, Nagpur, Maharashtra, 1998. Guide- P S G Kumar. 777

Design and development of information system for marine engineering libraries. Bakkannanava, Nagappa. University of Pune, Maharashtra, 2009. Guide- S K Patil. 778

Growth, development and structure of oceanographic information system in India: A critical study. Chowdhury, Nitai Roy. Vidyasagar University, West Bengal, 2008. Guide- J K Sarkhel. 779

Entry No.

INIS, AGRIS, DEVSIS and their impact on science and technology information systems and services in India: A study. Srivastava, Jagdamba Prasad. Dr B R Ambedkar University, Agra, Uttar Pradesh, 2001. Guide- U C Sharma. 780

Integrated information system for remotely sensed data. Murthy, E S. University of Pune, Maharashtra, 1992. Guide- S G Mahajan. 781

Planning and development of library and information system for medical colleges in Karnataka: An analysis of standards, mechanisms and models adaptable for an information network. Urs, Rama Raj. Bangalore University, Karnataka, 1996. Guide- M A Gopinath. 782

Role of BANSOC in scientific technical information system and services in Bangladesh. Basher, S A. Rashtrasant Tukadoji Maharaj Nagpur University, Nagpur, Maharashtra, 2004. Guide- P S G Kumar. 783

h. Statistics

Statistical information system for India. Shrivastava, S S. Jiwaji University, Madhya Pradesh, 1994. Guide- S M Tripathi & N R Satyanarayana. 784

Statistical information system in India: A proposed model. Goswami, Prakriti Ranjan. University of Delhi, Delhi, 1985. Guide- J L Sardana. 785

i. Web Resources

Designing a web based model for community information services through the public library system in West Bengal. Mukherjee, Parthasarathi. Jadhavpur University, West Bengal, 2007. Guide- Prabir Roy Choudhury. 786

Entry No.

INSTITUTIONAL REPOSITORIES

A study of manuscripts depository GNDU Amritsar. Harinder Singh. Guru Nanak Dev University, Amritsar, Punjab, 1993. Guide- Navjot Kaur. 787

Centralized model of institutional repository with special reference to universities in Gujarat. Oza, Nimesh D. Sardar Patel University, Gujarat, 2010. Guide- U A Thaker. 788

Design and development of national repository system for health information in India: A study. Surinder Kumar. Karnataka University, Karnataka, 2012. Guide- C R Karisiddappa. 789

Developing open access institutional repositories for scholarly communications: Role of university libraries in India. Chakravarty, Rupak. Panjab University, Chandigarh, Punjab, 2010. Guide- Preeti Mahajan. 790

Development of a model for university archives in India. Pal, Satnam Singh. Panjab University, Chandigarh, Punjab, 1989. Guide- J S Sharma. 791

Establishment and maintenance of web based institutional repository for scholarly contents: A model. Kataria, Sanjay. Makhanlal Chaturvedi National University of Journalism and Mass Communication, Madhya Pradesh, 2008. Guide- B S Nigam. 792

Institutional repositories in India: A study. Gadkari, Manjusha (Ms). Rashtrasant Tukadoji Maharaj Nagpur University, Nagpur, Maharashtra, 2011. Guide- M Hirwade. 793

Institutional repository initiatives in India: A status report. Sawant, Sarika (Ms). SNDT Women's University, Mumbai, Maharashtra, 2010. Guide- Bharati Sen. 794

Entry No.

Library as a repository of knowledge and preserver of values in a democratic society. De, Probhanjan Prasad. Ranchi University, Bihar, 1991. Guide- Anuradha Mishra. 795

Problems and perspectives in design and development of institutional repositories. Narayana, Poornima Rao. Kuvempu University, Shimoga, Karnataka, 2009. Guide- B S Biradar. 796

INTELLECTUAL PROPERTY

a. Laws

An ontological enquiry of cyberspace and intellectual property laws with special reference to India. Swain, Nirmal Kumar. Dr Hari Singh Gour Vishwavidyalaya, Sagar, Madhya Pradesh, 2011. Guide- K C Sahoo. 797

Legal aspects of information with special reference to India. Khobragade, Ashok. Rashtrasant Tukadoji Maharaj Nagpur University, Nagpur, Maharashtra, 2011. Guide- D Rajyalakshmi. 798

b. Patents

Importance of patent information in the socio-economic development of India (being a signatory of GATT Agreement). Mandal, Gorachand. Jadhavpur University, West Bengal, 2002. Guide- Bijoypada Mukherjee. 799

Patent document as a source of technical information for industrial development: Indian scenario. Ramachandran, R. Rashtrasant Tukadoji Maharaj Nagpur University, Nagpur, Maharashtra, 1997. Guide- P S G Kumar. 800

Patent information sources on Internet: An evaluation. Hirwade, Anil W (Ms). Rashtrasant Tukadoji Maharaj Nagpur University, Nagpur, Maharashtra, 2006. Guide- P S G Kumar. 801

Entry No.

Patent literature in chemical sciences: An analytical study of selected countries. Bhalchandra, Dahibhate Nandkumar. University of Pune, Maharashtra, 2011. Guide- S K Patil. 802

c. Rights

Intellectual Property Rights (IPRs) with special reference to copyright issues in electronic information age: Challenges and impact. Burman, Jogendra singh. Bundelkhand University, Jhansi, Uttar Pradesh, 2003. Guide- M T M Khan. 803

Intellectual Property Rights (IPR) information for R & D scientists in CSIR. Gupta, V K. University of Mysore, Karnataka, 2006. Guide- N B Pangannaya. 804

The impact of Intellectual Property Right (IPR) on biodiversity and biotechnology in India and designing a model biodiversity information system. Chaudhuri, Sabuj Kumar. Jadhavpur University, West Bengal, 2006. Guide- Chaitali Dutta. 805

INTERNATIONAL RELATIONS

Trans-national library relation: The Indo-American experience. Konnur, M R. University of Pune, Maharashtra, 1986. Guide- M R Riswadkar. 806

INTERNET RESOURCES

A model for mapping Internet resources for generation of web based information retrieval system: A case study of aerospace science and technology. Hatua, Sudip Ranjan. Vidyasagar University, West Bengal, 2008. Guide- Devika P Madalli. 807

Design, development and evaluation of Internet based educational information sources for the students in Andhra Pradesh. Madhusudan, M. Osmania University, Andhra Pradesh, 2004. Guide- V Vishwa Mohan. 808

Entry No.

Evaluation of Internet based defense related resources: Access reservation for digital library. Kanetkar, Jayashree. University of Pune, Maharashtra, 2008. Guide- N J Deshpande. 809

Impact of Internet on research: A study of selected universities of Andhra Pradesh. Kishore, A. Sri Venkateswara University, Tirupati, Andhra Pradesh, 2004. Guide- K Padmini. 810

Internet as an information source: A survey of engineering students in Nellore District. Sudharani, Y. Sri Venkateswara University, Tirupati, Andhra Pradesh, 2008. Guide- K Padmini. 811

Internet based resources and services in the fields of economics and commerce. Dinesh Kumar. Kurukshetra University, Haryana, 2006. Guide- Dinesh K Gupta. 812

Legal information sources on Internet. Punvetkar. Rashtrasant Tukadoji Maharaj Nagpur University, Nagpur, Maharashtra, 2012. Guide- S M Nikose. 813

a. Use and User Studies

Falling through the network: A case study on the use and application of Internet by the faculty of Annamalai University. Ragavan, P Srinivasaga. Annamalai University, Tamil Nadu, 2007. Guide- S Ravi. 814

Impact of Internet on library use: A study of universities in Karnataka. Naik, Umesha. Mangalore University, Karnataka, 2012. Guide- D Shivalingaiah. 815

Internet surfing and use by teachers and research scholars in universities of North Western India: An analytical study. Sharma, Chetan. Kurukshetra University, Haryana, 2003. Guide- Dinesh K Gupta. 816

Entry No.

Internet use among the faculty members of state universities in Tamil Nadu: A study. Sivasami, K. Annamalai University, Tamil Nadu, 2009. Guide- T Saravanan. 817

The usage of Internet among state university students in the North of Thailand. Pornparn, Srechaiwong. University of Pune, Maharashtra, 2005. Guide- S K Patil. 818

Use of Internet as an information source by engineering faculty and research scholars and impact on library and regional engineering colleges of India: A study. Jange, Suresh. Gulbarga University, Karnataka, 2004. Guide- Lalitha K Sami. 819

Use of Internet by the faculties of medicine in Yemeni Universities. Al-Subari, Munasar Ali Ahmed. University of Pune, Maharashtra, 2012. Guide- N J Deshpande. 820

Use of Internet in the major engineering and management institutions of Orissa: A critical study. Sahu, Nabin Kumar. Sambalpur University, Orissa, 2011. Guide- K C Panda. 821

Use of Internet resources and services in the engineering colleges of Punjab, Haryana and Himachal Pradesh: A survey. Rajeev Kumar. Guru Nanak Dev University, Amritsar, Punjab, 2005. Guide- Amritpal Kaur. 822

Use of Internet services in the university libraries of Assam: An evaluative study. Chkravorty, Suman. Gauhati University, Assam, 2010. Guide- Alaka Buragohain. 823

Utilization impact and relevance of Internet to the scientists working in various research institutes in Hyderabad. Damodhar, P. Osmania University, Andhra Pradesh, 2011. Guide- V Vishwa Mohan. 824

Entry No.

Utilization of Internet by the faculty, researchers and students of Madurai Kamaraj University, Tamil Nadu: A study. Kannan, K. Annamalai University, Tamil Nadu, 2007. Guide- T Saravanan. 825

IT APPLICATION IN LIBRARIES

A comparative study of the status awareness, use and effectiveness of information technology in libraries of agricultural universities and research institutes of Kenya and Karnataka (India). Raymond, Wafula Ongus. Bangalore University, Karnataka, 2008. Guide- T D Kemparaju. 826

A critical study of trends in growth and development of Indian library and information technology during the 20th century with a view to formulating guideline for future. Mishra, J K. Dr Hari Singh Gour Vishwavidyalaya, Sagar, Madhya Pradesh, 1997. Guide- R G Prasher. 827

Application of information and communication technology for rural development in Kerala. Suja, K. University of Calicut, Calicut, Kerala, 2009. Guide- V Jalaja. 828

Management and introduction of information technology (IT) in the libraries in India. Sen, Bharati (Ms). SNDT Women's University, Mumbai, Maharashtra, 1996. Guide- S R Ganpule. 829

Organizational framework of the academic libraries as a multimedia centers: Assessment and analysis of emerging trends in information sources and communication media. Naik, R R. Karnataka University, Karnataka, 2003. Guide- C R Karisiddappa. 830

Role of library and modern information technology in distance education with special reference to India. Kanjilal, Uma. Jiwaji University, Madhya Pradesh, 1993. Guide- S M Tripathi. 831

Entry No.

a. Academic Libraries

i. Academic Libraries – Colleges

Application of information technology in college libraries of Orissa: Problems and prospects. Mansingh, G. Utkal University, Orissa, 2003. Guide- C R Karisiddappa. 832

Application of information technology to college libraries in Punjab: A networking proposal. Gurmej Singh. Guru Nanak Dev University, Amritsar, Punjab, 2008. Guide- Sewa Singh. 833

Awareness and utilization of information and communication technology (ICT) among the faculty members of government engineering colleges in Tamil Nadu: A study. Maheswaran, K. Annamalai University, Tamil Nadu, 2011. Guide- M Aravinthan. 834

Contribution of information technology towards Pune University affiliated college libraries: A study. Marwade, R M. Dr Babasaheb Ambedkar Marathwada University, Aurangabad, Maharashtra, 2010. Guide- Shakuntala S Lomte. 835

Design and application of information technology in government college libraries in Uttar Pradesh: A feasibility study. Dubey, Tripurari Nath. Dr B R Ambedkar University, Agra, Uttar Pradesh, 2002. Guide- U C Sharma. 836

Problems and prospects of application of IT in college libraries of Western Uttar Pradesh. Kulshrestha, Shyam Babu. Jiwaji University, Madhya Pradesh, 2009. Guide- Hemant Sharma. 837

Strategic developmental plan for adoption of information and communication technology (ICT) in the college libraries of Mizoram. Sanjeev Kumar. Mizoram University, Mizoram, 2008. Guide- P K Rath. 838

Entry No.

Utilization of ICT among the faculty members of medical colleges in Puducherry. Kavitha, T. Annamalai University, Tamil Nadu, 2011. Guide- S Mohamed Esmail. 839

Utilization of information and communication technology among the B Ed college students in Cuddalore District. Sathiyamurthy, M D. Annamalai University, Tamil Nadu, 2011. Guide- M Aravinthan. 840

ii. Academic Libraries - Universities

Application of information and communication technologies in university libraries in West Bengal: The human resource perspective. Saha, Nimai Chand. University of Burdwan, Rajbati, Bardhaman, West Bengal, 2012. Guide- Subal Chandra Biswas. 841

Application of information technology (IT) in libraries of private universities of Bangladesh: An analytical study. Md Nazimuddin. Jadhavpur University, West Bengal, 2009. Guide- Krishnapada Majumder. 842

Consumers affectivity in changing information technological scenario at the libraries of the state universities in U P: A study. Sharma, Sanjeev K. Bundelkhand University, Jhansi, Uttar Pradesh, 2001. Guide- M T M Khan. 843

Coping with the new technology experience of university libraries in Maharashtra. Nikose, S M. Rashtrasant Tukadoji Maharaj Nagpur University, Nagpur, Maharashtra, 2004. Guide- D Rajyalakshmi. 844

Gujaratnan vishwavidyalaya granthalayaona vikaslakshi aayojanman mahitee pardhogiyekei no viniyog: Ek abhyas. Rana, Mahendrasingh Khetuba. Bhavnagar University, Gujarat, 2010. Guide- Kirit M Vyas. 845

Entry No.

Information technology application in university libraries in M P. Boria, Raj. Vikram University, Madhya Pradesh, 2009. Guide- Sonal Singh. 846

Madhya Pardesh ke vishwavidyalayin evam mahavidyalyin pustkalyo mei suchna pardhogiyekei upyog ka samiksha adhyayan: suchna evam pustakalaya network ke sandharbh mei. Tiwari, Sunil Kumar. Awadhesh Pratap Singh University, Madhya Pradesh, 2011. Guide- R K Sharma. 847

Madhya Pradesh ke viswavidyalaya granthalayao mein suchna evam produghiki ka upyog: suchna evam pustkalaya networking Kendra ke sandarabh mein. Pateriya, Shailendra. Jiwaji University, Madhya Pradesh, 2006. Guide- B K Sharma & Hemant Sharma. 848

Modernization of university libraries in India. Rawal, Chandrakant N. Sardar Patel University, Gujarat, 2001. Guide- M K R Naidu. 849

Organization of information technology (IT) units of the university libraries in West Bengal with special reference to the Calcutta University Library System. Maiti, Arabinda. University of Calcutta, West Bengal, 2011. Guide- Biplab Chakrabarti. 850

Use of information technology in central university libraries in India. Venkata Ramana, P. Osmania University, Andhra Pradesh, 2002. Guide- V Chandrasekhara Rao. 851

Use of information technology in some selected university libraries of Bangladesh: An analytical study. Rahman, Md Anisur. University of Burdwan, Rajbati, Bardhaman, West Bengal, 2010. Guide- A K Bandyopadhyay. 852

Use of information technology in university libraries in India: A study. Patil, D B. Mangalore University, Karnataka, 2002. Guide- V G Talwar. 853

Entry No.

b. Engineering Libraries

Application of information and communication technology in the engineering college libraries in Tamil Nadu: A critical study. Muthusamy, C. Annamalai University, Tamil Nadu, 2004. Guide- S Ravi. 854

Application of information technology in selected engineering college libraries in Rayalaseema area of Andhra Pradesh: A study. Naidu, K Nataraja. Sri Krishnadevaraya University, Andhra Pradesh, 2012. Guide- P Rajarathnam Chetty. 855

Application of IT in the engineering college libraries with special reference to Vidharbha Region. Tirpude, C R. Rashtrasant Tukadoji Maharaj Nagpur University, Nagpur, Maharashtra, 2009. Guide- D R Deshpande. 856

Prospects of ICT in engineering college libraries of Haryana: A study. Praveen Kumar. Jiwaji University, Madhya Pradesh, 2010. Guide- J N Gautam. 857

Vartmaan viksit suchna prodyogiki paridrashya mein polytechnic granthalayaon ki prabhavsheelta: Uttar Pradesh ke polytechnic granthalayaon ki seva paddati ka adhyayan. Sharma, Brahmdutt. Dr B R Ambedkar University, Agra, Uttar Pradesh, 1999. Guide- V K Sharma. 858

c. Industries

Adoption and utilization of information and communication technologies in small scale industries in Tamil Nadu with special reference to Tirunevel District. Suriyanarayanan, S. Annamalai University, Tamil Nadu, 2001. Guide- M Nagarajan. 859

Utilization of information and communication technologies in small scale industries in Cuddalore District. Kavitha, S. Annamalai University, Tamil Nadu, 2011. Guide- M Nagarajan. 860

Entry No.

d. Medical Sciences

A study of the application of information technology in tribal medicine in Kerala with regard to forest medicinal plants. Asha, B (Ms). University of Calicut, Calicut, Kerala, 2004. Guide- Raju M Mathew. 861

A study on the application of information and communication technology in health care profession. Natarajan, N O. Annamalai University, Tamil Nadu, 2010. Guide- M Aravinthan. 862

Role of information communication technology in dental health awareness programme: A study. Manimozhi, R. Annamalai University, Tamil Nadu, 2009. Guide- M Suriya. 863

Study of the application of information technology in the treatment, preparation of medicine in ayurveda with special reference to Kerala. Nair G, Hemachandran. University of Calicut, Calicut, Kerala, 2005. Guide- Raju M Mathew. 864

e. Special Libraries

Application of information and communication technologies in special libraries in Kerala. Haneefa K, Mohamed. University of Calicut, Calicut, Kerala, 2005. Guide- M Bavakutty. 865

Application of information and communication technology in management institutions: A comparative study of libraries of management institutions of Orissa and IIM, Lucknow. Gouda, Prakash. Berhampur University, Orissa, 2011. Guide- R K Mahapatra. 866

Application of information technology in library and information centers in Chennai: A study. Kashi Rao, V. University of Madras, Tamil Nadu, 2002. Guide- B Ramesh Babu. 867

Entry No.

Application of information technology in major R & D libraries of Delhi: A study. Sharma, Pawan Kumar. Dr Hari Singh Gour Vishwavidyalaya, Sagar, Madhya Pradesh, 2008. Guide- K C Sahoo. 868

Application of information technology in science and technology libraries in Northern India: An evaluative study. Gaur, Rupesh. Kurukshetra University, Haryana, 2010. Guide- Dinesh K Gupta. 869

Application of IT in the special libraries of Bangladesh: Problems and prospects. Islam, Anwar ul. Sambalpur University, Orissa, 2008. Guide- K C Panda. 870

Information technology in libraries of science and technology (S & T) organisations: A comparative study. Shujat Husain. Bundelkhand University, Jhansi, Uttar Pradesh, 2001. Guide- M T M Khan. 871

Information technology vis-à-vis information handling in special libraries of Rajasthan with reference to information access and transfer: A critical study. Meena, Ramesh Lal. University of Rajasthan, Jaipur, Rajasthan, 2006. Guide- Dabir Singh. 872

Role of libraries and information centres in technology transfer for arid and semi arid regions of Rajasthan. Ojha, Dinesh Kumar. University of Rajasthan, Jaipur, Rajasthan, 1987. Guide- C D Sharma. 873

Status of social science libraries in India- a state-of-art with special reference to IT application in select social science libraries and information centres of India: A study. Kakkar, Anuradha. Bundelkhand University, Jhansi, Uttar Pradesh, 2005. Guide- M T M Khan. 874

Use of ICT in pharmacology and allied sciences libraries and information centers of Iran. Salami, Maryam. University of Pune, Maharashtra, 2010. Guide- S N Singh. 875

Entry No.

Use of information technology in select research libraries in Karnataka. Vijaya Kumar, N. Kuvempu University, Shimoga, Karnataka, 2005. Guide- B U Kannappanavar. 876

Use of IT in the libraries of IITs and IIMs in India: A comparative study. Maharana, Bulu. Sambalpur University, Orissa, 2009. Guide- K C Panda. 877

IT IMPACT ON LIBRARIES

a. Academic Libraries

Impact of emerging enabling technologies on academic library and information centers: Assessment of the state of the art. Hanchinal, Vidya Veeresh. Shivaji University, Kolhapur, Maharashtra, 2007. Guide- C R Karisiddappa. 878

Impact of information technology in self financing engineering college libraries in Chennai: A survey. Kanniyappan, E. Anna University, Chennai, Tamil Nadu, 2010. Guide- K Nithyanandam & R Raju. 879

Prospects of application of information technology in academic libraries in Assam. Sarma, Mukut. Gauhati University, Assam, 2008. Guide- Alaka Buragohain. 880

Research and information technology: A case study of the University Library King Fahad; University of Petroleum and Minerals, Dhahran, Saudi Arabia. Qureshi, Jamil Ahmad. Jamia Millia Islamia, Delhi, 1992. Guide- M Abu Baker & Herton. 881

b. Medical Libraries

Impact of information technology in the development of medical libraries and information centers in IMSU, Iran. Asefeh, Asemi. University of Pune, Maharashtra, 2006. Guide- N J Deshpande. 882

Entry No.

Impact of information technology in the functions of medical libraries of Northern India. Malvinder Kaur (Ms). University of Jammu, Jammu and Kashmir, 2007. Guide- I V Malhan. 883

Impact of information technology on biomedical information centres and libraries in India: A critical evaluation. Singh, S N. University of Rajasthan, Jaipur, Rajasthan, 2001. Guide- B S Garg. 884

c. Special Libraries

Impact of information technology on libraries of leading management institutes of India with special reference to Indian Institutes of Management. Sajjad, Zaufishan. University of Rajasthan, Jaipur, Rajasthan, 2010. Guide-Purnima Kaushik. 885

Impact of information technology on libraries of software industries in Karnataka: A study. Kattimani, Parashuram S. Gulbarga University, Karnataka, 2010. Guide- V T Kamble. 886

Impact of information technology on the libraries of institutes of management studies in Haryana: A study. Geeta (Ms). Kurukshetra University, Haryana, 2012. Guide-Ashu Shokeen. 887

Information transfer technology: Its impact on Indian libraries and information centres with special reference to scientific and technical libraries. Goyal, Bharat Kumar. University of Rajasthan, Jaipur, Rajasthan, 1998. Guide- S C Verma. 888

Use of information and communication technology by scientists and its impacts on special libraries in Tamil Nadu: A study. Ramesh Babu, V. Annamalai University, Tamil Nadu, 2006. Guide- M Nagarajan. 889

Entry No.

IT INFRASTRUCTURE FACILITIES

ICT facilities in autonomous Christian colleges in TN: A Study. Franklin. Bishop Heber College, Bharathidasan University, Tamil Nadu, 2012. Guide- S Ally Sornam. 890

Information communication technology (ICT) infrastructure facilities in self financing engineering college libraries in Tamil Nadu. Dhanavandan, S. Annamalai University, Tamil Nadu, 2011. Guide- S Mohamed Esmail. 891

Information infrastructure in the area of appropriate technology transfer for rural development: A micro study of the Mysore District. Achutha Rao, H R. Karnataka University, Karnataka, 1996. Guide- C R Karisiddappa. 892

Information support system in relation to infrastructural facilities and their utilization in Indian university libraries. Amar Nath. Panjab University, Chandigarh, Punjab, 2005. Guide- Ranjana Vohra. 893

Infrastructural problems of information technology application in Iranian university libraries. Davarpanah, Mohammad Raza. Panjab University, Chandigarh, Punjab, 2001. Guide- Ranjana Vohra. 894

KNOWLEDGE AUDIT

Developing a model of information audit for engineering college librarians. Pradhan, Amita Sachin. University of Pune, Maharashtra, 2012. Guide- N J Deshpande. 895

Knowledge audit: An analytical study. Balu, Gangadhar Mukhadal. Dr Babasaheb Ambedkar Marathwada University, Aurangabad, Maharashtra, 2011. Guide- Ashwini Anand Vaishnav. 896

Entry No.

KNOWLEDGE MANAGEMENT

An approach to knowledge management (KM) - problems and solutions for Indian situations: A conceptual / operational model for library KM. Datta, Sarmistha (Ms). University of Calcutta, West Bengal, 2006. Guide- Biplab Chakrabarti. 897

Problems and prospects of implementing knowledge management in central universities in India. Mohd Nazim. Banaras Hindu University, Uttar Pradesh, 2012. Guide- B Mukharjee. 898

LAW LIBRARIES

A study of organization, administration and services of supreme court library and MP high court libraries to propose a model judicial library system. Saraf, Sanjiv. Dr Hari Singh Gour Vishwavidyalaya, Sagar, Madhya Pradesh, 2000. Guide- H S Sengar. 899

Kanooni granthalayitva avam paschim Bharatna uttch nayalaya na granthalayao: Ek abhyas. Rawal, Ajaykumar Mukundbhai. Hemchandracharya North Gujarat University, Gujarat, 2012. Guide- M K Prajapati. 900

Organization and services of high court libraries in Northern India: An evaluative study. Khan, Kamran Ahmad. University of Kashmir, Jammu and Kashmir, 2011. Guide- S M Shafi. 901

Use of e resources among legal professionals of the Madras High Court: A study. Thanuskodi, S. Annamalai University, Tamil Nadu, 2010. Guide- M Aravinthan. 902

LIBRARY ADMINISTRATION AND MANAGEMENT

A study of administrative problems of university libraries in India with special reference to M P. Rajput, D S. Dr Hari Singh Gour Vishwavidyalaya, Sagar, Madhya Pradesh, 2000. Guide- B P Shrivastava. 903

Entry No.

A study of management and working of IIT Libraries in India. Agrawal, D K. Dr Hari Singh Gour Vishwavidyalaya, Sagar, Madhya Pradesh, 2001. Guide- B P Shrivastava. 904

A survey of organization, administration and utilization of the university libraries in Kerala, with special reference to Calicut University Library System. Veeran, M C K. University of Calicut, Calicut, Kerala, 2005. Guide- Rosamma Joseph. 905

Centralization and decentralization in university library system in Punjab and Chandigarh: with special to departmental libraries. Arora, Kanu (Ms). Panjab University, Chandigarh, Punjab, 2005. Guide- Ranjana Vohra. 906

Chattisgarh ke vishwavidyalayin pustakalayon ki sanrachna evam prabandham: Ek adhyayan. Yadav, Ram Gopal. Guru Ghasidas University, Chhattisgarh, 1998. Guide- J L Saini. 907

Condition and prospects of libraries of self financial institutions, affiliated to Dr Bhim Rao Ambedkar University, Agra. Anil Kumar. Dr B R Ambedkar University, Agra, Uttar Pradesh, 2002. Guide- B K Sharma. 908

Disaster planning prospectless recovery for libraries of national information in Delhi. Arora, Jyotsna. Jiwaji University, Madhya Pradesh, 2008. Guide- Rochana Shrivastava & J N Gautam. 909

Effects of participative decision making process on staff satisfaction of Indian university libraries and its impact on library services and patrons' satisfaction: A study using Merchant's Performance Measurement Model. Jaspal Singh. Panjab University, Chandigarh, Punjab, 1994. Guide- U K Tikku. 910

Entry No.

Gujarat rajayanan vishwavidyalaya granthalayaon ki antarika vibhagoneekaryasaranee ane sahyog: Uttar Gujarat vishwavidyalaya granthalayao sandarbhman. Patel, Yogesh Kumar. Hemchandracharya North Gujarat University, Gujarat, 2002. Guide- S M Charan. 911

Gujarat rajya vishwavidyalaya granthalaya privartan samasyao hetu prasashan Uttar Gujarat vishwavidyalaya granthalayao vishesh sandarbh. Patel, Ghanshyambhai Gandabhai. Hemchandracharya North Gujarat University, Gujarat, 2003. Guide- S M Charan. 912

Ikkisvin sadi mein pustakalaya prabandh, samasyayen evam samadhan: Chattisgarh ke vishwavidyalaya pustakalyon ke vishesh sandarbh mein. Verma, Karuna. Guru Ghasidas University, Chhattisgarh, 2006. Guide- U N Singh. 913

Library administration in Assam. Sharma, Ramesh Chandra. Gauhati University, Assam, 1990. Guide- V Venkata Rao. 914

Management and organizational pattern of university libraries in Madhya Pradesh. Sharma, C K. Pt Ravishankar University Raipur, Chhattisgarh, 1977. Guide- Madhusudan Dubey. 915

Management of college libraries with special references to Aurangabad Districts. Jagtap, Tara P (Ms). Dr Babasaheb Ambedkar Marathwada University, Aurangabad, Maharashtra, 1993. Guide- B B Pahurkar. 916

Management of distance education libraries: An analytical study. Pradeep Kumar. Panjab University, Chandigarh, Punjab, 1989. Guide- Ranjana Vohra. 917

Management of the libraries of degree colleges for minority communities in Andhra Pradesh: A study. Rani, Syamalamba(Ms). Andhra University, Andhra Pradesh, 2007. Guide- N David Livingstone. 918

Entry No.

Management of university libraries in West Bengal since Independence with special reference to collection development and manpower planning. Gupta, Anup Kumar. University of Calcutta, West Bengal, 1998. Guide- A Dasgupta. 919

Managerial role of chief academic librarians in India: A study using Mintzberg's Model. Goel, Preeti (Ms). Panjab University, Chandigarh, Punjab, 1992. Guide- H R Chopra. 920

Organization and administration of monastic libraries in ancient India. Barua, Pulin. University of Calcutta, West Bengal, 1985. Guide- Sukumar Sengupta. 921

Organization and management of police academy libraries of India: A critical study. Gupta, Meena. Guru Ghasidas University, Chhattisgarh, 2011. Guide- Brajesh Tiwari. 922

Organization of medical college libraries in Andhra Pradesh. Chengoni, Ravi Kumar. Osmania University, Andhra Pradesh, 2012. Guide- S Sudarshan Rao. 923

Organization of university libraries in Rayalaseema. Reddy, N Thulasirami. Sri Venkateswara University, Tirupati, Andhra Pradesh, 2000. Guide- N Guruswamy Naidu. 924

Perceptions of library management of central school libraries in A P: A study. Surya Prakasha Rao, K. Andhra University, Andhra Pradesh, 2011. Guide- P Bhaskara Rao. 925

Public libraries as community information centres in relation to e governance projects in India: A study with special reference to M P. Kala, Chitresh Kumar. Vikram University, Madhya Pradesh, 2010. Guide- S Kumar. 926

Sakshnik pustakalayo mei prabandh ki bhumika: M P ke vishwavidyalaya kei vishesh samdarbh mei. Mishra, Shiv Kant. Awadhesh Pratap Singh University, Madhya Pradesh, 2007. Guide- R K Sharma. 927

Entry No.

Strategic management of engineering college libraries in Karnataka: A study. Dinesh, K S. University of Mysore, Karnataka, 2008. Guide- Khaiser Nikam. 928

Study of organization, working and utility of the agricultural university libraries of Northern India. Prasher, Ram Gopal. Panjab University, Chandigarh, Punjab, 1985. Guide- J S Sharma. 929

The delegation of authority in university libraries with special reference to Andhra Pradesh: A study. Ramchander, M. Sri Krishnadevaraya University, Andhra Pradesh, 2004. Guide- P Kamaiah. 930

The planning function in management of university libraries in Andhra Pradesh. Chandran, D. Sri Venkateswara University, Tirupati, Andhra Pradesh, 1995. Guide- N Guruswamy Naidu. 931

University libraries in Iran: Their development, organization and services. Moarrefzadeh, Abdol Hamid. University of Delhi, Delhi, 2001. Guide- P B Mangla. 932

a. Comparative Studies

A comparative and critical study of the university library organizations in Gujarat State. Bhavsar, Vaishaliben L (Ms). Sardar Patel University, Gujarat, 2000. Guide- S M Charan. 933

A critical and comparative study of organization, administration and services of libraries of colleges of education in India with special reference to M P. Pandey, Prabhat Kumar. Dr Hari Singh Gour Vishwavidyalaya, Sagar, Madhya Pradesh, 2000. Guide- B P Shrivastava. 934

Working of libraries in multi-faculty colleges affiliated to Andhra University: A comparative study. Sudhakara Rao, U. Andhra University, Andhra Pradesh, 2000. Guide- P Soma Raju. 935

Entry No.

b. Evaluative Studies

Bhartiya rastriya granthalayaon ki vyavastha padhti: Ek alochnatmak adhyayan evam mulyankan. Kalpana Singh. Dr B R Ambedkar University, Agra, Uttar Pradesh, 2011. Guide- B K Sharma. 936

Management of university libraries in India with special reference to Orissa and West Bengal: A critical study. Rout, Ratnakar. University of Burdwan, Rajbati, Bardhaman, West Bengal, 1988. Guide- Pulin Behari Barua. 937

University management and engineering college libraries in Andhra Pradesh: An evaluative study. Krishna Murthy, M. Andhra University, Andhra Pradesh, 2001. Guide- P Soma Raju. 938

Uttar Pradesh ke sangrahalaya prachar aur jansambandh: Ek vivechanatmak adhyayan. Yadav, Hira Lal. Banaras Hindu University, Uttar Pradesh, 1990. Guide- S K Srivastava. 939

c. IT Impact

A study of impact of information technology on the effective management of library operations with special reference to Assam. Singh, Sanjay Kumar. Gauhati University, Assam, 2006. Guide- Alaka Buragohain. 940

Dynamics of change in the management of academic libraries - an approach towards management information system (MIS) development: A study. Singh, Satya Pal. Bundelkhand University, Jhansi, Uttar Pradesh, 2001. Guide- M T M Khan. 941

Impact of computerization on library management: A study of selected libraries of Chhattisgarh. Singh, Vinay Kumar. Guru Ghasidas University, Chhattisgarh, 2010. Guide- Brajesh Tiwari. 942

Entry No.

Impact of information technology on the provision and promotion of professional activities in the university libraries of Rajasthan: An analysis. Mehra, Vinay. Mohan Lal Sukhadia University, Udaipur, Rajasthan, 2010. Guide- L N Verma. 943

Management of technological change in library: A study of select agricultural institutions. Lalotra, Seema (Ms). University of Jammu, Jammu and Kashmir, 2012. Guide- Sangita Gupta. 944

The impact of information technology on management of libraries: A comparative study of selected libraries in Chhattisgarh. Sharma, Manish. Guru Ghasidas University, Chhattisgarh, 2010. Guide- Brajesh Tiwari. 945

The impact of IT on the organization and services of the libraries in Christian congregations and seminaries in Kerala. Muhammed Salih, T K. University of Calicut, Calicut, Kerala, 2005. Guide- Rosamma Joseph. 946

d. Personnel Problems

A study of personnel problems in library management with special reference to university libraries in West Bengal. Sain, Chittaranjan. University of Burdwan, Rajbati, Bardhaman, West Bengal, 1995. Guide- Pulin Behari Barua. 947

Personnel problem in public library management: A case study in zilla granthalaya samsthas of Andhra Pradesh. Rama Subbaiah, K. Sri Krishnadevaraya University, Andhra Pradesh, 2007. Guide- P Kamaiah. 948

Personnel problems in library management: A study of the university and post graduate centre libraries in the north eastern region of India. Singh, Naorem Giridhari. Manipur University, Manipur, 1992. Guide- M R Kumbhar. 949

Entry No.

Personnel problems in library management: A study of the university libraries in Andhra Pradesh, India. Kamaiah, P. Karnataka University, Karnataka, 1986. Guide- M R Kumbhar. 950

Problems and prospects of SC/ST professional staff in the university libraries in India. Kamble, V T. Gulbarga University, Karnataka, 1996. Guide- S R Gunjal. 951

Uttar Pradesh me rajya vishwavidyalaya granthalayaon ki karmik samasyayein: Tulnatmak vastustithi ka adhyayan. Sharma, Yogesh. Dr B R Ambedkar University, Agra, Uttar Pradesh, 2002. Guide- V K Sharma. 952

LIBRARY ASSOCIATIONS

Indian Libraries Association: A critical evaluation of its contribution to the library and information science profession in India. Vijaya Sudha, V (Ms). Andhra University, Andhra Pradesh, 1995. Guide- G V S L Narasimha Raju. 953

Library associations: Their role in the promotion of library and information science with special reference to India. Srivastava, Mukesh Kumar. University of Rajasthan, Jaipur, Rajasthan, 1990. Guide- S C Verma. 954

National library associations in India: Evaluation of their actuaries and achievements in changing environment. Pandey, Arpita. Dr B R Ambedkar University, Agra, Uttar Pradesh, 2004. Guide- U C Sharma. 955

Role played by ILA and IASLIC in the development of librarianship. Paradkar, Parag. Rashtrasant Tukadoji Maharaj Nagpur University, Nagpur, Maharashtra, 2010. Guide- P S G Kumar. 956

Entry No.

LIBRARY AUTOMATION

An enquiry into man computer interaction in library automation environment: An ergonomical study. Chaturvedi, Kiran (Ms). Banaras Hindu University, Uttar Pradesh, 2002. Guide- H N Prasad. 957

a. Academic *Libraries*

Automation and networking at Delhi base of academic library under D A V Management: A study. Khanna, Babita. Bundelkhand University, Jhansi, Uttar Pradesh, 2005. Guide- Pandey S K Sharma. 958

Automation in the libraries of Indian Institutes of Technology: A study. Khare, V P. Bundelkhand University, Jhansi, Uttar Pradesh, 2002. Guide- M T M Khan. 959

i. Academic Libraries - Colleges

A feasibility study of automation and networking of college libraries affiliated to Sri Venkateswara University and Sri Krishnadevaraya University, Andhra Pradesh, Tirupati. Anuradha, P (Ms). Sri Venkateswara University, Tirupati, Andhra Pradesh, 2003. Guide- V Pulla Reddy. 960

A study of library automation and networking in dental college libraries affiliated to Rajiv Gandhi University of Health Sciences, Bangalore. Kemdarne, Suryakant Balbhim. Tilak Maharashtra Vidyapeeth, Maharashtra, 2012. Guide- Namita B Khot. 961

Computerization of education college libraries in West Bengal. Mondal, Manik. Sambalpur University, Orissa, 2007. Guide- K C Panda. 962

Entry No.

ii. Academic Libraries - Universities

Computerization in university libraries of India: A critical study. Munshi, Amita (Ms). Rashtrasant Tukadoji Maharaj Nagpur University, Nagpur, Maharashtra, 2007. Guide- D Rajyalakshmi. 963

Computerization of university libraries in Gujarat State: A plan. Thaker, Urmila Ben A (Ms). Sardar Patel University, Gujarat, 2002. Guide- M K R Naidu. 964

Library automation in university libraries of Uttaranchal State: A study. Gayakwad, Kalpana(Ms). Dr Hari Singh Gour Vishwavidyalaya, Sagar, Madhya Pradesh, 2009. Guide- B P Shrivastava. 965

Professional attitude towards library computerization: A study of university and special libraries in Andhra Pradesh. Vijaya kumar, J. Andhra University, Andhra Pradesh, 1995. Guide- G V S L Narasimha Raju. 966

University library automation: An analytical study. Bansode, Sadanand Y. Dr Babasaheb Ambedkar Marathwada University, Aurangabad, Maharashtra, 2007. Guide- Ashwini Anand Vaishnav. 967

b. Problems and Prospects

Post automation problems: A study of libraries in Gujarat. Rathod, Meeta (Ms). M S University, Baroda, Gujarat, 2011. Guide- Shyama Rajaram. 968

Problems and prospects of automation in Indian libraries and information centers. Kumar, P S G. Gulbarga University, Karnataka, 1984. Guide- S R Gunjal. 969

Problems and prospects of automation in selected university libraries of Madhya Pradesh and Rajasthan: A comparative study. Tiwari, Brij Kishore. Dr Hari Singh Gour Vishwavidyalaya, Sagar, Madhya Pradesh, 2008. Guide- K C Sahoo. 970

Entry No.

Problems and prospects of automation in special libraries of M P: A study. Thapa, Neelam (Ms). Dr Hari Singh Gour Vishwavidyalaya, Sagar, Madhya Pradesh, 2005. Guide- K C Sahoo. 971

Problems and prospects of automation in the libraries of Bundelkhand Region: A study. Gautam, Vinod. Bundelkhand University, Jhansi, Uttar Pradesh, 2007. Guide- M T M Khan. 972

Problems and prospects of library automation in university libraries of Delhi, Haryana, Himachal Pradesh and Punjab: An analytical study. Prabha, Neelam. Sambalpur University, Orissa, 2003. Guide- K C Panda. 973

c. Special Libraries

An evaluative study of automation in selected special libraries in South India. Harinarayana, N S. University of Mysore, Karnataka, 1995. Guide- H A Khan. 974

Computer application in the libraries of Indian Council of Social Science Research Institutes: An evaluative study. Chokse, Shivsindhu. Vikram University, Madhya Pradesh, 2003. Guide- S Kumar. 975

Computer technology - its application in libraries and information centers in the Western India region: A status study. Abraham, Philips. University of Pune, Maharashtra, 2001. Guide- M B Konnur. 976

State of automation in major newspaper libraries in Delhi City: A study. Jose, Bino. Berhampur University, Orissa, 2005. Guide- K C Panda. 977

LIBRARY BUILDINGS

University library buildings in India. Rajwant Singh. University of Rajasthan, Jaipur, Rajasthan, 1981. Guide- S N Srivastava. 978

Entry No.

University library buildings in Iran: A critical study. Mogaddam, Hadi Sharif. Panjab University, Chandigarh, Punjab, 2002. Guide- H R Chopra. 979

a. Planning

Planning and design of university level library buildings. Misra, V N. Karnataka University, Karnataka, 1988. Guide- K S Deshpande. 980

Planning and utilization of space in university library buildings in Karnataka: An evaluation. Lalitamba, G. University of Mysore, Karnataka, 1993. Guide- H A Khan. 981

Space planning in the university libraries of Maharashtra in the changing information technology scenario: A study. Mohammad Biyle, Siray. Bundelkhand University, Jhansi, Uttar Pradesh, 2003. Guide- Shabahat Husain. 982

LIBRARY CATALOGUE

a. Use and User Studies

Evaluation of catalogue use: A study of Dr V S Krishna Library, Andhra University. Gandhi, T M K. Andhra University, Andhra Pradesh, 1993. Guide- K Siva Reddy. 983

Use of catalogue in university libraries in Karnataka: An evaluation study. Chandrashekara, M. University of Mysore, Karnataka, 2003. Guide- V G Talwar. 984

LIBRARY HISTORY

A study of organization and development of libraries and learning centre in ancient and medieval India. Gupta, Rakhi. Jiwaji University, Madhya Pradesh, 2009. Guide- Hemant Sharma. 985

History of libraries and librarianship in modern India, since 1850. Mishra, Jogesh. Ranchi University, Bihar, 1973. Guide- N A. 986

Entry No.

History of libraries in ancient India down to 1200 AD. Sahay, S. Tilka Manjhi Bhagalpur University, Bihar, 1977. Guide- A K Verma. 987

History of library development in Orissa since early times. Panda, Budhadev. Utkal University, Orissa, 1991. Guide- P K Mishra. 988

Libraries and librarianship during Muslim rule in India: An analytical study. Shaikh, Allaudin. Sambalpur University, Orissa, 1993. Guide- R K Rout. 989

Libraries and librarianship of ancient and medieval India from earliest times to 1850 AD. Dutta, Bimal Kumar. University of Calcutta, West Bengal, 1963. Guide- Nihar Ranjan Ray. 990

Libraries in medieval India. Prasad, Anirudh. Tilka Manjhi Bhagalpur University, Bihar, 1977. Guide- A K Verma. 991

Libraries in medieval India. Ahmad, Sardar. University of Patna, Bihar, 1996. Guide- Qeyamuddin Ahmad. 992

LIBRARY LEGISLATION

Bharatiya rajyon ke pustakalaya adhiniyamon ka adhyayan: Madhya Pradesh mein pustakalaya adhiniyam kee anivaryata evam bhavishya. Tiwari, Ramkirtan. Guru Ghasidas University, Chhattisgarh, 1999. Guide- Brajesh Tiwari. 993

Effect of library legislation on public library development in Andhra Pradesh. Narasimha Raju, G V S L. Andhra University, Andhra Pradesh, 1983. Guide- K Ramakrishna Rao. 994

Impact of Kerala Granthasala Sangham on the formulation of Kerala Public Libraries Act 1989. Nasirudheen, T P O. University of Calicut, Calicut, Kerala, 2004. Guide- M Bavakutty. 995

Entry No.

Impact of library legislation on public library development in Maharashtra. Balekar, R S. Rashtrasant Tukadoji Maharaj Nagpur University, Nagpur, Maharashtra, 1994. Guide- P S G Kumar. 996

Impact of public library legislation on the socio-economic development of West Bengal: A critical study of West Bengal Public Libraries Act, 1979. Konar, Satyangsusekhar. University of Burdwan, Rajbati, Bardhaman, West Bengal, 1990. Guide- Pulin Behari Barua. 997

Library legislation in India. Mittal, R L. Gauhati University, Assam, 1972. Guide- V Venkata Rao. 998

Madhya Pradesh mein grathalaya adhiniyam hetu prayas: Ek atihasik sinhavalokan evam bhavi sambhavnion. Mishra, Jagdish Kumar. Vikram University, Madhya Pradesh, 2010. Guide- Surendra Singh. 999

Model Public Libraries Act for N C T of Delhi: A study. Sharma, Priti. Bundelkhand University, Jhansi, Uttar Pradesh, 2006. Guide- Pandey S K Sharma. 1000

Public libraries legislation in Goa: A critical study. Naik, K Ashok. University of Pune, Maharashtra, 2008. Guide- M B Konnur. 1001

a. Comparative Studies

Comparative study of Public Libraries Acts of various states of India with special reference to the Gujarat Public Libraries Act and its impact on development of the public libraries in Gujarat. Jani, Kanakbala Arvindkumar. Hemchandracharya North Gujarat University, Gujarat, 2010. Guide- M K Prajapati. 1002

Public Libraries Acts in India: A comparative study. Shirke, Pravati (Ms). Rashtrasant Tukadoji Maharaj Nagpur University, Nagpur, Maharashtra, 2011. Guide- U P Nahle. 1003

Entry No.

Public Library Acts in India: A comparative study. Majumdar, Swapna (Ms). University of Calcutta, West Bengal, 2003. Guide- Pijush Kanti Mahapatra. 1004

LIBRARY MANAGEMENT SOFTWARE

A study of effective use of integrated library software in engineering college libraries in Karnataka. Mulla, K R. University of Mysore, Karnataka, 2009. Guide- M Chandrashekara. 1005

A study of library software used in health science college libraries in Maharashtra. Kude, N S. Rashtrasant Tukadoji Maharaj Nagpur University, Nagpur, Maharashtra, 2010. Guide- U P Nahle. 1006

An investigation of the effective use of integrated library software in Indian university libraries. Basavanyappa, K P. Karnataka University, Karnataka, 2007. Guide- S L Sangam. 1007

Application and implication of library software in college libraries affiliated to Nagpur University, Nagpur: A critical study. Lihitkar, R S. Rashtrasant Tukadoji Maharaj Nagpur University, Nagpur, Maharashtra, 2011. Guide- Ashwini P Paradkar. 1008

Application of library software in technical universities of U P with special reference to Roorkee and Pantnagar: A critical study. Vinod Kumar. Hemawati Nandan Bahuguna, Uttranchal, 2009. Guide- N A. 1009

Commercial library software in India: An evaluation of selected packages. Gopalakrishnan, S. University of Madras, Tamil Nadu, 2001. Guide- K S Raghavan. 1010

Critical study of library management software. Katkar, M. Swami Ramanand Teerth Marathwada University, Maharashtra, 2012. Guide- S P Satarkar. 1011

Entry No.

Feasibility of library software packages for library automation in higher educational institutes of Assam: A critical study. Barman, Hemanta Kumar. Gauhati University, Assam, 2007. Guide- Alaka Buragohain. 1012

Library software packages: Their availability, applicability and utility in S & T libraries. Dinesh Kumar. Kurukshetra University, Haryana, 1999. Guide- Ashu Shokeen. 1013

Marketing strategies of library management software (LMS) vendors in T N: A Study. Chitradhavaputhalvi. Bishop Heber College, Bharathidasan University, Tamil Nadu, 2012. Guide- S Ally Sornam. 1014

Status of library management software application in India: An evaluative study. Ansari, Mahtaab. Jiwaji University, Madhya Pradesh, 2009. Guide- J N Gautam. 1015

a. Open Sources

An analytical study of open source software (OSS) for college libraries. Sunil, M V. University of Mysore, Karnataka, 2012. Guide- N S Harinarayana. 1016

An evaluation of open source software for building digital libraries. Barve, Sunita. University of Pune, Maharashtra, 2009. Guide- A R D Prasad. 1017

b. Software Development

Design and development of software packages for information retrieval and SDI using micro-computer. Vyasamoorthy, P. Gulbarga University, Karnataka, 1990. Guide- S R Gunjal. 1018

Developing user friendly software for library and information centre management. Prasad, R C. Tilka Manjhi Bhagalpur University, Bihar, 1998. Guide- S Sahay. 1019

Entry No.

LIBRARY PERSONNEL

A study of the para professional staff their co-operation and conflict in university libraries in India based on survey of university of MP, Haryana and Delhi. Chaudhary, Poonam. Jiwaji University, Madhya Pradesh, 1995. Guide- S M Tripathi & S R Gupta. 1020

Personnel in the public library system in Tamil Nadu: A case study of District Central Library. Geetha, V (Ms). University of Madras, Tamil Nadu, 2005. Guide- B Ramesh Babu. 1021

Professionals in organizations: A study of trained librarians in university, public and special libraries. Jayaswal, P K. Jawaharlal Nehru University, Delhi, 1989. Guide- T K Oomen. 1022

Public librarians in Kenya: An analytical study. Samsung, Henry. Dr Babasaheb Ambedkar Marathwada University, Aurangabad, Maharashtra, 2010. Guide- Ashwini Anand Vaishnav. 1023

Recruitment of managerial personnel in public undertakings: A case study of Hindustan Steel Ltd. Indwar, R P. Ranchi University, Bihar, 1978. Guide- R N Trivedi. 1024

Solo librarians in Mumbai: A study. Powdwal, Sushama (Ms). SNDT Women's University, Mumbai, Maharashtra, 2007. Guide- Harsha Parekh. 1025

a. Attitude Towards IT

A study of the attitude of librarians in Kerala towards the use of information technology in library and information activities. Somanathan Nair, K P. University of Kerala, Kerala, 1991. Guide- C V Rajan Pillai. 1026

Entry No.

Attitude towards IT: A study of professionals in research and academic libraries in Hyderabad and Secundrabad. Nirikshna Babu, V. Andhra University, Andhra Pradesh, 2004. Guide- K Somasekhara Rao. 1027

Attitudes of academic and research library professionals towards information technology and its relationship with library and information science courses in India. Temjen, T. North East Hill University, Shillong, Meghalaya, 2003. Guide- Veena Saraf. 1028

Professional attitude of librarians towards IT: A survey of polytechnic libraries in Andhra Pradesh. Nageswara Rao, C. Andhra University, Andhra Pradesh, 2004. Guide- K Somasekhara Rao. 1029

Professional attitude of library personnel of technological libraries in India with special reference to Indian Institutes of Technology. Singh, Bibhuti Narayan. Banaras Hindu University, Uttar Pradesh, 1986. Guide- S N Singh. 1030

Professionals attitude towards library computerization: A study of university and college libraries in Vidharbha Region. Gabhane, D R. Rashtrasant Tukadoji Maharaj Nagpur University, Nagpur, Maharashtra, 2009. Guide- D R Deshpande. 1031

b. Career Advancement

A comparative study of career advancement of library professionals in university libraries in Punjab, Haryana, Madhya Pradesh and Uttar Pradesh. Singh, Dev Raj. University of Delhi, Delhi, 1991. Guide- Krishan Kumar. 1032

Aptitude test index: An analytical study of some theoretical and empirical issues. Tank, Kokila Tribhuvanbhai. Saurashtra University, Rajkot, Gujarat, 2011. Guide- Harsha Parekh. 1033

Entry No.

Construction and standardization of an aptitude test for the librarians of Gujarat State. Kantaria, Nileshkumar Mansukhal. Saurashtra University, Rajkot, Gujarat, 2010. Guide- M C Nandani. 1034

Personnel in public library system in Andhra Pradesh: A study of career development. Reddy, J Yadagiri. Osmania University, Andhra Pradesh, 1997. Guide- A A N Raju. 1035

Professional staff in the university libraries of A P: A study of their career growth and development. Yadagiri, S. Osmania University, Andhra Pradesh, 2005. Guide- S Sudarshan Rao. 1036

c. Conflict Management

A study of the professional staff concerning their co-operation and conflicts in university libraries in Thailand. Chalaragse, Pariot. University of Delhi, Delhi, 1996. Guide- S R Gupta. 1037

Conflict management in university libraries of Delhi. Abbas, Syed Mohd. University of Delhi, Delhi, 2004. Guide- S R Gupta. 1038

d. Development

Developing managerial skills for digital environment in engineering college libraries in Gujarat. Patel, Chandrakank K. Sardar Patel University, Gujarat, 2010. Guide- C N Rawal. 1039

Human resource development and work efficiency in university and special libraries: A comparative study. Anand, Vindu (Ms). Kurukshetra University, Haryana, 1997. Guide- J K Khanna. 1040

Human resource development in Indian Institutes of Technology (IITs) and National Institutes of Technology (NITs) libraries in Northern India: An evaluative study. Kadyan, Sanjiv. Kurukshetra University, Haryana, 2010. Guide- Ashu Shokeen. 1041

Entry No.

Human resource development in the institutions of higher education in Assam with automated libraries: A critical study. Barua, Niraj. Gauhati University, Assam, 2012. Guide- R K Barman. 1042

Human resource development in university libraries of Delhi with special reference to Delhi University; Jawaharlal Nehru University and Jamia Milia Islamia: A critical appraisal. Ansari, Mohd Murtaza Ali. Dr B R Ambedkar University, Agra, Uttar Pradesh, 2000. Guide- U C Sharma. 1043

Human resource development in university libraries of Punjab, Haryana, Himachal Pradesh and Chandigarh. Manjit Kaur (Ms). Guru Nanak Dev University, Amritsar, Punjab, 2008. Guide- Sewa Singh. 1044

Human resource development of library and information professionals in science and technology (S & T) libraries in Delhi. Taneja, Krishan Kumar. University of Delhi, Delhi, 2007. Guide- Shashi Prabha Singh. 1045

Human resource development of library personnel in the perspective of IT: A study of university libraries in Maharashtra. Wagh, Nilesh. Sant Gadge Baba Amravati University, Maharashtra, 2008. Guide- D Rajyalakshmi. 1046

Human resources development in information technology scenario: A study with special reference to university libraries in Uttar Pradesh. Yadav, Satish Kumar. North Maharashtra University, Jalgaon, Maharashtra, 2012. Guide- Shamkant J Deshmukh. 1047

Human resources development in university libraries of Andhra Pradesh: A study. Babu Rao, G. Andhra University, Andhra Pradesh, 1997. Guide- G V S L Narasimha Raju. 1048

Entry No.

Impact of academic libraries in development of human resource: With special reference to Arunachal Pradesh and Nagaland (colleges and universities) 1971 to1999. Yadav, Ramvir Singh. Gauhati University, Assam, 2008. Guide- Alaka Buragohain. 1049

Professional library manpower development for college libraries in Kerala in the IT environment. Mohana Kumar, T. University of Kerala, Kerala, 2008. Guide- C V Rajan Pillai. 1050

e. Interpersonal Relations

Human relations in librarianship: A study of interaction with the users. Rajaram, Shyama. University of Pune, Maharashtra, 2002. Guide- M B Konnur. 1051

Human relations in university libraries in Kerala. M Meena, V (Ms). University of Calicut, Calicut, Kerala, 2007. Guide- V Jalaja. 1052

Liaison relationship among librarians of Christian colleges in Tamil Nadu. Manalan. Bishop Heber College, Bharathidasan University, Tamil Nadu, 2011. Guide- B S Swaroop Rani. 1053

Library public relations: An analytical study of Karnataka Public Library System. Konnur, P V. Karnataka University, Karnataka, 1994. Guide- S L Sangam. 1054

Power strategies in interpersonal relationship among Indian library professionals. Hangsing, P. North East Hill University, Shillong, Meghalaya, 2003. Guide- Veena Saraf. 1055

f. IT Impact

An analysis of the impact of automation on library staff. Kurahatti, Basavaraj Tammanna. Mangalore University, Karnataka, 2003. Guide- A K Baradol. 1056

Entry No.

Impact of information communication technology (ICT) on professional development and educational needs of library professionals in the universities of Kerala. Mathew, Susan. Cochin University of Science & Technology, Kerala, 2011. Guide- M D Baby. 1057

Impact of information technology on information professionals after the World War II till 1990. Moity, Chandana. Vidyasagar University, West Bengal, 1993. Guide- M A Gopinath & Ashok Basu. 1058

Impact of information technology on library personnel: An analytical study of university and engineering college libraries in Tamil Nadu and Pondicherry. Nithyanandam, K. University of Madras, Tamil Nadu, 1996. Guide- Manorama Srinath. 1059

Impact of information technology on the skills and working of library personnel in selected libraries: A comparative study of Delhi and J & K. Wani, Manzoor Ahmad. University of Kashmir, Jammu and Kashmir, 2010. Guide- S M Shafi. 1060

Role of ICT in academic libraries and its impact on their professional staff: A study of selected central university libraries of North India. Agarwal, Anil. Mohan Lal Sukhadia University, Udaipur, Rajasthan, 2012. Guide- T D Tilwani. 1061

g. Job Performance Evaluation

A study of employee motivation and work performance among library professionals in colleges affiliated to Mangalore University. Shailarani, B (Ms). Mangalore University, Karnataka, 2012. Guide- K M Khan. 1062

Evaluation of professional competencies of the library professionals working in agricultural science university libraries in India and training needs analysis. Kumbar, Pravin Kumar Irappa. Kuvempu University, Shimoga, Karnataka, 2008. Guide- B U Kannappanavar. 1063

Entry No.

Factors related to employee performance: A study in library organization. Bhooshan Lal. Indian Institute of Technology, Delhi, Delhi, 1984. Guide- Purnima Mathur. 1064

Job performance evaluation of library personnel in university system: A study of libraries of Chandigarh, Himachal Pradesh, Haryana and Punjab. Sharma, Neelam. North East Hill University, Shillong, Meghalaya, 2007. Guide- A S Chandel. 1065

M P ke uchch shiksha vibhag me karyarat shekshnik evam granthalaya karmiyon ki yogyata, vetanman evam estar ka tulnatamak adhyayan. Mishra, Shiv Partap. Awadhesh Pratap Singh University, Madhya Pradesh, 2009. Guide- N R Satyanarayana. 1066

Motivation and performance level of library personnel in university libraries. Pradhan, Sanghamitra. M S University, Baroda, Gujarat, 2008. Guide- Kautilya Shukla. 1067

Motivation and performance of library professionals: A study with reference to the Karnataka State university libraries. Mallaiah, T Y. Mangalore University, Karnataka, 2005. Guide- M K Bhandi. 1068

Motivational dynamic and work efficiency in the university libraries. Khanna, Jugal Kishore. Panjab University, Chandigarh, Punjab, 1978. Guide- J S Sharma. 1069

Organizational commitment and work performance in academic and special libraries: A comparative study. Shokeen, Ashu. Jiwaji University, Madhya Pradesh, 1993. Guide- S M Tripathi. 1070

h. Job Satisfaction

An evaluative study of motivation and job satisfaction among non government college librarians in West Bengal. Jana, Lakshmi Kanta (Ms). Vidyasagar University, West Bengal, 2006. Guide- P K Panigrahi. 1071

Entry No.

Hemchandracharya North Gujarat University, Patan affiliated college librarians' job satisfaction. Patel, Krupa Kantilal. Hemchandracharya North Gujarat University, Gujarat, 2010. Guide- Gitaben S Patel. 1072

Job involvement and job satisfaction among professionals in university and college libraries in Delhi. Bajpai, Saroj Kumar. University of Delhi, Delhi, 1999. Guide- Krishan Kumar. 1073

Job satisfaction among library professionals in Karnataka State university libraries. Shivarai, Kumbhar Nagratna. Kuvempu University, Shimoga, Karnataka, 2009. Guide- B S Biradar. 1074

Job satisfaction among library professionals: A study of public. academic and special libraries in Andhra Pradesh. Ramanaiah, K. Karnataka University, Karnataka, 1999. Guide- S L Sangam. 1075

Job satisfaction among the library professionals in engineering and technological colleges in Rayalaseema Region of A P. Devendra Reddy, K. Sri Krishnadevaraya University, Andhra Pradesh, 2012. Guide- D Ravinder. 1076

Job satisfaction among the professional employees of the library: A study. Prasad, H N. Banaras Hindu University, Uttar Pradesh, 1991. Guide- S N Singh. 1077

Job satisfaction among the professionals working in the engineering and technology libraries in Karnataka: A study. Sirumath, S S. Bangalore University, Karnataka, 1997. Guide- P Sadashivmurthy. 1078

Job satisfaction amongst librarians working in engineering institutions in Maharashtra State. Hambarde, Govind. Swami Ramanand Teerth Marathwada University, Maharashtra, 2012. Guide- S P Satarkar. 1079

Entry No.

Job satisfaction and motivation among industrial library personnel of Orissa: A case study. Dash, Babita. Utkal University, Orissa, 2008. Guide- Pushpanjali Jena. 1080

Job satisfaction of library professional staff. Pulla Reddy, V. Sri Venkateswara University, Tirupati, Andhra Pradesh, 1992. Guide- Self Adjudication. 1081

Job satisfaction of LIS professionals in the academic libraries in Dakshina Kannada: A study. Gowda, Purushothama M. Mangalore University, Karnataka, 2005. Guide- D Shivalingaiah. 1082

Manpower management in university libraries in India: A survey of job satisfaction. Navalani, K. Karnataka University, Karnataka, 1985. Guide- K S Deshpande. 1083

Personality and job satisfaction of librarians of universities of Delhi and Rajasthan: A multivariate study. Garg, B S. University of Rajasthan, Jaipur, Rajasthan, 1986. Guide- Krishan Kumar. 1084

Status and job satisfaction of librarians in colleges and university libraries of Orissa: An evaluation in Indian context. Parida, Baman. Utkal University, Orissa, 1993. Guide- Manoranjan Mahapatra. 1085

i. Job Stress

Measuring job related stress among the library professionals of Orissa: An empirical investigation. Pradhan, Suchitra. Utkal University, Orissa, 2011. Guide- Pushpanjali Jena. 1086

Organizational role stress, work environment and job involvement among library professionals of colleges and universities in Delhi. Sharma, Lokesh. University of Rajasthan, Jaipur, Rajasthan, 1993. Guide- Usha Pawan. 1087

Entry No.

Organizational role stress: A comparative study of job involvement and job satisfaction of university libraries in libraries of agricultural and other universities of Punjab, Haryana and Himachal Pradesh. Ajit Singh. Punjabi University, Patiala, Punjab, 1997. Guide- K Navalani. 1088

Stress and burnout among library professionals in the universities and colleges of Punjab, Haryana and Chandigarh. Awasthi, Neeru (Ms). Panjab University, Chandigarh, Punjab, 2003. Guide- H R Chopra. 1089

Techno stress among library professionals of engineering colleges of Anna University , Tamil Nadu. Mahalakhsmi. Bishop Heber College, Bharathidasan University, Tamil Nadu, 2012. Guide- S Ally Sornam. 1090

j. Leadership Styles

Leadership behaviour of college librarians of Haryana: A study. Nirmala Devi. Dr B R Ambedkar University, Agra, Uttar Pradesh, 2004. Guide- U C Sharma. 1091

Leadership styles and their effectiveness in management of university libraries in India. Saraf, Veena. North East Hill University, Shillong, Meghalaya, 1995. Guide- J C Binwal. 1092

Leadership styles strategies for success: A study of
university libraries in the state of Haryana. Siwatch, Ajit 1093
Singh. Maharshi Dayanand University, Rohtak, Haryana, 2000. Guide- Daleep Singh & J K Khanna.

k. Management

A comparative study of staff management in different types of libraries in Manipur. Arambam, Hileima Devi. Manipur University, Manipur, 2012. Guide- Purnima Devi. 1094

Human resource management in libraries in Tamil Nadu: A case study. Parthiban, M. University of Madras, Tamil Nadu, 2012. Guide- Manorama Srinath. 1095

Entry No.

Madhya Pradesh ke viswavidyalaya granthalayao mein karmik prabandh. Sahu, Laxman Singh. Pt Ravishankar University Raipur, Chhattisgarh, 1994. Guide- A K Varma. 1096

Management of library personnel in the university libraries of J & K, Punjab, Haryana, Himachal Pradesh and Chandigarh. Dhar, Meghna (Ms). University of Jammu, Jammu and Kashmir, 2005. Guide- I V Malhan. 1097

Manpower utilization in the university libraries of Kerala: An evaluation. Vijaya Kumari, K P. University of Kerala, Kerala, 1991. Guide- K A Isaac. 1098

Personnel administration in university libraries in north eastern region with special reference to Assam. Barman, Rajani Kanta. Gauhati University, Assam, 1991. Guide- Niru Hazarika. 1099

Personnel management in college libraries under jurisdiction of Sholapur University, Sholapur. Vasudeorao, Adaskar Pravin. North Maharashtra University, Jalgaon, Maharashtra, 2012. Guide- Shamkant J Deshmukh. 1100

Personnel management in public libraries in Karnataka: A study. Venkatesh, A. Mangalore University, Karnataka, 2001. Guide- V G Talwar. 1101

Personnel management of university libraries: A study of organizational climate. Manorama Raju, O R. University of Madras, Tamil Nadu, 1989. Guide- P Gangadhara Rao. 1102

l. Management-Problems and Prospects

Problems and prospects of human resource management in university libraries in Karnataka and Tamil Nadu: A study. Sivasubramanian, V. University of Mysore, Karnataka, 2009. Guide- Khaiser Nikam. 1103

Entry No.

Professional manpower management in the public library system in Karnataka: Problems and prospects. Chandanagoudar, S H. Karnataka University, Karnataka, 1992. Guide- S R Ijari. 1104

m. Need Analysis

An analysis of the manpower in college libraries in U P and its impact on library services: A study. Suresh Chandra. Bundelkhand University, Jhansi, Uttar Pradesh, 2002. Guide- M T M Khan. 1105

Demands of the library and information science professionals in the industrial organizations in India in the present perspective: An evaluative study. Salam, S K Abul. University of Calcutta, West Bengal, 2012. Guide- Biplab Chakrabarti. 1106

Human resource development needs as depicted by the survey of automation of scientific and technical libraries in India. Sangita Rani (Ms). University of Jammu, Jammu and Kashmir, 1994. Guide- I V Malhan. 1107

Job dimensions and educational needs of university libraries in Rajasthan and Delhi. Gupta, Pawan Kumar. University of Rajasthan, Jaipur, Rajasthan, 1994. Guide- S N Srivastava. 1108

Madhya Pradesh ke viswavidyalaya granthalayao mein manav shakti niyojan evam karya vishleshan. Sahu, Harish Kumar. Pt Ravishankar University Raipur, Chhattisgarh, 2002. Guide- A K Varma. 1109

Manpower requirements of library and information science personnel in special libraries and library information science education with special reference to Kerala. Baby, M D (Ms). University of Calicut, Calicut, Kerala, 1994. Guide- M Bavakutty. 1110

Entry No.

Professional manpower needs in university and college libraries of Delhi, Punjab and Madhya Pradesh and their implication on library and information science education. Rewadikar, Shalini (Ms). University of Delhi, Delhi, 1984. Guide- P B Mangla. 1111

n. Planning

Human resource planning for academic libraries of Orissa: A study. Satpathy, Sunil Kumar. Sambalpur University, Orissa, 2002. Guide- R K Rout. 1112

Human resource planning in university libraries in Sri Lanka. Weersooriya, W A. University of Pune, Maharashtra, 2008. Guide- N J Deshpande. 1113

Manpower planning in university libraries in Andhra Pradesh. Muralikrishna, C. Sri Venkateswara University, Tirupati, Andhra Pradesh, 1998. Guide- N Guruswamy Naidu. 1114

o. Professional Image

An assessment of the image of the library and information professionals. Samyuktha, R (Ms). University of Madras, Tamil Nadu, 1995. Guide- K S Raghavan. 1115

Faculty perception of academic library professionals in the universities of Haryana: A study. Joshi, Manoj K. Kurukshetra University, Haryana, 2006. Guide- Ashu Shokeen. 1116

Image of library and information science professionals - perception and attitudes: A study in Vishakhapatnam. Satya Radhadevi, G (Ms). Andhra University, Andhra Pradesh, 2009. Guide- R S R Varalakshmi. 1117

p. Self Assessment

Self-assessment of professionals in special libraries in Hyderabad and Secunderabad - Andhra Pradesh (India): A study. Venkata Rao, K. Andhra University, Andhra Pradesh, 2009. Guide- K Somasekhara Rao. 1118

Entry No.

Self-assessment of professionals in university and special libraries in Secunderabad and Hyderabad - A P (India): A comparative study. Achamamba, V (Ms). Andhra University, Andhra Pradesh, 2012. Guide- K Somasekhara Rao. 1119

Self-assessment of professionals in university libraries: A study on university libraries of Andhra Pradesh (India). Prabhakar, G. Andhra University, Andhra Pradesh, 2007. Guide- K Somasekhara Rao. 1120

q. Skill Development

Development of professional skills of library information service personnel for special libraries in India: A survey and implication to library and information science schools. Kemparaju, T D. Bangalore University, Karnataka, 1993. Guide- M A Gopinath. 1121

Expertise and qualities required of special library staff in India. Marolia, Perin V. SNDT Women's University, Mumbai, Maharashtra, 1996. Guide- V A Kamath. 1122

Information literacy skills of LIS professionals in self financing engineering institutions in Tamil Nadu: A study. Hariharan, A. Annamalai University, Tamil Nadu, 2010. Guide- M Suriya. 1123

IT skills among LIS professionals of medical libraries in India and Iran: A comparative study. Farahi, Mina Tavassoli. University of Mysore, Karnataka, 2012. Guide- R T D Ramesh Gandhi. 1124

Provision and effectiveness of staff development programmes for professionals in university libraries in India with special reference to Bihar, Orissa and West Bengal. Arun Kumar. University of Delhi, Delhi, 2008. Guide- Shailendra Kumar & S R Gupta. 1125

Entry No.

Training and development facilities available for professional staff in university libraries in Karnataka: An analysis. Kalaivani, T. Bangalore University, Karnataka, 2001. Guide- Lalitha Aswath. 1126

r. Staffing Pattern

Staffing pattern in the college libraries: Case study of the Maharashtra. Satarkar, S P. Swami Ramanand Teerth Marathwada University, Maharashtra, 1999. Guide- S R Ganpule. 1127

Study of staffing pattern in university libraries of U P in the context of total quality management. Singh, Rajesh Kumar. Babasaheb Bhimrao Ambedkar University, Lucknow, Uttar Pradesh, 2008. Guide- K L Mahawar. 1128

s. Work Ethics

Work values of library professionals of universities of Punjab, Haryana and Himachal Pradesh. Kaur, Prit Pal. Punjabi University, Patiala, Punjab, 2005. Guide- Jagtar Singh. 1129

t. Work Life Quality

Job environment and life style of library professionals of Orissa: A socio-economic study. Nanda, Jhunu. Utkal University, Orissa, 2011. Guide- Baman Parida. 1130

Quality of work life among library professionals in the CSIR libraries in Northern India: A study. Verma, Shilpi (Ms). Babasaheb Bhimrao Ambedkar University, Lucknow, Uttar Pradesh, 2011. Guide- K L Mahawar. 1131

Quality of work life in the public libraries in Andhra Pradesh. Pratapa Reddy, B. Sri Krishnadevaraya University, Andhra Pradesh, 2005. Guide- P Rajarathnam Chetty. 1132

Entry No.

Quality of work life in the university libraries of Andhra Pradesh: A case study. Rajarathnam Chetty, Pakala. Sri Krishnadevaraya University, Andhra Pradesh, 1999. Guide- P Kamaiah. 1133

LIBRARY POLICIES

A study of state policy and administration of libraries of collegiate education in Andhra Pradesh. Narasimha Murthy, G. Osmania University, Andhra Pradesh, 1999. Guide- D B Eshwara Reddy. 1134

Evaluation of planning policies of central libraries in the Ministry of Higher Education and Culture Government (IRAN). Riahina, Nosrat (Ms). University of Delhi, Delhi, 2000. Guide- C P Vashishth. 1135

Personnel management policies and practices in the university libraries of Tamil Nadu: An analytical study. Lawrance mary, A. Annamalai University, Tamil Nadu, 2003. Guide- M Nagarajan. 1136

Role of university libraries in U P in the context of new education policy: A study with particular reference to formulating new standards. Sharma, Brij Kishor. Jiwaji University, Madhya Pradesh, 1993. Guide- S M Tripathi. 1137

University Grants Commission policies for university libraries: A study of Madhya Pradesh university libraries. Dubey, Priyadirshi. Jiwaji University, Madhya Pradesh, 2001. Guide- J N Gautam. 1138

Use of information resources in U N depository centres in South India: A study with special reference to the formulation of policies, procedures and plan of action in view of the growth and development of Internet. Raghunandana, M. Karnataka University, Karnataka, 2009. Guide- C R Karisiddappa. 1139

Entry No.

LIBRARY PROFESSION

Emerging trends in library and information science sector: Issues, challenges and dimensions. Byadgi, G G. Karnataka University, Karnataka, 2012. Guide- C R Karisiddappa. 1140

Libraries in the making: A study in professional socialization of library and information science students in North India. Neera (Ms). Panjab University, Chandigarh, Punjab, 1994. Guide- G C Bansal. 1141

Role of librarians in India from 12th century to 18th century: An analytical study. Roy, Dipak Kumar. University of Burdwan, Rajbati, Bardhaman, West Bengal, 1995. Guide- Aloke Mitra. 1142

a. Career Choice and Guidance

Conjoint analysis of users preferences for library science. Manathrachira, Varghese A. North East Hill University, Shillong, Meghalaya, 2003. Guide- J C Binwal. 1143

Librarianship as a profession: A study of socio-economic background and professional orientation of the libraries in Delhi. Chopra, Hans Raj. Panjab University, Chandigarh, Punjab, 1985. Guide- A K Anand & J S Sharma. 1144

b. LIS Conferences /Seminars

Changing trends in LISC: An analysis of theme of LIS conference /seminar, etc. Pendam, Gopal. Rashtrasant Tukadoji Maharaj Nagpur University, Nagpur, Maharashtra, 2011. Guide- K B Kale. 1145

LIBRARY RESOURCES AND SERVICES

A study of library resources and services with reference to users of colleges and universities of J & K State. Gupta, Urmil (Ms). University of Jammu, Jammu and Kashmir, 1999. Guide- I V Malhan. 1146

Entry No.

A survey of resources and services of polytechnic colleges libraries of Punjab and Chandigarh. Gurmeet Singh. Guru Nanak Dev University, Amritsar, Punjab, 2011. Guide- H S Chopra. 1147

A survey on the resources and services provided by the libraries of film and television training institutes in Maharashtra with special reference to WWII library, Mumbai and their utilization by interested students, professionals of film institute of Ori. Padhi, Satyajit. Berhampur University, Orissa, 2010. Guide- R K Mahapatra. 1148

Collection development, organization and services of central universities libraries U P. Khan, Abdul Mannan. Aligarh Muslim University, Uttar Pradesh, 2009. Guide- S M K Q Zaidi. 1149

Information sources, services and user survey of B Ed college libraries in Andhra Pradesh. Swarna Kumari, P (Ms). Andhra University, Andhra Pradesh, 2004. Guide- R S R Varalakshmi. 1150

Library resources and services for the blind in Orissa: An analytical study. Dani, Paresh Chandra. Dr Hari Singh Gour Vishwavidyalaya, Sagar, Madhya Pradesh, 2007. Guide- K C Sahoo. 1151

Resources and services of theological libraries of Goa and Coastal Karnataka. Anuradha, V (Ms). Mangalore University, Karnataka, 2012. Guide- A K Baradol. 1152

Study of the information sources and services of agricultural extension offices with special reference to technology transfer in agriculture. Ishwara Reddy, D B. Karnataka University, Karnataka, 1983. Guide- K S Deshpande. 1153

Entry No.

a. Evaluative Studies

Assessment of resources, facilities and services in libraries of forest institutions of India: A proposal for resource sharing and networking. Arjun Singh. University of Rajasthan, Jaipur, Rajasthan, 2003. Guide- S P Sood. 1154

Evaluation of library resources and services of the self financing engineering universities in Tamil Nadu: A study. Sarangapani, R. Annamalai University, Tamil Nadu, 2010. Guide- S Ravi. 1155

b. IT Environment

Changing information environment- the impact of technology innovation on resources and services of libraries: A study with special reference to institutes of management studies in Mumbai. Kanamadi, S T. Karnataka University, Karnataka, 2005. Guide- B D Kumbhar. 1156

Resources and services in the ICT environment: A comparative study of law college libraries of Orissa and National University of Judicial Science Library, Kolkata (West Bengal). Panda, Ajit Kumar. Berhampur University, Orissa, 2012. Guide- R K Mahapatra. 1157

c. Medical Colleges

A survey of collection and services of medical college libraries in U P: Prospects, problems and proposal for their modernization. Siddiqui, Mohammad Azeem. Babasaheb Bhimrao Ambedkar University, Lucknow, Uttar Pradesh, 2010. Guide- K L Mahawar. 1158

Medical college libraries in Punjab and Chandigarh: A study of their resources, services and users with a proposal for setting up a library and information network. Lamba, Navneet (Ms). Guru Nanak Dev University, Amritsar, Punjab, 2009. Guide- Amritpal Kaur. 1159

Entry No.

Reading material and services of allopathic, ayurvedic and homeopathic medical college libraries of Gujarat: The necessity and scope of new medical colleges at North Gujarat University. Trivedi, Mayank Kumar. Hemchandracharya North Gujarat University, Gujarat, 2005. Guide- S M Charan. 1160

Resources and services of medical college libraries of A P and Orissa. Pradhan, Purushottam. Berhampur University, Orissa, 2005. Guide- K C Panda. 1161

d. Use and User Studies

A survey of users' attitude towards the resources and services of three university libraries in Rajasthan. Kwatra, P S. University of Rajasthan, Jaipur, Rajasthan, 1988. Guide- Pushpa Dhyani. 1162

Study of users' attitude towards the resources and services of university libraries in Karnataka. Kumbar, Mallinath. Karnataka University, Karnataka, 1995. Guide- S L Sangam. 1163

Use of information resources and services by health professionals: A study of Manipal Academy of Higher Education. Bhat, Shivanand. University of Mysore, Karnataka, 2002. Guide- M A Gopinath. 1164

Use of resources and services in the university libraries of Orissa: An evaluation. Choudhury, Bijaya Kumar. Utkal University, Orissa, 1993. Guide- K Siva Reddy. 1165

Utilization of information resources and services of rural development institutions in Andhra Pradesh. Padmaja, M. University of Mysore, Karnataka, 2010. Guide- Mallinath Kumbar. 1166

LIBRARY SERVICES

A critical study of public library services in Madhya Pradesh: Model plan for resource sharing and networking. Sharma, Ramakant. Guru Ghasidas University, Chhattisgarh, 1999. Guide- Brajesh Tiwari. 1167

Entry No.

A study of knowledge, skills and attitude of users to services in academic libraries in Tehran (Iran). Tajdaran, Mansour. University of Pune, Maharashtra, 2006. Guide- S N Singh. 1168

A study of library services for disabled persons in India with special reference to visually handicapped in Madhya Pradesh. Bajpai, Poonam (Ms). Maharani Laxmi Bai Govt. College of Excellence, Jiwaji University, Madhya Pradesh, 2010. Guide- Neerja Verma. 1169

An in-depth evaluation of development of libraries and information services in the United Arab Emirates (UAE) after its independence: Possibilities, problems and current boundaries of building up an effective library and information service system. Kalburgi, L B. Karnataka University, Karnataka, 1992. Guide- C R Karisiddappa. 1170

Bharatvarsh me gramin pustkalaya seva: Madhya Pradesh ke vishes sandarbh me ek alochnatmak adhyayan. Bajpai, Raghubansh. Mahatma Gandhi Chitrakoot Gramodaya Vishwavidyalaya, Satna, Madhya Pradesh, 1998. Guide- H S Sengar. 1171

Circulation services in the university libraries in Karnataka. Kumbar, S S. Mangalore University, Karnataka, 1997. Guide- A K Baradol. 1172

College library services in Marathwada. Ghumre, Shivshankar. Dr Babasaheb Ambedkar Marathwada University, Aurangabad, Maharashtra, 2012. Guide- D K Veer. 1173

Critical study of the organization and administration of library services in Kamrup District and its impact on adult education. Nath, Premada Bora. Gauhati University, Assam, 1994. Guide- L Das. 1174

Entry No.

Gwalior and Chambal sambagh me shastriya mahavidhalya ke granthalya ke saghtan pravandan and sevaon mein vivechanatmak study. Gautam, Devendra Kumar. Jiwaji University, Madhya Pradesh, 2001. Guide- Hemant Sharma. 1175

Higher secondary school libraries in Jammu and Kashmir: Operations and services. Sofi, Zahoor Ahmad. University of Kashmir, Jammu and Kashmir, 2011. Guide- S M Shafi. 1176

Libraries and library services in Thanjavur District. Padmanaban. T. University of Madras, Tamil Nadu, 1998. Guide- K S Raghavan. 1177

Library and information utility centers in the context of library services in universities of Karnataka State. Ramesha. Karnataka University, Karnataka, 2003. Guide- B D Kumbhar. 1178

Library facilities and services of tirumala tirupati devasthanamse educational institutions in information technology environment: A survey. Srinivasulu, R. Sri Venkateswara University, Tirupati, Andhra Pradesh, 2010. Guide- D Chandran. 1179

Library facilities in colleges in Karnataka. Shivalingaiah, D. Mangalore University, Karnataka, 1995. Guide- V G Talwar. 1180

Library services in financial institutes of Assam. Hazarika, Anu. Gauhati University, Assam, 2009. Guide- Narendra Lahkar. 1181

Library services to the hospitalised patients in Chandigarh and Delhi: A study and proposed model. Harjeet Singh. Panjab University, Chandigarh, Punjab, 2008. Guide- H R Chopra. 1182

Library services to the prisoners in Himachal Pradesh: A study and proposed model. Anupama (Ms). Panjab University, Chandigarh, Punjab, 2002. Guide- H R Chopra. 1183

Entry No.

Library services to the visually challenged persons in Northern India: A study. Preeti Sharda (Ms). Panjab University, Chandigarh, Punjab, 2005. Guide- H R Chopra. 1184

Library support services to distance learners in India. Anjaiah, M. Osmania University, Andhra Pradesh, 2006. Guide- S Sudarshan Rao. 1185

Nature of public library services in relation to users and their needs: A study of public libraries in Chikmagalur District (Karnataka). Ramakrishnagowda, K C. University of Mysore, Karnataka, 1996. Guide- H A Khan. 1186

Networked services of NIT libraries in India: An analytical study. Srinivas Rao, Y. Sambalpur University, Orissa, 2010. Guide- B K Choudhury. 1187

Promoting library services in colleges: Potentials and barriers. Tikam, Madhuri (Ms). SNDT Women's University, Mumbai, Maharashtra, 2008. Guide- Bharati Sen. 1188

Public libraries services and community analysis in an urban setting: A study of the District Central Library of Vishakhapatnam and its communities. Satyanarayana, M. Andhra University, Andhra Pradesh, 1994. Guide- K Sarada. 1189

Public library facilities and services for children in Karnataka: A study of their provision and evolution. Venkatesh, Y. University of Mysore, Karnataka, 2002. Guide- V G Talwar. 1190

Public library services in North East India. Sarkar, Pranab. Gauhati University, Assam, 2011. Guide- R K Barman. 1191

Public library system and services in Tamil Nadu: A case study of users of urban and rural libraries. Ashok Kumar, S K. University of Madras, Tamil Nadu, 2006. Guide- B Ramesh Babu. 1192

Entry No.

Readers' services in university libraries of North India. Gautam, Anil Kumar. University of Rajasthan, Jaipur, Rajasthan, 1995. Guide- S C Verma. 1193

Role of public library as community centres and their services to society in Vidharbha Region of Maharashtra State. Tankar, Amit. Sant Gadge Baba Amravati University, Maharashtra, 2007. Guide- D Rajyalakshmi. 1194

Role of UNESCO in the development of library and information services in India. Bar, Narendra Kumar. University of Burdwan, Rajbati, Bardhaman, West Bengal, 2006. Guide- Pulin Behari Barua. 1195

Rural library services and community analysis: A study of an Andhra village. Sarada, K. Andhra University, Andhra Pradesh, 1984. Guide- K Siva Reddy. 1196

Study of libraries and their services of the rehabilitation institutes for the disabled in Gujarat and Maharashtra State. Fulmali, S R (Ms). Rashtrasant Tukadoji Maharaj Nagpur University, Nagpur, Maharashtra, 2006. Guide- D Rajyalakshmi. 1197

Study of the readers services in the university libraries of Bangladesh with special reference to the services in the Dhaka and the Rajsahi university libraries to suggest a model for university library system of Bangladesh. Mostafa, Md Golam. University of Burdwan, Rajbati, Bardhaman, West Bengal, 2004. Guide- A K Bandyopadhyay. 1198

The status of library and information facilities and services in engineering colleges of Andhra Pradesh: An evaluative study. Nagaratnamani, G. Andhra University, Andhra Pradesh, 2009. Guide- C Sasikala. 1199

Entry No.

University libraries in North East India: A comparative study of their services with suggestion for their networking. Prodhani, M A. Jiwaji University, Madhya Pradesh, 1997. Guide- J N Gautam. 1200

University library ki prabhav shilta Madhya Pradesh ke university libraries ki seva prapti ki ek study. Acharya, Shailesh. Jiwaji University, Madhya Pradesh, 1994. Guide- S M Tripathi & H S Sengar. 1201

User services in the university libraries of Madhya Pradesh: A survey. Mahawar, K L. University of Rajasthan, Jaipur, Rajasthan, 1997. Guide- S P Sood. 1202

Uttar Pradesh ke viswavidyalaya ke granthaliya ke sansadhanon ki sevaon ka vishleshnatmak adhyayan. Vajpai, Rajkumar. Jiwaji University, Madhya Pradesh, 2006. Guide- Hemant Sharma. 1203

Viswavidyalaya pustkalaya mei sevaon ka prabandhan Aligadh Muslim Viswavidyalaya evam Luknow Viswavidyalaya kei sandarbh mei. Sharma, Kushum Lata. Awadhesh Pratap Singh University, Madhya Pradesh, 2008. Guide- R K Sharma. 1204

a. Evaluative Studies

An assessment of public library systems and services in Darjeeling District of West Bengal from information marketing point of view. Pradhan, Debasish. University of Burdwan, Rajbati, Bardhaman, West Bengal, 2009. Guide- Tridib Tripathi. 1205

Evaluation of library services of non agricultural university libraries in Maharashtra with special reference to Jayakar Library, University of Pune. Patil, S K. University of Pune, Maharashtra, 1999. Guide- S G Mahajan. 1206

Entry No.

Madhya Pradesh ke shiksha mahavidyalayon me granthalaya sevaen: Ek samikshatmk adhyayan. Patidar, Amit Kumar. Vikram University, Madhya Pradesh, 2003. Guide- G D Bhargava. 1207

Public library services in different continents of world: An evaluative study, suggesting a suitable model in West Bengal. Samanta, Ranjan. Jadhavpur University, West Bengal, 2012. Guide- Udayan Bhattacharya. 1208

b. IT Application

A critical study of library services and their modernization in university libraries of Madhya Pradesh. Sahu, Mukesh Kumar. Dr Hari Singh Gour Vishwavidyalaya, Sagar, Madhya Pradesh, 2011. Guide- B P Shrivastava. 1209

Application of information technology in the services of libraries of the Indian Council of Agricultural Research Institutions: A study. Pratap Singh. Dr B R Ambedkar University, Agra, Uttar Pradesh, 1999. Guide- U C Sharma. 1210

Application of information technology in university library services: A case study of Mumbai University and SNDT Women's University. Dash, Rajlaxmi. Berhampur University, Orissa, 2011. Guide- R K Mahapatra. 1211

ICT facilities and services in libraries of medical education institutions in Tamil Nadu: An analytical study. Ravi Sankar, G. University of Madras, Tamil Nadu, 2009. Guide- B Ramesh Babu. 1212

c. IT Environment

An assessment of the services of college libraries in the context of changing information scenario with special reference to Mizoram. Hnamte, Lalbiaksanga. Mizoram University, Mizoram, 2011. Guide- R N Mishra. 1213

Entry No.

Effectiveness of library services and user satisfaction in the changing information technology environment. Sharma, T Ramabhadra. Osmania University, Andhra Pradesh, 2009. Guide- S Sudarshan Rao. 1214

d. IT Impact

Impact of information technology on library services in private institutions of Western U P importing professional education: An evaluative study. Sharma, Sudeep. Bundelkhand University, Jhansi, Uttar Pradesh, 2009. Guide- M T M Khan. 1215

Impact of information technology on the provision and promotion of university library services in developing countries: A comparative study of university libraries in Kenya and Karnataka (India). Nyamboga, Constantine M. Bangalore University, Karnataka, 2004. Guide- T D Kemparaju. 1216

Madhya Pradesh ke mahavidyalayin evam granthalya seva mei suchna prodhyogiki ka parbhav: Ek mulyankan. Mishra, Bhartendu. Awadhesh Pratap Singh University, Madhya Pradesh, 2012. Guide- R K Sharma. 1217

LIBRARY STANDARDS

Benchmarking. Muralidher, S. Annamalai University, Tamil Nadu, 2004. Guide- M Suriya. 1218

Decision support system for the implementation of ISO 9001:2000 Standard in university library. Thulasi Kavitha Yadav, S (Ms). University of Madras, Tamil Nadu, 2003. Guide- Manorama Srinath. 1219

Diffusion and utilization of standards and specifications in defense research development organizations in Bangalore. Divyananda, K. Karnataka University, Karnataka, 1997. Guide- S L Sangam. 1220

Entry No.

Quality management approaches in library and information science sector in India with particular reference to ISO 9000 standards and T Q M concepts. Verma, Ramesh Kumar. Kurukshetra University, Haryana, 2002. Guide- Ashu Shokeen. 1221

Use of standards in the medical and dental college libraries in Karnataka. Ravichandra. Mangalore University, Karnataka, 2010. Guide- A K Baradol. 1222

LIBRARY STUDIES

Library as a social system. Mohal, Snehalata M (Ms). Dr Babasaheb Ambedkar Marathwada University, Aurangabad, Maharashtra, 1997. Guide- B L Joshi. 1223

Library facilities, information seeking and the development of curricular activities in secondary schools with special reference to Ganjam District of Orissa. Das, K C. Berhampur University, Orissa, 1992. Guide- Manoranjan Mahapatra. 1224

Prak-palashi banglaye janasamaje siksha-o-granth-agar byabasthar provab (1700 A D-1757 A D). Bose, Sreekanta. University of Burdwan, Rajbati, Bardhaman, West Bengal, 2003. Guide- Subal Chandra Biswas. 1225

Study of growth, development and use of National Library, Kolkata and Khuda Baksh Library, Patna. Akhtar Husain. Aligarh Muslim University, Uttar Pradesh, 2011. Guide- Nishat Fatima. 1226

a. Academic Libraries

An evaluative study of school libraries in and around Kolkata. Mukhopadhyay, Lopita (Ms). University of Calcutta, West Bengal, 2010. Guide- Subir K Sen. 1227

Entry No.

Autonomous college libraries in Andhra Pradesh, India: A study. Prasada Rao, G A. Andhra University, Andhra Pradesh, 2004. Guide- K Somasekhara Rao. 1228

Autonomous college libraries in India: An assessment of the impact of autonomous status on the development of college libraries. Singh, Satya Prakash. University of Lucknow, Uttar Pradesh, 2003. Guide- N R Satyanarayana. 1229

College libraries in M P: An evaluation. Goyal, Sheila. Awadhesh Pratap Singh University, Madhya Pradesh, 2001. Guide- N R Satyanarayana. 1230

College libraries in Punjab: A statistical analysis of their problems. Jasmer Singh. Guru Nanak Dev University, Amritsar, Punjab, 1990. Guide- Sewa Singh. 1231

Comparative study of libraries of Dr Ambedkar chairs in India with special reference to Delhi, Madhya Pradesh, Maharashtra, Uttar Pradesh and Uttaranchal. Chouhan, Sunita. Vikram University, Madhya Pradesh, 2009. Guide- Sonal Singh. 1232

Deviance in academic libraries: A sociological study with reference to Assam. Nabajyoti Das. Gauhati University, Assam, 2009. Guide- N N Sharma. 1233

Higher education libraries in the state of Tripura: An analytical study. Chakraborty, H S. Andhra University, Andhra Pradesh, 1999. Guide- P Soma Raju. 1234

Junior university libraries in Andhra Pradesh: Emergence, services, trends and problems. Somasekhara Rao, K. Andhra University, Andhra Pradesh, 1993. Guide- K Siva Reddy. 1235

Libraries in senior secondary schools: A critical study in Madhya Pradesh. Singh, Om Vir. Jiwaji University, Madhya Pradesh, 2003. Guide- Hemant Sharma. 1236

Entry No.

Organization pattern of autonomous college libraries in M P with a view to formulate a model. Khan, Mohd Akil. Dr Hari Singh Gour Vishwavidyalaya, Sagar, Madhya Pradesh, 2000. Guide- B P Shrivastava. 1237

Problems and prospects of college libraries affiliated to Mysore University. Nalini, K R. University of Mysore, Karnataka, 1995. Guide- B Nagappa. 1238

Status of libraries of higher secondary school with special reference to Vidharbha Region. Bhimanwar, V K. Rashtrasant Tukadoji Maharaj Nagpur University, Nagpur, Maharashtra, 2011. Guide- P Dakhole. 1239

The libraries system of Andhra Pradesh open universities: Evaluation of library facilities, resources and services. Raju, A P S V V S N L N. Andhra University, Andhra Pradesh, 1994. Guide- B Vijayalakshmi. 1240

The status of academic libraries in India: A survey. Tiwari, Rajani (Ms). Banaras Hindu University, Uttar Pradesh, 2001. Guide- H N Prasad. 1241

University libraries in Gujarat. Shukla, K. Vikram University, Madhya Pradesh, 1990. Guide- A Tejomurty. 1242

University libraries in Madhya Pradesh. Tejomurty, A. University of Rajasthan, Jaipur, Rajasthan, 1984. Guide- S C Verma. 1243

University libraries in Rajasthan: Their development and management. Sood, S P. University of Rajasthan, Jaipur, Rajasthan, 1993. Guide- S N Srivastava. 1244

Uttar Gujarat vishwavidyalaya granthasayanu snatak ane anusnatak shikshanam yogadana. Patel, C M. Hemchandracharya North Gujarat University, Gujarat, 2002. Guide- S M Charan. 1245

Entry No.

b. Engineering Libraries

A study of the libraries of government polytechnics in Andhra Pradesh. David Livingstone, N. Andhra University, Andhra Pradesh, 1995. Guide- B Vijayalakshmi. 1246

Indian Institute of Technology (IIT) libraries in India: An evaluative study of their growth, development, and services. Singh, Shashi Prabha (Ms). University of Delhi, Delhi, 1993. Guide- J L Sardana. 1247

The IIT libraries: A study of their resources, services, and users, with proposal for setting up a library and information network. Bhaskara Rao, P. Andhra University, Andhra Pradesh, 1993. Guide- B Vijayalakshmi. 1248

Uttar Pradesh ke polytechnical colleges mein pustakalayo: A vayvharik adhyayan. Tripathi, Manish. Jiwaji University, Madhya Pradesh, 2009. Guide- Hemant Sharma & B K Sharma. 1249

c. National Libraries

National Library of Bangladesh: Retrospect and prospect. Nahar, Nurun. University of Kerala, Kerala, 1985. Guide- K A Isaac. 1250

d. Public Libraries

British library experience in India: A retrospective and prospective analysis. Khan, K M. University of Mysore, Karnataka, 2003. Guide- N B Pangannaya. 1251

Functioning of regional public libraries in Andhra Pradesh: A study. Chandrasekhar Rao, L V. Andhra University, Andhra Pradesh, 2006. Guide- P Bhaskara Rao. 1252

Entry No.

Organization, administration, resources, services and utilization of the public libraries in Malabar: An evaluative study. S Sudha, A (Ms). University of Calicut, Calicut, Kerala, 2008. Guide- Rosamma Joseph. 1253

Present status and future needs of public libraries in Bangladesh. Ullah, Mohd Ahsan. University of Pune, Maharashtra, 2007. Guide- N J Deshpande. 1254

Problems and prospects of public libraries in four library law states in India. Khan, H A. Karnataka University, Karnataka, 1985. Guide- K S Deshpande. 1255

Rural libraries in Madhya Pradesh: An evaluation. Jayant, Jaswant Singh. Maharani Laxmi Bai Govt. College of Excellence, Jiwaji University, Madhya Pradesh, 2011. Guide- Arvind Kumar Sharma. 1256

Status of state central libraries in India: An analytical study. Ramasamy, R. Sambalpur University, Orissa, 2002. Guide- K C Panda. 1257

e. Special Libraries

A critical study of law college libraries in the region of Marathwada and Vidarbha. Sulsule, Shobha Rajabhau (Ms). Dr Babasaheb Ambedkar Marathwada University, Aurangabad, Maharashtra, 2010. Guide- Shakuntala S Lomte. 1258

A survey of medical college libraries in Andhra Pradesh, India. Srinivasulu, P. Sri Venkateswara University, Tirupati, Andhra Pradesh, 2009. Guide- V Pulla Reddy. 1259

Aided and unaided physical education colleges in Maharashtra: A study. Jahulkar, S. Rashtrasant Tukadoji Maharaj Nagpur University, Nagpur, Maharashtra, 2012. Guide- P Dakhole. 1260

Entry No.

Anaupcharik shiksha ke vikas mein granthalayaon kee bhoomika: Chhattisgarh ke vishesh sandarbh mein. Sahu, Shaila. Guru Ghasidas University, Chhattisgarh, 2004. Guide- J L Saini. 1261

Assessment of library and information resources, facilities and services in the management schools in India to ascertain the feasibilities of their coordination and standardization for effective resource sharing and networking. Raina, R L. Dr Hari Singh Gour Vishwavidyalaya, Sagar, Madhya Pradesh, 1995. Guide- R G Prasher. 1262

Industrial libraries of Andhra Pradesh: A study. Sasikala, C (Ms). Andhra University, Andhra Pradesh, 1992. Guide- K Siva Reddy. 1263

Industrial libraries: Case study of Maharashtra. Aghav, Udhav R. Swami Ramanand Teerth Marathwada University, Maharashtra, 2007. Guide- S P Satarkar. 1264

Madhya Pardesh ke kendriya karagar ke garnthalyon ki istithi evam vikas: Ek adhyayan. Shrivastava, Suchita. Awadhesh Pratap Singh University, Madhya Pradesh, 2012. Guide- R K Sharma. 1265

Maharashtril krushi mahavidyalayin granthalayachi vadh vikas ek sarvekshan. Chone, Sachin Narayan. Dr Babasaheb Ambedkar Marathwada University, Aurangabad, Maharashtra, 2012. Guide- Shakuntala S Lomte. 1266

Maharastratil Krushi Vidyapith ek sarveskhan. Dahifale, Vikram Uttamrao. Dr Babasaheb Ambedkar Marathwada University, Aurangabad, Maharashtra, 2006. Guide- S M Mohal. 1267

Medical college libraries in West Bengal: Present status and a plan for future development. Md Musleuddin. University of Burdwan, Rajbati, Bardhaman, West Bengal, 2010. Guide- Tridib Tripathi. 1268

Entry No.

Medical college libraries of Andhra Pradesh: A study. Varalakshmi, R S R (Ms). Andhra University, Andhra Pradesh, 1991. Guide- K Siva Reddy. 1269

Medical college libraries of Orissa: A comparative study. Routray, B (Ms). Utkal University, Orissa, 2006. Guide- Pushpanjali Jena. 1270

Music libraries in India. Rajendra, Aparna. University of Pune, Maharashtra, 2008. Guide- M B Konnur. 1271

Role of special libraries in Assam and its socio-economic impact on societies: A study. Bharali, Bhrigu Ram. Gauhati University, Assam, 2000. Guide- N N Sharma. 1272

Status of medical college libraries in Karnataka and Maharashtra: A comparative study. Vasantha Kumar, M. Shivaji University, Kolhapur, Maharashtra, 2011. Guide- P V Konnur. 1273

The role of information and knowledge centers in comprehensive development of Kachchh: A study. Mehta, Varsha Bhagvatidas. Kachchh University, Gujarat, 2012. Guide- M K Prajapati. 1274

The role of special libraries in the field of art and culture in India with special reference to national academics. Choudhury, Ashok Kumar. Utkal University, Orissa, 2003. Guide- Baman Parida. 1275

LIS EDUCATION

A study of library and information science education in Indian universities with a view to formulate norms in M P. Shrivastava, B P. Dr Hari Singh Gour Vishwavidyalaya, Sagar, Madhya Pradesh, 1992. Guide- H S Sengar. 1276

Entry No.

Analysis for learning library and information science at graduate level in India with special reference to northern region. Ghulam Ali. University of Jammu, Jammu and Kashmir, 1995. Guide- A N Sadhu & I V Malhan. 1277

Analytical study of multiple intelligences and information and communication skills among the students of LIS schools in South India. Baskaran, S. University of Madras, Tamil Nadu, 2011. Guide- B Ramesh Babu. 1278

Continuing education of library and information science faculty in Indian universities: An appraisal of modes and methods. Gursharnjit Singh. Punjabi University, Patiala, Punjab, 1998. Guide- Jagtar Singh. 1279

Impact of information and communication technology (ICT) on library information science education with special reference to the institutions in Tamil Nadu and Pondicherry. Baskar, M. Annamalai University, Tamil Nadu, 2004. Guide- M Suriya. 1280

Infrastructure and facilities of library and information science departments of Indian universities with special emphasis on universities in Maharashtra. Wadnerkar, Vaishali (Ms). Sant Gadge Baba Amravati University, Maharashtra, 2008. Guide- D Rajyalakshmi. 1281

Job satisfaction among LIS teachers in India. Sangeeta. Gulbarga University, Karnataka, 2011. Guide- V T Kamble. 1282

Library and information science education and professional manpower needs of special libraries of Northern India in the light of application of information technology. Mohd Yusuf. University of Rajasthan, Jaipur, Rajasthan, 2002. Guide- M R Rawtani. 1283

Entry No.

Library and information science education in Gujarat. Surati, Daksha (Ms). SNDT Women's University, Mumbai, Maharashtra, 2000. Guide- M K R Naidu. 1284

Library and information science education in north east region: A critical study. Lalngaizuali. Mizoram University, Mizoram, 2010. Guide- P K Rath. 1285

Library education in India. Dalbir Singh. University of Rajasthan, Jaipur, Rajasthan, 1991. Guide- S N Srivastava. 1286

Off-campus LIS education programmes in South India: An evaluative study. Sugathri Devi, K (Ms). Andhra University, Andhra Pradesh, 2001. Guide- R S R Varalakshmi. 1287

Status of library and information science education in India: An evaluative study. Mishra, Vishvambhari (Ms). Banaras Hindu University, Uttar Pradesh, 2012. Guide- H N Prasad. 1288

Teaching of library science in Indian universities: Problems and prospects. Khan, Habib-ur-Rehman. Aligarh Muslim University, Uttar Pradesh, 2002. Guide- S M K Q Zaidi. 1289

Trends in library and information science education and training in India: A study. Sharma, Anil Kumar. Panjab University, Chandigarh, Punjab, 2007. Guide- Ranjana Vohra. 1290

a. Comparative Studies

Library science education in India and United Kingdom: A comparative study since 1947. Batta, Rashmi (Ms). Panjab University, Chandigarh, Punjab, 1989. Guide- U K Tikku. 1291

Library science education in Islamic Republic of Iran and India: A comparative study. Khoozestani, Hassan Kiani. Panjab University, Chandigarh, Punjab, 2000. Guide- G C Bansal. 1292

Entry No.

b. Curriculum Development

A study of curriculum requirements towards improving IT skills of library professionals. Yadav, Akhilesh Kumar Singh. Mizoram University, Mizoram, 2010. Guide- S N Singh. 1293

Application of teaching techniques to library and information science education with reference to Curriculum Development Committee Report, 2001. Siddiqui, Eraj Azeeza Zulfekharuddin. Swami Ramanand Teerth Marathwada University, Maharashtra, 2007. Guide- S P Satarkar. 1294

Curricula and methods of teaching and evaluation in library and information science education in the universities of Iran and India and their relationship to the role of professionals: A study. Bagheri, Mansoureh(Ms). Panjab University, Chandigarh, Punjab, 2003. Guide- G C Bansal. 1295

Curriculum development and program for continuing education in the field of library and information science in India: A survey and evaluation. Shivanna, R. Bangalore University, Karnataka, 1998. Guide- M A Gopinath. 1296

India's response to new competencies for library and information science education with special reference to adoption of CDC Report 2001 in Northern India. Shabir Ahmad. University of Kashmir, Jammu and Kashmir, 2011. Guide- W A Alvi. 1297

Information technology components in library and information science curriculum. Jayanna, R. University of Mysore, Karnataka, 2010. Guide- C P Ramasesh. 1298

c. Historical Development

Library and information science in India in the 1990s. Sengupta, Shivani. University of Pune, Maharashtra, 1992. Guide- M R Riswadkar. 1299

Entry No.

Library science education in Karnataka since 1900: A critical study. Sadashiva Murthy, P. Gulbarga University, Karnataka, 1991. Guide- S R Gunjal. 1300

d. IT Application

The use of information technology in academic departments of library and information science in Iranian universities. Zal Zdeh, Ibrahim. University of Pune, Maharashtra, 2008. Guide- S N Singh. 1301

Use of IT in library and Information science schools in India. Patil, Harsha (Ms). Sant Gadge Baba Amravati University, Maharashtra, 2008. Guide- P S G Kumar. 1302

e. NAAC Assessment

Accreditation of library and information science courses on establishing standards for accreditation in Indian universities with special emphasis on establishing standards. Baba, Abdul Majeed. University of Kashmir, Jammu and Kashmir, 1995. Guide- M L Wali. 1303

Organization, collection and services of college libraries affiliated to the North Maharashtra University Jalgaon: With special reference to assessment by NAAC. Patil, Vinay B. University of Pune, Maharashtra, 2010. Guide- S K Patil. 1304

LIS LITERATURE

Contributions of library professionals in Maharashtra in the publication of literature on LIS. Deshmukh, Sonali (Ms). Sant Gadge Baba Amravati University, Maharashtra, 2012. Guide- M R Kherde. 1305

Granthalaya evam suchna vigyan ka Hindi me adhyayan tatha Hindi bhasha me uplabdh pathya samagri ka alochnatmak adhyayan. Dharamveer Singh. Dr B R Ambedkar University, Agra, Uttar Pradesh, 2002. Guide- U C Sharma. 1306

Entry No.

Publication of library science literature in Telugu: A critical evaluation. Sarada, P. Sri Krishnadevaraya University, Andhra Pradesh, 2003. Guide- P Kamaiah. 1307

Web content management (WCM) for library and information science: A study. Date, Dhanashree (Ms). University of Mumbai, Maharashtra, 2007. Guide- P A Gokhale. 1308

LITERACY MOVEMENT

A study of public library and literacy movement in India with special reference to Delhi, Haryana and Rajasthan. Verma, Sahab Singh. University of Delhi, Delhi, 2000. Guide- S R Gupta & D S Aggarwal. 1309

Collaboration of public libraries and literacy programme for rural development in the tribal district of Orissa. Satapathy, Bhabani Kumar. Berhampur University, Orissa, 2012. Guide- K C Das. 1310

Grameen vikas evam saksharata abhyan mein pustakalaya kee bhumika: Ek anusheelan. Naidu, P Saraswati. Guru Ghasidas University, Chhattisgarh, 2002. Guide- J L Saini. 1311

Libraries in promotion of literacy and adult education in India with special reference to Punjab: A model. Kathuria, Kiran (Ms). Guru Nanak Dev University, Amritsar, Punjab, 2009. Guide- M P Satija. 1312

LITERATURE GROWTH STUDIES

A study on growth and development of literature in Naga languages. Ao, Shashilemla. Gauhati University, Assam, 2012. Guide- Narendra Lahkar. 1313

An analysis of structural and system dynamics of specialization biotechnology area: An empirical study of literature experiments, specialization in the field of animal cell technology. Ramakrishna, N V. University of Mysore, Karnataka, 2002. Guide- N B Pangannaya. 1314

Entry No.

Fifty years of Bengali feature films: Filmography and history with a trend analysis. Chatterjee, Gautam. Jadhavpur University, West Bengal, 2002. Guide- Prabir Roy Choudhury. 1315

Growth and development of children's literature in Hindi published in independent India. Gupta, Vijaya (Ms). University of Delhi, Delhi, 1991. Guide- D S Aggarwal. 1316

Hindi me sandarbh sahitya ka udbhav evam vikas: Alochnatmak adhyayan. Sharma, Ajay Kumar. Jiwaji University, Madhya Pradesh, 1988. Guide- S M Tripathi. 1317

Historical development of legal literature on customary laws in Assam: A critical study. Rahman, Md Wakidur. Gauhati University, Assam, 2003. Guide- Alaka Buragohain & A Hussain. 1318

Recent directions of growth of biomedical knowledge: An analytical study based on observed changes in the scientific impact of serial publications. Sengupta, Indranaryan. University of Calcutta, West Bengal, 1983. Guide- Self Adjudication. 1319

Swadhinottar bangla sishu sahityer gati o prakiti, 1947-1986. Chaudhuri, Priti. Jadhavpur University, West Bengal, 1995. Guide- Prabir Roy Choudhury. 1320

a. Language Periodicals

Bardhaman jelay prakashita samayik patrika panjir bishlesanatmak samiksha: 1960-85. Mukhopadhyay, Kabita (Ms). University of Burdwan, Rajbati, Bardhaman, West Bengal, 1991. Guide- Pulin Behari Barua. 1321

Origin and development of periodical literature in English language in India up to 1947: A survey. Kumar, Ramesh Pal. Panjab University, Chandigarh, Punjab, 1978. Guide- J S Sharma. 1322

Entry No.

The development pattern of Tamil periodicals with special reference to the consumer periodicals: A descriptive study in historical perspectives. Shanmugam, S P. Madurai Kamaraj University, Tamil Nadu, 1997. Guide- S Nakkiran. 1323

b. Science Periodicals

Growth and development of science and technology journals in India since independence: An evaluative study. Shafi, Muzammil. Aligarh Muslim University, Uttar Pradesh, 2006. Guide- Shabahat Husain. 1324

Growth of ethno-botanical journal literature and dictionary pattern of ethno-botanists in India: A study. Dhiman, Anil Kumar. Jiwaji University, Madhya Pradesh, 2009. Guide- Hemant Sharma. 1325

Indian scientific periodicals: A study of their origin and development up to 1900. Sen, Bimal Kanti. Jadhavpur University, West Bengal, 1995. Guide- Prabir Roy Choudhury. 1326

MANUSCRIPTS

Buddhist manuscripts in Arunachal Pradesh: Preservation, restoration and digitization. Maltesh, M. Gauhati University, Assam, 2010. Guide- Narendra Lahkar. 1327

Buddhist manuscripts in Thailand: Survey, analysis and use. Nuchanarth, P Lert. Banaras Hindu University, Uttar Pradesh, 1984. Guide- P N Kaula. 1328

Manuscripts of Manipur: A study in the modern perspective. Devi, Thiyam Satyabati (Ms). Manipur University, Manipur, 2006. Guide- Purnima Devi. 1329

Organization and management of Marathi manuscripts in India with special reference to Maharashtra. Pharande, C P. University of Pune, Maharashtra, 1998. Guide- S G Mahajan. 1330

Entry No.

Study of Tamil Christian literacy manuscripts and the government oriental manuscripts. Soundarapandian, S. University of Madras, Tamil Nadu, 1991. Guide- S Innasi. 1331

MARKETING

Marketing of information services to industries in Andhra Pradesh. Chandraiah, I. Sri Venkateswara University, Tirupati, Andhra Pradesh, 2000. Guide- N Guruswamy Naidu. 1332

Marketing orientation of university libraries of Kerala in information dissemination. Vinod, V M. University of Calicut, Calicut, Kerala, 2006. Guide- V Jalaja. 1333

a. Information Products and Services

Effectiveness of marketing of information in British Council Library Network. Bhat, I M. Karnataka University, Karnataka, 2002. Guide- S L Sangam. 1334

Exploring the marketing library service: A study on foreign libraries in India. Tyagi, Deepak. Jiwaji University, Madhya Pradesh, 2008. Guide- Hemant Sharma. 1335

Marketing and processing of electronic digital information products in developing and distribution mechanism in NRI. Bhattacharya, Prabha Kalian. Jiwaji University, Madhya Pradesh, 2009. Guide- J N Gautam. 1336

Marketing of information of non conventional energy sources. Yesudoss, P. University of Madras, Tamil Nadu, 2007. Guide- Manorama Srinath. 1337

Marketing of information product and information services by libraries and information centres in Jordon. Fadial Jamil, Abdul Khalil. Jiwaji University, Madhya Pradesh, 1993. Guide- S M Tripathi & Noorul Hasan khan. 1338

Entry No.

Marketing of information product in the state university libraries in Uttar Pradesh: An evaluative study. Sharma, Renu. Bundelkhand University, Jhansi, Uttar Pradesh, 2009. Guide- V P Khare. 1339

Marketing of information products and services in agriculture sector: A study of marketing management of the libraries of agricultural research institutes of ICAR. Rathore, Jagmohan. University of Rajasthan, Jaipur, Rajasthan, 2003. Guide- Dabir Singh. 1340

Marketing of information products and services in select libraries and documentation centres in NCR: A survey. Choudhary, Pravin Kumar. Kurukshetra University, Haryana, 2012. Guide- Ashu Shokeen. 1341

Marketing of information products and services in university libraries of Punjab and Chandigarh: A study. Sarita Rani (Ms). Guru Nanak Dev University, Amritsar, Punjab, 2007. Guide- Amritpal Kaur. 1342

Marketing of library and information products and service : Present trends and future perspectives. Rama Patnaik, K (Ms). Andhra University, Andhra Pradesh, 2002. Guide- C Sasikala. 1343

Marketing of library information products and services: A study in designing economic models with reference to capital markets in India. Hiremath, C V. Karnataka University, Karnataka, 2003. Guide- C R Karisiddappa. 1344

Marketing of medical information products in libraries: A feasibility study. Kambaraman, B. University of Madras, Tamil Nadu, 2009. Guide- Manorama Srinath. 1345

New awareness for marketing of library and information services and product in the libraries in India: A feasibility study. Jitendra Kumar. Jiwaji University, Madhya Pradesh, 2012. Guide- B K Sharma & Hemant Sharma. 1346

Entry No.

Prospects of library marketing in North East India: A study. Sarma, Kishor. Gauhati University, Assam, 2011. Guide- Narendra Lahkar. 1347

Public relations and marketing of information: A state of art study with proposal of P R model with central university libraries of Delhi. Lohia, Jaswant Singh. Dr B R Ambedkar University, Agra, Uttar Pradesh, 2001. Guide- U C Sharma. 1348

Public relations and marketing of library and information science in public libraries in Punjab. Banerjee, Sushanta (Ms). Panjab University, Chandigarh, Punjab, 2006. Guide- H R Chopra. 1349

The role of marketing in the field of libraries and information service: A future implications. Mohan, K. University of Rajasthan, Jaipur, Rajasthan, 1998. Guide- Pushpa Dhyani. 1350

MEDIA LIBRARIES

A study of telecast media libraries in India. Thakur, Ranjeet Singh. University of Delhi, Delhi, 2005. Guide- Shailendra Kumar. 1351

An investigation in the development of computer based multimedia library system with special reference to voice data. Singh, Anand Pratap. Jiwaji University, Madhya Pradesh, 1997. Guide- J N Gautam & TAV Murthy. 1352

Educational media libraries: Their organization and services. Amjad Ali. University of Rajasthan, Jaipur, Rajasthan, 2002. Guide- M R Rawtani. 1353

Information management in akashwani and doordarshan kendra of Madhya Pradesh: Bhopal, Indore, Gwalior and Jabalpur. Pant, Prem Prakash. Jiwaji University, Madhya Pradesh, 2009. Guide- B K Sharma & Hemant Sharma. 1354

Entry No.

NATIONAL INFORMATION CENTRES

National information centre for sugar industry: A development plan. Divatankar, N I. Shivaji University, Kolhapur, Maharashtra, 2007. Guide- S R Gunjal. 1355

Perspective and plan for the establishment of national information centre on petroleum. Kawale, A V. Rashtrasant Tukadoji Maharaj Nagpur University, Nagpur, Maharashtra, 1999. Guide- P S G Kumar. 1356

NATIONAL INFORMATION SYSTEMS

A comparative study of the national information systems in education in UK and USA with a view to developing a model for India. Verma, Sunder Lal. University of Delhi, Delhi, 1989. Guide- D S Aggarwal. 1357

A study of growth and development of physical education of sport libraries in India: A proposed model for national information system for physical educational and sport science in India. Bedi, Manmohan Singh. Jiwaji University, Madhya Pradesh, 1997. Guide- J N Gautam. 1358

Design and development of multilingual information system with numeric MARK. Tripathi, Aditya. University of Pune, Maharashtra, 2005. Guide- A R D Prasad. 1359

National information systems: A comparative study with special reference to UK, USA, USSR and India. Dharma, Neelimesh. Dr Hari Singh Gour Vishwavidyalaya, Sagar, Madhya Pradesh, 1986. Guide- H S Sengar. 1360

a. Sciences

Conceptual framework for an Indian national agricultural information system (INAGRIS). Subbaiah, Revuru. University of Kerala, Kerala, 1986. Guide- K A Isaac. 1361

Entry No.

Design and development of a national information system for marine fisheries in India. Johnson, E. University of Kerala, Kerala, 1989. Guide- K A Isaac. 1362

Design and development of a national information system in nutrition science for India (Nisnuts): A study. Chary, K Sampatha. Osmania University, Andhra Pradesh, 1999. Guide- A A N Raju. 1363

Design and development of Indian national information system for ayurveda. George, Joshi P. University of Kerala, Kerala, 2001. Guide- G Devarajan. 1364

NETWORKS AND CONSORTIA

a. Library Consortia

A comparative study of available consortia in India. Jawahar Lal. Banaras Hindu University, Uttar Pradesh, 2012. Guide- H N Prasad. 1365

Administration of electronic journals through consortia: A model for science and technology libraries in India. Christina, Louis (Ms). Andhra University, Andhra Pradesh, 2005. Guide- B Vijayalakshmi. 1366

Collaborative approach towards e resources from acquisition to use: A study. Sinha, Abhijeet. University of Delhi, Delhi, 2012. Guide- Shashi Prabha Singh. 1367

Design and development of consortium among fishery libraries in Kerala. Ancy Jais. Bishop Heber College, Bharathidasan University, Tamil Nadu, 2012. Guide- S Ally Sornam. 1368

Development of library consortium for engineering colleges in Kerala. Abdul Azeez, T A. University of Calicut, Calicut, Kerala, 2007. Guide- M Bavakutty. 1369

Entry No.

E journals access and management: Consortia model for India. Goudar, I R N. Karnataka University, Karnataka, 2006. Guide- S L Sangam. 1370

Effectiveness of INDEST Consortium in providing e access to scholarly journals and databases at special libraries in Delhi: A critical study. Chidambaram, S Siva. University of Rajasthan, Jaipur, Rajasthan, 2012. Guide- M R Rawtani. 1371

Feasibility of consortium of e journals in medical college libraries in Madhya Pradesh. Agrawal, Vivek. Vikram University, Madhya Pradesh, 2010. Guide- S S Chandel & S Kumar. 1372

Satisfying end users through consortia based systems: A model for collaboration among engineering libraries in Western India. Ghosh, Maitrayee Mondal (Ms). University of Burdwan, Rajbati, Bardhaman, West Bengal, 2009. Guide- Subal Chandra Biswas. 1373

Use of UGC INFONET e journal consortium: Its impact on the academic community and the libraries in universities of Karnataka. Vishala, B K (Ms). Mangalore University, Karnataka, 2008. Guide- M K Bhandi. 1374

b. Library Networks

A study of an integrated library network and consortium of central university libraries in north east region. Lamzuala, C. Mizoram University, Mizoram, 2012. Guide- R N Mishra. 1375

AGRILIBNET (Agricultural Libraries Network): A prototype web portal. Rathinasabapathy, G. University of Madras, Tamil Nadu, 2006. Guide- A Amudavalli. 1376

An information network for linguistics and Indian languages: A proposal including a study of its problems and prospects. Murthy, Sulochana S. University of Mysore, Karnataka, 1998. Guide- H A Khan. 1377

Entry No.

Barriers of resource sharing in library networks: An analysis of DELNET. Kaul, H K. University of Pune, Maharashtra, 1998. Guide- M B Konnur. 1378

Creating network and digital library of social science institutions in National Capital Region, Delhi. Malviya, Rama Nand. Jiwaji University, Madhya Pradesh, 2008. Guide- J N Gautam. 1379

Design and development of cost effective intranet model for sharing electronic information resources: Consortia based study with reference to IIM libraries. Pandian, M P. Karnataka University, Karnataka, 2005. Guide- C R Karisiddappa. 1380

Design of an online bibliographic network for multi unit R & D organizations. Murthy, S S. Gulbarga University, Karnataka, 1990. Guide- S R Gunjal. 1381

Designing a network for resource sharing among the health science libraries in West Bengal. Satpathi, Jatindranath. Jadhavpur University, West Bengal, 1999. Guide- M L Chakraborty. 1382

Development and management of health science library network of the state of Karnataka, India. Pathan, A M. Karnataka University, Karnataka, 1991. Guide- C R Karisiddappa. 1383

Electronic resources accessible through University of Delhi campus network: A study of the use of e resources by research scholars and faculty members. Lalita. Dr B R Ambedkar University, Agra, Uttar Pradesh, 2010. Guide- U C Sharma. 1384

Impact of INFLIBNET in the development of university libraries with special reference to university libraries of Uttar Pradesh and Uttarakhand. Shrivastava, Anurag. Babasaheb Bhimrao Ambedkar University, Lucknow, Uttar Pradesh, 2011. Guide- K L Mahawar. 1385

Entry No.

Impact of INFLIBNET programme on its oriented services in U P: An evaluative study. Upadhyay, Archana. Bundelkhand University, Jhansi, Uttar Pradesh, 2005. Guide- M T M Khan. 1386

Impact of information and library network on university library services in special reference to the universities of M P. Prince, Dashrath Parsad. Awadhesh Pratap Singh University, Madhya Pradesh, 2012. Guide- N R Satyanarayana. 1387

Indian university libraries network: A status survey and guidelines for library automation. Kumbar, T S. Gulbarga University, Karnataka, 1995. Guide- S L Sangam. 1388

Indian web resources offered by various library networks: With special reference to DELNET. Singh, Byanktesh Narain. Jiwaji University, Madhya Pradesh, 2006. Guide- Hemant Sharma. 1389

Information and Library Network (INFLIBNET): A case study of university libraries and information centres in Gujarat. Saha, Ananta Lal. Sambalpur University, Orissa, 2002. Guide- B K Choudhury. 1390

Information networks in India: Problems and prospects. Bose, Kaushik. Vikram University, Madhya Pradesh, 1992. Guide- T A V Murthy. 1391

Information village for small scale industries in North East India: A model. Yanthan, Zuchamo. University of Delhi, Delhi, 2009. Guide- Shailendra Kumar. 1392

Knowledge discovery through library networks: Methodology for developing knowledge based model library network for India. Kaul, Sangeeta. University of Pune, Maharashtra, 2009. Guide- M B Konnur. 1393

Entry No.

Library networks in India: Policy analysis, implementation and management. Mondal, Bhriguram. Jadhavpur University, West Bengal, 2003. Guide- M L Chakraborty. 1394

Metropolitan network for Nagpur City. Prakashe, Veena (Ms). Rashtrasant Tukadoji Maharaj Nagpur University, Nagpur, Maharashtra, 2008. Guide- P S G Kumar. 1395

National disability information network. Reddy, H S. Karnataka University, Karnataka, 1997. Guide- C R Karisiddappa. 1396

Network of college libraries under Visvesvaraya Technological University: A perspective plan. Bachalapur, M M. Karnataka University, Karnataka, 2005. Guide- B D Kumbhar. 1397

Network of university libraries in Iraq. Aboud, Azhar M (Ms). Sardar Patel University, Gujarat, 2011. Guide- U A Thaker. 1398

Organizational and attitudinal factors in the development of local library networks in India. Mishra, Sanjaya. University of Delhi, Delhi, 1998. Guide- C P Vashishth. 1399

Problems and prospects in implementing INFLIBNET program in university libraries of M P. Sarwan, Jay Prakash. Vikram University, Madhya Pradesh, 2010. Guide- S S Chandel & S Kumar. 1400

Resources and services of Indian library networks with special reference to DELNET: A study. Chaurasia, Neeraj Kumar. Dr Hari Singh Gour Vishwavidyalaya, Sagar, Madhya Pradesh, 2009. Guide- B P Shrivastava. 1401

Role of library networks. Mathur, Shishir. Dr B R Ambedkar University, Agra, Uttar Pradesh, 2002. Guide- B K Sharma. 1402

Rural public library network in Punjab: A study (1947-1980). Jagtar Singh. Panjab University, Chandigarh, Punjab, 1985. Guide- J S Sharma. 1403

Entry No.

The information and library network programme: A case study of Manipur. Singh, R K Joteen. Manipur University, Manipur, 2008. Guide- Madhuri Devi. 1404

Use of networks by library and information science faculty in India, U K and U S A: A study. Kalra, Harinder Pal Singh. Punjabi University, Patiala, Punjab, 2005. Guide- Jagtar Singh. 1405

c. Library Networks Model

A proposal for model network of art libraries and information centres in India. Gakhar, A P. Dr B R Ambedkar University, Agra, Uttar Pradesh, 2002. Guide- U C Sharma. 1406

Bridging the information divide among engineering college libraries in Tamil Nadu: A network design based on library resources, facilities and services. Sivaraj, S. Annamalai University, Tamil Nadu, 2010. Guide- S Mohamed Esmail. 1407

Cost effective network model for science and engineering college libraries in Gujarat. Tandel, Kailash. Sardar Patel University, Gujarat, 2012. Guide- U A Thaker. 1408

Development of cost effective network model for optimum utilization of resources in polytechnic libraries of Karnataka: A study. Shirur, S S. Karnataka University, Karnataka, 2005. Guide- B D Kumbhar. 1409

Network model for resource sharing in Indian universities. Singh, Kewal Jeet. Panjab University, Chandigarh, Punjab, 1985. Guide- U K Tikku. 1410

Networking model for pharmacy colleges in Gujarat. Modi, Bipinchandra Jayantilal. Hemchandracharya North Gujarat University, Gujarat, 2009. Guide- C N Rawal. 1411

Plan proposal for the establishment of network of libraries in North East India. Christina, Doibila (Ms). University of Delhi, Delhi, 2006. Guide- Shailendra Kumar. 1412

Entry No.

Rural development information network (RDIN): A model integrated information system for the development of community. Raju, K A. Karnataka University, Karnataka, 2000. Guide- C R Karisiddappa. 1413

NEWSPAPER LIBRARIES

A study of libraries information needs and use of information sources in newspaper establishments in Kerala. Joseph, Rosamma (Ms). University of Calicut, Calicut, Kerala, 1991. Guide- M Bavakutty. 1414

Integrated information network for newspaper libraries in Karnataka. Bankapur, Vinayak M. Karnataka University, Karnataka, 1998. Guide- S L Sangam. 1415

Management and utilization of newspaper libraries in Chandigarh, Delhi and Punjab. Parveen Kumar. Panjab University, Chandigarh, Punjab, 2011. Guide- Preeti Mahajan. 1416

Newspaper libraries in Andhra Pradesh (India): A study on emergence, services and professional attitude towards automation. Riajuddin, Md Gouse. Sri Venkateswara University, Tirupati, Andhra Pradesh, 2010. Guide- D Chandran. 1417

Newspaper libraries in information dissemination. Pandit, Surekha. Vikram University, Madhya Pradesh, 2007. Guide-Sonal Singh. 1418

ONLINE PUBLIC ACCESS CATALOGUE

Authority control of romanized arabic names in online public access catalogue. Veerankutty, Chelatayakkot,. University of Calicut, Calicut, Kerala, 2006. Guide- V Jalaja. 1419

Computerization of library catalogue and OPAC services of institutes of higher learning in Maharashtra. Bhongade, Devendra. Rashtrasant Tukadoji Maharaj Nagpur University, Nagpur, Maharashtra, 2008. Guide- D Rajyalakshmi. 1420

Entry No.

OPACs in South Indian libraries: A study of their facilities and features. Thamizhchelvan, M. University of Madras, Tamil Nadu, 2004. Guide- B Ramesh Babu. 1421

Subject access to OPACs: Problems and possible solutions. Shabahat Hussain. University of Lucknow, Uttar Pradesh, 2010. Guide- N R Satyanarayana. 1422

a. Use and User Studies

A study of users' attitude towards online public access catalogue (OPAC). Kaliyaperumal, K. University of Madras, Tamil Nadu, 2000. Guide- B Ramesh Babu. 1423

Usability assessment of qualitative methodology in OPAC search. Guha, Tamal Kumar. North East Hill University, Shillong, Meghalaya, 2003. Guide- Veena Saraf. 1424

Use of online public access catalogue in university libraries of Chandigarh and Punjab: A study. Shiv Kumar. Panjab University, Chandigarh, Punjab, 2011. Guide- Ranjana Vohra. 1425

OPEN ACCESS RESOURCES

Evaluation of free online e resources in library and information science: A study of their facilities and features. Kaushal. Berhampur University, Orissa, 2012. Guide- R K Mahapatra. 1426

Impact of open access (OA) publications on library and information science community in Bangkok metropolitan universities in Thailand: A study. Thaotip, Laksana. University of Pune, Maharashtra, 2010. Guide- S K Patil. 1427

Open source initiatives in Indian libraries: A critical study. Mete, Mahindra. Sant Gadge Baba Amravati University, Maharashtra, 2011. Guide- P S G Kumar. 1428

Entry No.

Scholarly communication on the web: An investigation of open access electronic journals in library and information science. Mukherjee, Bhaskar. Banaras Hindu University, Uttar Pradesh, 2007. Guide- H N Prasad. 1429

The scope and dissemination of open access in university libraries of Gujarat State in the special context of North Gujarat University Library. Patel, Manubhai Gopaldas. Hemchandracharya North Gujarat University, Gujarat, 2003. Guide- S M Charan. 1430

ORGANIZATIONAL EFFECTIVENESS

A comparative study of performance measurement of R & D and special libraries. Parikh, Shreyansi Kanchanlal. Gujarat University Ahmedabad, Gujarat, 2011. Guide-Shailendra Kumar. 1431

Adjudication of the performance by the library users in the colleges affiliated to Bharathiar University: A study. Kavitha, E S. Annamalai University, Tamil Nadu, 2012. Guide- K Vijayakumar. 1432

Effect of organizational characteristics on the performance of university libraries in Rajasthan: A critical study. Meena, Rakesh. Mohan Lal Sukhadia University, Udaipur, Rajasthan, 2003. Guide- L N Verma. 1433

Effectiveness of college libraries: A case study of Meghalaya. Challam, Medalda. North East Hill University, Shillong, Meghalaya, 2007. Guide- A S Chandel. 1434

Effectiveness of the university libraries in education and research: A case study of Punjab and Punjabi universities. Devinder Kaur. Punjabi University, Patiala, Punjab, 2002. Guide- S.P. Narang 1435

Effectiveness of university libraries in research: A users study: Sharma, Permanand. University of Rajasthan, Jaipur, Rajasthan, 1990. Guide-S C Verma 1436

Entry No.

Factors related to organizational effectiveness: A study based on special and academic libraries. Saha, Karuna. Indian Institute of Technology, Delhi, Delhi, 1987. Guide- Purnima Mathur. 1437

Library effectiveness in material science in research institutions in Delhi during 1980-92. Dhawan, Surinder Mohan. University of Delhi, Delhi, 1998. Guide- J L Sardana. 1438

Measuring effectiveness of university libraries: A case study of Bangladesh. Islam, Mezbah. North East Hill University, Shillong, Meghalaya, 2003. Guide- Veena Saraf. 1439

Measuring library effectiveness. Ganpule, S R. University of Pune, Maharashtra, 1987. Guide- M R Riswadkar. 1440

Organization structure and work efficiency in universities in Haryana, Punjab and Delhi. Aboot, Neelam. Jiwaji University, Madhya Pradesh, 1994. Guide- S M Tripathi & J K Khanna. 1441

Performance evaluation of engineering college libraries and their information services in Coimbatore District of Tamil Nadu. Kanagaraj, M. Annamalai University, Tamil Nadu, 2003. Guide- M Nagarajan. 1442

Performance evaluation of university libraries in Tamil Nadu: An application cost effectiveness analysis. Suriya, M. Annamalai University, Tamil Nadu, 1990. Guide- V Durairajan. 1443

Performance of colleges: A critical study of college libraries under the jurisdiction of Nagpur University. Jain, P B. Rashtrasant Tukadoji Maharaj Nagpur University, Nagpur, Maharashtra, 2007. Guide- P S G Kumar. 1444

PUBLIC LIBRARIES

A study of the socio-cultural aspects of library support for non-financial learning in Assam. Buragohain, Alaka. Gauhati University, Assam, 1996. Guide- Self Adjudication. 1445

Entry No.

An assessment of the role of state and district libraries for the socio-cultural and educational development of Mizoram. Ngurtinkhuma, R K. Mizoram University, Mizoram, 2007. Guide- P K Rath. 1446

Assessment of contribution of a public library to the society with special reference to cultural and literary development: A case study of Mumbai Marathi Granth Sasngrahalaya. Karnik, P N. University of Pune, Maharashtra, 2005. Guide- S P Ganpule. 1447

District libraries in Punjab and Haryana: A comparative study. Gursharan Kaur. Punjabi University, Patiala, Punjab, 2009. Guide- Jagtar Singh. 1448

Public libraries and tribal community: A study in Andhra Pradesh. Chandra Sekhar Rao, V. Andhra University, Andhra Pradesh, 1992. Guide- K Sarada. 1449

Public libraries for the disadvantaged: A study of special component plan libraries in Andhra Pradesh with a special reference to Scheduled Caste. Keshalu, P. Sri Krishnadevaraya University, Andhra Pradesh, 2006. Guide- P Rajarathnam Chetty. 1450

Public libraries in a multicultural society and their role in promoting social harmony: A critical study with special reference to Assam. Hussain, Mahatab. Gauhati University, Assam, 2009. Guide- N N Sharma. 1451

Role of libraries in development and maintaining cultural relations: An analysis of effectiveness of the British Council Libraries in India. Jayarajan, P. Vidyasagar University, West Bengal, 1993. Guide- M A Gopinath & Ashok Basu. 1452

Role of libraries in the upliftment of education in the rural areas with special reference to the tribal areas of Rajasthan. Sharma, Pushkar Lal. Mohan Lal Sukhadia University, Udaipur, Rajasthan, 2007. Guide- L N Verma. 1453

Entry No.

Role of public libraries in creating social consciousness and in promoting the prospect of functional literacy: A study in the Burdwan District. Ganguly, Pranab Kumar. Vidyasagar University, West Bengal, 2005. Guide- A Sengupta & P K Jana. 1454

Role of village libraries in development: A case study in Mizoram. Lalremsiami. North East Hill University, Shillong, Meghalaya, 2008. Guide- P Hangsing & A S Chandel. 1455

PUBLIC LIBRARY MOVEMENT

Bangiya granthagar parishad of paschim banga sadaran granthagar andolan. Majumder, Krishnapada. Jadhavpur University, West Bengal, 2002. Guide- Prabir Roy Choudhury. 1456

Library movement in Gujarat and Madhya Pradesh: A comparative evaluation. Charan, Shivdanbhai Mekranbhai. Sardar Patel University, Gujarat, 1990. Guide- G D Bhargava. 1457

Public library movement in India with special reference to Madhya Pradesh. Tomar, Surendra Singh. Vikram University, Madhya Pradesh, 1989. Guide- S S Agarwal. 1458

The role of district libraries in the development of public library movement in Maharashtra. Deshpande, N J (Ms). University of Pune, Maharashtra, 1998. Guide- S G Mahajan. 1459

a. Historical Development

History of library movement in Western Maharashtra, 1901-1947. Adhikari, Pan Singh. Allahabad University, Uttar Pradesh, 1966. Guide- V Venkata Rao. 1460

Entry No.

History of public library movement in Vidharbha Region of Maharashtra wef 1850-1970. Gajway, P M. Sant Gadge Baba Amravati University, Maharashtra, 2001. Guide- V M Bhagvatkar. 1461

History of the public library movement in Western Maharashtra, 1805-1921. Mahajan, S G. University of Pune, Maharashtra, 1979. Guide- A R Kulkarni. 1462

Public library movement in Kerala: A historical analysis. Joseph, K S. University of Pune, Maharashtra, 1991. Guide- S J Verma. 1463

Public library system and socio-cultural, political movement during freedom movement in circa, Andhra Pradesh: A Study. Vijaya Kumari, J (Ms). Andhra University, Andhra Pradesh, 2007. Guide- Self Adjudication. 1464

PUBLIC LIBRARY SYSTEM

A study of public library system as community information centers in Nagaland: Realities and challenges. Imchen, A Takatemsu. Gauhati University, Assam, 2008. Guide- N N Sharma. 1465

Design and development of multi type rural public library system in Andhra Pradesh (India): A case study. Venkateswarlu, Y Ch. Sri Krishnadevaraya University, Andhra Pradesh, 2008. Guide- P Kamaiah. 1466

Development of an integrated public library system for Bangladesh with reference to a Model Public Library Bill. Sarkar, Nikhil Chandra. Jadhavpur University, West Bengal, 2006. Guide- Bijoypada Mukherjee & J K Sarkhel. 1467

Public library system for Delhi. Balbir Singh. Jiwaji University, Madhya Pradesh, 1994. Guide- S M Tripathi & J L Sardana. 1468

Entry No.

Public library system in Bangladesh: Its origin, growth and future prospects. Sarkar, Utpal. Jadhavpur University, West Bengal, 2001. Guide- M L Chakraborty. 1469

Public library system in Bhutan: A systematic approach for future development. Kannan, S. Gauhati University, Assam, 2009. Guide- Narendra Lahkar. 1470

Public library system in Madhya Pradesh. Nandwana, H B. Vikram University, Madhya Pradesh, 1994. Guide- A Tejomurty. 1471

Public library system in Manipur and how to develop it by library legislation. Singh, Thounaojam Khomdon. Manipur University, Manipur, 1991. Guide- M R Kumbhar. 1472

Public library systems in Haryana, Jammu & Kashmir and Punjab: Development and assessment. Wani, Zahid Ashraf. University of Kashmir, Jammu and Kashmir, 2007. Guide- M L Wali. 1473

Restructuring the public library system in Karnataka. Krishnamurthy, C V. Karnataka University, Karnataka, 2010. Guide- B D Kumbhar. 1474

a. Development Plan

A study of system science and further development plans in the public libraries of northern region of India. Malik, Satendar. Awadhesh Pratap Singh University, Madhya Pradesh, 2010. Guide- N R Satyanarayana. 1475

Development plan for public library system in the Karnataka State. Ijari, S R. Karnataka University, Karnataka, 1983. Guide- M R Kumbhar. 1476

Public libraries and community information centers: A developmental plan for Andaman and Nicobar Islands. Ganesh, Y. Guru Ghasidas University, Chhattisgarh, 2007. Guide- Brajesh Tiwari. 1477

Entry No.

Public library system for Gujarat State: A development plan. Patel, P F. Gujarat University Ahmedabad, Gujarat, 1978. Guide- M R Kumbhar. 1478

Public library system in Orissa: A developmental plan. Patel, Ananta Kumar. Sambalpur University, Orissa, 1997. Guide- R K Rout. 1479

PUBLISHING PATTERN

Evaluation of time lag between publication of information and its use in university libraries in Maharashtra. Kene, Neeta (Ms). Sant Gadge Baba Amravati University, Maharashtra, 2011. Guide- M R Kherde. 1480

Pattern of literature growth and publishing output in information technology (IT) with special reference to major LIS periodicals in India: An analytical study. Neena (Ms). Sambalpur University, Orissa, 2005. Guide- K C Panda. 1481

Publication status and pattern of India and China on chemistry. Padmavathi, K P. University of Madras, Tamil Nadu, 2004. Guide- A Amudavalli. 1482

Publishing pattern of scientists in India with special reference to astronomers and astrophysicists. Vageswari, G (Ms). Andhra University, Andhra Pradesh, 1998. Guide- B Vijayalakshmi. 1483

Studies on the characteristics of publication in the field of electronics with special reference to semiconductor device technology and their role in information flow in research, development and industry. Talawar, V G. Karnataka University, Karnataka, 1985. Guide- M R Kumbhar. 1484

RANGANATHAN STUDIES

An investigation into the research methodology of S R Ranganathan and his style of writing. Satija, M P. Guru Nanak Dev University, Amritsar, Punjab, 1990. Guide- K Navalani. 1485

Entry No.

Dr S R Ranganathan on Internet: An analytical study. Syed, Ruhina Kauser. Rashtrasant Tukadoji Maharaj Nagpur University, Nagpur, Maharashtra, 2012. Guide- Ashwini P Paradkar. 1486

Impact of Ranagnathan on AACR 2. Rajyalakshmi, D (Ms). Rashtrasant Tukadoji Maharaj Nagpur University, Nagpur, Maharashtra, 1992. Guide- P S G Kumar. 1487

Ranganathaner granthagar o tathyabigyan bhabnay Sanskrit sahityer prabhab: Ekti barnanamulak samiksha. Kundu, Shyam Sundar. University of Burdwan, Rajbati, Bardhaman, West Bengal, 2006. Guide- Subal Chandra Biswas & S N Mukherjee. 1488

READING HABITS

Enquiry into reading interests of pupil of standard VIII to X. Goswami, Renu. M S University, Baroda, Gujarat, 1983. Guide- M M Shah. 1489

Investigation into the reading interests and habits of the first year degree course of Marathi students studying in colleges affiliated to the University of Poona. Dhunake, A R. University of Pune, Maharashtra, 1978. Guide- B K Sohoni. 1490

Promotion of reading habits among school going children: A case study in Vishakhapatnam District. Bhaskara kumar, B S. Andhra University, Andhra Pradesh, 1999. Guide- P Soma Raju. 1491

Reading habits among science college teachers in Vidharbha Region. Ugle, Vaishali (Ms). Rashtrasant Tukadoji Maharaj Nagpur University, Nagpur, Maharashtra, 2009. Guide- D R Deshpande. 1492

Reading habits and literature use by botanists. Shrivastava, Rochana. Jiwaji University, Madhya Pradesh, 1993. Guide- B Guha. 1493

Entry No.

Reading habits of college students in Dakshina Kannada District: A study. Sudha, S T. University of Mysore, Karnataka, 2008. Guide- N S Harinarayana. 1494

Reading habits of library user in Bundelkhand University and Jiwaji University: A comparative study. Vyas, Shalini. Bundelkhand University, Jhansi, Uttar Pradesh, 2005. Guide- V P Khare. 1495

Reading habits of the university and college teachers with respect to their field of specialization and study. Verma, Sarita. Jiwaji University, Madhya Pradesh, 2001. Guide- S M Tripathi. 1496

Reading interests of children in India. Chandel, A S. University of Lucknow, Uttar Pradesh, 1984. Guide- L S Chopra. 1497

Role of kendriya vidyalaya librarians in inculcating reading habits among the students. Shaikh, Irshad Mohammad. Vikram University, Madhya Pradesh, 2006. Guide- Surendra Singh. 1498

a. IT Impact

Impact of electronic media on reading habits in Karnataka State university libraries. Patil, F G. Mangalore University, Karnataka, 2009. Guide- M K Bhandi. 1499

Impact of surfing on reading habits: A case study of students of Kashmir Valley. Lone, Fayaz Ahmad. University of Kashmir, Jammu and Kashmir, 2011. Guide- S M Shafi. 1500

Influence of information technology on the reading habits of the students in degree college libraries affiliated to Acharya Nagarjuna University, Andhra Pradesh. Kodal, Krishna Mohan. Sri Krishnadevaraya University, Andhra Pradesh, 2006. Guide- P Kamaiah. 1501

Entry No.

RESEARCH ROLE OF UNIVERSITY LIBRARIES

A comparative study of the role of libraries of the University of Delhi and Jawaharlal Nehru University in their research programmes in social sciences. Kamlesh, Vinayak (Ms). University of Delhi, Delhi, 1993. Guide- P B Mangla. 1502

Guru Ghasidas vishwavidyalaya ke anusuchit jati evam janjati kei shetro ke uchch shiksha mein granthalayaon ki bhumika: Ek mulyankan, 1983-1996. Chandel, Vivek Singh. Guru Ghasidas University, Chhattisgarh, 2004. Guide- J L Saini. 1503

Role of library in enhancing agricultural research and education. Perumalaswamy, K. Karnataka University, Karnataka, 1994. Guide- S R Ijari. 1504

Role of the university library in supporting research: A case study of Andhra University. Soma Raju, P. Andhra University, Andhra Pradesh, 1985. Guide- A Neelameghan. 1505

Role of university libraries in research in Kerala: A case study. S Sheeja, N K. University of Calicut, Calicut, Kerala, 2007. Guide- V Jalaja. 1506

Role of university libraries in support of social science research: A comparative study of Panjab, Punjabi and Guru Nanak Dev Universities. Kulvir Kaur. Guru Nanak Dev University, Amritsar, Punjab, 2012. Guide- Amritpal Kaur. 1507

RESOURCE SHARING AND NETWORKING

Bhartiya prabandh sansadhanon ke pustakalya mein suchna sansadhan sahabaghita evam networking: Ek adhyayan. Sandeep Kumar. Jiwaji University, Madhya Pradesh, 2008. Guide- Hemant Sharma & B K Sharma. 1508

Entry No.

Library cooperation in India. Verma, Subhash. University of Rajasthan, Jaipur, Rajasthan, 1978. Guide- S N Srivastava. 1509

Networking of libraries in Puducherry: A prototype design. Nagalingam, U. University of Madras, Tamil Nadu, 2008. Guide- B Ramesh Babu. 1510

Resource sharing and networking of ministerial libraries. Rao, Y Avinindranath. Mahatma Gandhi Chitrakoot Gramodaya Vishwavidyalaya, Satna, Madhya Pradesh, 2012. Guide- R P Bajpai. 1511

a. Academic Libraries

A feasibility study of resource sharing among university libraries of Rajasthan: A proposed plan. Khatter, Nandini. University of Rajasthan, Jaipur, Rajasthan, 2003. Guide- Usha Pawan. 1512

A study of resource sharing and networking of North West Indian university libraries. Iqbal Singh. Punjabi University, Patiala, Punjab, 2007. Guide- Jagtar Singh. 1513

A study of resource sharing and networking of university libraries in Andhra Pradesh. Sujatha, G (Ms). Andhra University, Andhra Pradesh, 1996. Guide- K Sarada. 1514

Information sharing in university libraries in U P with special reference to networking. Sharma, Satyendra Kumar. Jiwaji University, Madhya Pradesh, 2008. Guide- Hemant Sharma. 1515

Multitype library resource sharing and network with special reference to university libraries of Orissa. Panda, K C. Berhampur University, Orissa, 1991. Guide- C R Karisiddappa. 1516

Networking of autonomous college libraries in Tamil Nadu: A prototype design. Nageswara Rao, P. University of Madras, Tamil Nadu, 2009. Guide- B Ramesh Babu. 1517

Entry No.

Networking of JNTU libraries of Andhra Pradesh: A prototype design based on information needs and information seeking behaviour of faculty. Doraswamy Naik, B R. Sri Venkateswara University, Tirupati, Andhra Pradesh, 2012. Guide- D Chandran. 1518

Networking of sanskrit vidyapeetha libraries in India: A prototype design based on information needs and information seeking behaviour of Sanskrit faculty. Gopal Reddy, G. University of Madras, Tamil Nadu, 2004. Guide- B Ramesh Babu. 1519

Resource sharing among university and college libraries in Jammu and Kashmir with a proposed model. Alvi, W A. University of Kashmir, Jammu and Kashmir, 1994. Guide- Self Adjudication. 1520

Resource sharing and networking of college libraries affiliated to Gulbarga University, Gulbarga: A study. Biradar, G S. Karnataka University, Karnataka, 2012. Guide- R R Naik. 1521

b. Engineering Libraries

A study of co-operation and networking among engineering and technological libraries in India. Saibaba, Bathala. University of Burdwan, Rajbati, Bardhaman, West Bengal, 1992. Guide- Pulin Behari Barua. 1522

An automated library network for resource sharing among the engineering colleges of Uttar Pradesh: A study. Prasad, Neelam (Ms). Banaras Hindu University, Uttar Pradesh, 2002. Guide- H N Prasad. 1523

Electronic information sources, services and the possibility of networking for resource sharing in the libraries of the Indian Institutes of Technology: An evaluation. Sutradhar, Bablu. Vidyasagar University, West Bengal, 2005. Guide- J K Sarkhel. 1524

Entry No.

Networking of government engineering college libraries: A perspective plan. Mandaliya, Shishir H. Sambalpur University, Orissa, 2008. Guide- K C Panda. 1525

c. Medical Libraries

Resource sharing and national information system in medical libraries with a plan for such a network in India. Trivedi, Satish Chandra. University of Rajasthan, Jaipur, Rajasthan, 1994. Guide- S C Verma. 1526

Virtual resource sharing centre for medical institutions in Chennai: A model. Jayamani, N C. University of Madras, Tamil Nadu, 2002. Guide- Manorama Srinath. 1527

d. Special Libraries

Collection development of participating libraries: An evaluative study of resources sharing in physical sciences. Jain, S P. Jiwaji University, Madhya Pradesh, 1997. Guide- T A V Murthy & J N Gautam. 1528

Growth and development of Indian financial and banking sector libraries and resource sharing through a proposed library networks (BANKLIBNET): A critical appraisal. Ahuja, Jatinder Pal Singh. University of Rajasthan, Jaipur, Rajasthan, 2010. Guide- M R Rawtani. 1529

Impact of information technology on resource sharing with special reference to hydropower sector libraries in India. Rakesh Parshad. Panjab University, Chandigarh, Punjab, 2008. Guide- Preeti Mahajan. 1530

Networking agricultural libraries for effectively meeting information needs of researchers. Murthy, Lakshmi (Ms). University of Lucknow, Uttar Pradesh, 2007. Guide- N R Satyanarayana. 1531

Entry No.

Networking of National Institute of Fashion Technology (NIFT) resource centers in India: A prototype design based on information seeking pattern by the NIFT faculty. Gopalakrishnan, S. University of Madras, Tamil Nadu, 2004. Guide- B Ramesh Babu. 1532

Opportunities for science libraries in managing and resource sharing through consortia approach in Karnataka. Vasantha, N. Mangalore University, Karnataka, 2009. Guide- M V Mudhol. 1533

Resource sharing among special libraries of Bhopal. Raghuvanshi, Ajay Singh. Vikram University, Madhya Pradesh, 2010. Guide- Surendra Singh & Sonal Singh. 1534

Resource sharing among special libraries of Indore. Mathur, Seema. Vikram University, Madhya Pradesh, 2004. Guide- Surendra Singh & Sonal Singh. 1535

Resource sharing in electronic environment in science and technology libraries in U P. Upadhyay, Sunil Kumar. Dr B R Ambedkar University, Agra, Uttar Pradesh, 2009. Guide- B K Sharma. 1536

Resource sharing in scientific and technical libraries in India: A study. Gurdev Singh. University of Jammu, Jammu and Kashmir, 1998. Guide- I V Malhan. 1537

Resource sharing in the Internet era: A conceptual model for Indian social science libraries. Manjunath, G K. Karnataka University, Karnataka, 2009. Guide- S L Sangam. 1538

Resource sharing in vernacular language librarians in India. Siddiqui, Ayesha (Ms). Osmania University, Andhra Pradesh, 2011. Guide- V Vishwa Mohan. 1539

Entry No.

Role of the Internet in enhancing the resource sharing and enriching the information resources in the special libraries in India: An investigation. Sreekumar, M G. University of Calicut, Calicut, Kerala, 2005. Guide- Raju M Mathew. 1540

Study of select libraries of management institutes in India with special reference to institutions within the jurisdiction of University of Pune with relevance to networking accessibility and services to the users. Oak, Meenal. University of Pune, Maharashtra, 2011. Guide- S K Patil. 1541

ROLE OF UGC

A critical study of the University Grants Commission's contribution to development of university libraries in Western India. Khot, Namita Babasaheb. University of Pune, Maharashtra, 2003. Guide- M B Konnur. 1542

The role of University Grants Commission in the development of university libraries of Gujarat State: A study. Ankuya, Babulal Jivabhai. Hemchandracharya North Gujarat University, Gujarat, 2012. Guide- M K Prajapati. 1543

The role of UGC's contribution in the development of Hemchandracharya North Gujarat University Library and libraries of the affiliated colleges to the University: A study. Chaudhari, Bhagavanbhai Kuberbhai. Hemchandracharya North Gujarat University, Gujarat, 2012. Guide- M K Prajapati. 1544

The role of University Grants Commission (India) in the development of university libraries: A critical appraisal of university libraries in Northern India. Panwar, Sarbjit Singh. University of Rajasthan, Jaipur, Rajasthan, 1996. Guide- Usha Pawan. 1545

Entry No.

RTI ACT AND CENSORSHIP

Impact of RTI Act and Censorship in library and information science: A study in perspective. Srivastava, Pravi (Ms). University of Lucknow, Uttar Pradesh, 2012. Guide- N R Satyanarayana. 1546

SCIENTOMETRIC STUDIES

A scientometric study of Ph D theses submitted in botany in universities in U P during 1998-2007. Pachori, Narandra Kumar. Jiwaji University, Madhya Pradesh, 2009. Guide- Hemant Sharma & B K Sharma. 1547

A study of the scientific productivity and information use pattern of scientists in the context of new information technology with special reference to universities in Kerala. Soman, K N. University of Calicut, Calicut, Kerala, 2003. Guide- Raju M Mathew. 1548

An analytical study of research output of Jamia Milia Islamia in the field of natural sciences (1971-2004). Naqvi, Shehbaz Husain. University of Delhi, Delhi, 2010. Guide- Shailendra Kumar. 1549

Bibliographic analysis of the citations of doctoral theses on science submitted to North Bengal University. Rahman, Md Ziaur. Jadhavpur University, West Bengal, 2011. Guide- Udayan Bhattacharya. 1550

Biotechnology research in India and China: A scientometrics analysis. Adinarayanan, K. Annamalai University, Tamil Nadu, 2004. Guide- S Ravi. 1551

Citation analysis of Indian metallurgists and scientist in the field of powder metallurgy during 1970 to 1990: A study. Hafiz, Aftaabh. Jiwaji University, Madhya Pradesh, 1994. Guide- Noorul Hasan Khan & J N Gautam. 1552

Entry No.

Contributions of University of Burdwan in pure sciences research in West Bengal: An analytical study. Nandi, Amitava. University of Burdwan, Rajbati, Bardhaman, West Bengal, 2012. Guide- A K Bandyopadhyay. 1553

Contributions to medical journals by Indian medical professionals: A study. Sarama, T N G. Osmania University, Andhra Pradesh, 2007. Guide- V Chandrasekhara Rao. 1554

Evolution of materials science and engineering: A scientometric study. Koteswara Rao, Mamidi. University of Madras, Tamil Nadu, 2006. Guide- K S Raghavan. 1555

History of science communication of Bengal (1947-2005): Review and analysis of information sources. Banerjee, Arnab Kumar. Jadhavpur University, West Bengal, 2011. Guide- Subarna Kumar Das. 1556

Indicators in the field of chemical sciences with special reference to India: A scientometric study. Meera. Karnataka University, Karnataka, 2008. Guide- S L Sangam. 1557

Indicators in the field of marine engineering: A scientometric analysis. Agadi, K B. Karnataka University, Karnataka, 2009. Guide- S L Sangam. 1558

Life and works of Dr Raja Rammana: A scientometric study. Kademani, Basavaraj. Karnataka University, Karnataka, 2008. Guide- B D Kumbhar. 1559

Metallurgy and material science research in India (1985-94): A scientometric study. Sandha, D P. Utkal University, Orissa, 2001. Guide- Pitambar Padhi. 1560

Productometric analysis of research contributions made in the field of metallurgy and material science: A case study of NML (CSIR). Mishra, Paras Nath. Sambalpur University, Orissa, 2010. Guide- K C Panda. 1561

Entry No.

Publications in science and technology by faculty members in universities of Jordan: A scientometric study. Al-Jaradat, Omar Mohammad Hussien. Aligarh Muslim University, Uttar Pradesh, 2009. Guide- Shabahat Husain. 1562

Research productivity analysis in life sciences. Kaliyaperumal, R. Annamalai University, Tamil Nadu, 1999. Guide- P Pichappan. 1563

Research productivity and use of literature by agriculture scientists in Orissa, 1985-93. Kaul, Rama (Ms). Utkal University, Orissa, 2007. Guide- G Mahapatra. 1564

Science indicators to study and analyze the scientific literature with an emphasis on CFTRI's research publications. Seetharaman, Geetha. University of Mysore, Karnataka, 1997. Guide- I K Ravichandra Rao. 1565

Scientific research productivity in India: An empirical analysis using selected indicators. Buchandiran, G. Annamalai University, Tamil Nadu, 2008. Guide- P Pichappan. 1566

Scientometric analysis of literature on aerospace based on *SCOPUS* bibliographic database. Shanthi, J (Ms). University of Madras, Tamil Nadu, 2011. Guide- B Ramesh Babu. 1567

Scientometric analysis of research output in medicinal plants in *Biological Abstracts* from the year 2000-2008: A study. Sridhar, Daya. AVVM Sri Pushpam College, Bharathidasan University, Tamil Nadu, 2009. Guide- A Ganesan. 1568

Scientometric study of chemical literature cited in the doctoral theses of chemistry submitted to the University of Jammu. Sachar, Anita (Ms). University of Jammu, Jammu and Kashmir, 1999. Guide- I V Malhan. 1569

Entry No.

Scientometric study of research output in chemistry: A comparative study of selected central and state universities of U P from 2000 to 2009. Dwivedi, Sandhya (Ms). Dr Hari Singh Gour Vishwavidyalaya, Sagar, Madhya Pradesh, 2012. Guide- K C Sahoo. 1570

Trends of chemistry research in India, 2000-2009: An empirical analysis. Veeramani, K. Annamalai University, Tamil Nadu, 2012. Guide- P Sivaraman. 1571

a. Agriculture Sciences

A study of the trend of growth of agricultural literature in North Eastern India from 1976 to 1996 and its impact upon higher studies in agricultural science. Syiem, M D. Gauhati University, Assam, 2005. Guide- Alaka Buragohain. 1572

Growth of Indian horticultural literature during 1980-89 and the contribution of Indian horticultural scientists in foreign horticultural periodicals: A quantitative analysis. Humayun Kabir, S. Bangalore University, Karnataka, 1996. Guide- A Y Asundi. 1573

Productometric study of Oil Seed Crops Research Institutes of Indian Council of Agricultural Research (ICAR). Surendra Kumar. Vikram University, Madhya Pradesh, 2010. Guide- S Kumar. 1574

b. Computer Science

A scientometric study of literature in software studies in India with a comparison to the world literature. Sahoo, Bibhuti Bhusan. University of Pune, Maharashtra, 2007. Guide- I K Ravichandra Rao. 1575

Mapping the research productivity of computer communication: A scientometric analysis. Amutha, M. Annamalai University, Tamil Nadu, 2012. Guide- M Suriya. 1576

Entry No.

Research activities on neural network in Asian countries: A scientometric analysis. Kasilingam, K. Annamalai University, Tamil Nadu, 2012. Guide- P Ravichandran. 1577

Research productivity in artificial intelligence in G 8 countries with special reference to India: A bibliometric analysis. Ushadevi, P. Annamalai University, Tamil Nadu, 2011. Guide- P Sivaraman. 1578

c. Medical Sciences

Bibliographic study on liver transplantation, 1999-2003. Yadav, Abhishek. Aligarh Muslim University, Uttar Pradesh, 2004. Guide- Mehtab Alam Ansari. 1579

Indian literature on health sciences: A scientometric study. Krishnamoorthy, G. University of Madras, Tamil Nadu, 2004. Guide- A Amudavalli. 1580

Research output performance of G 8 countries in cardiology: A scientometric analysis. Baskaran, C. Annamalai University, Tamil Nadu, 2010. Guide- M Sadik Batcha. 1581

Scientometric analysis of literature on hepatitis: A study based on bibliographic databases. Ramakrishnan, J. University of Madras, Tamil Nadu, 2007. Guide- B Ramesh Babu. 1582

Scientometric analysis of medical science research in India. Mohan Kumar, L. Annamalai University, Tamil Nadu, 2010. Guide- S Ravi. 1583

d. Periodical Literature

Analytical study of contributions in Bengali scientific periodicals originated in West Bengal (1947-2001). Chatterjee, Sunil Kumar. Jadhavpur University, West Bengal, 2005. Guide- Prabir Roy Choudhury. 1584

Entry No.

Growth of literature and citation pattern among the Indian journals in the field of botany, 1950-1980. Mahapatra, Manoranjan. University of Burdwan, Rajbati, Bardhaman, West Bengal, 1984. Guide- Bijoynath Mukherjee. 1585

Impact of informatics on information storage and retrieval in libraries and information centers: A scientometric study of periodical literature since 1981. Hashemzadeh, Mohammad Javed. University of Delhi, Delhi, 2006. Guide- Shailendra Kumar & S R Gupta. 1586

Information sources in history of science in India: A scientometric study of periodical literature. Shailendra Kumar. University of Rajasthan, Jaipur, Rajasthan, 1992. Guide- B S Garg. 1587

e. Physical Sciences

A scientometric analysis of literature on fiber optics: A study based on bibliographic databases. Rajendran, P. University of Madras, Tamil Nadu, 2007. Guide- B Ramesh Babu. 1588

Growth informetrics and indicators of superconductivity research and literature, 1911-2000. Sarma, Hari Prasad. University of Calcutta, West Bengal, 2006. Guide- Subir K Sen. 1589

Mapping of the subject physics: A study of research in India during 20th century. Ravi, B. University of Mysore, Karnataka, 2004. Guide- V G Talwar. 1590

Physics research in middle level countries: A scientometric analysis of high tech physicists in India, Australia, Canada and Israel. Singh, U N. Birla Institute of Technology, Mesra, Ranchi, Bihar, 1994. Guide- R C Gupta. 1591

Entry No.

Scientometric study of laser research in India during 1970-94. Garg, K C. Utkal University, Orissa, 2002. Guide- Pitambar Padhi. 1592

Trends in scientific communication in India through historic, sociometric and bibliographic analysis of the scientific journals in physical sciences especially physics and astronomy. Ratnakar, A. Karnataka University, Karnataka, 1992. Guide- M R Kumbhar. 1593

f. Social Sciences

Research evaluation on gender studies in informatics: An application of scientometric indicators and mapping techniques. Sambandam, C. Annamalai University, Tamil Nadu, 2006. Guide- M Suriya. 1594

Scientometric analysis of social science research in India. Keshav. Karnataka University, Karnataka, 2003. Guide- S L Sangam. 1595

TECHNICAL PROCESSING, TOOLS AND TECHNIQUES

Application of modern information technology to information processing in India. Sathyanarayan, R. Gulbarga University, Karnataka, 1992. Guide- S R Gunjal. 1596

Retro-conversion of documents in Central Secretariat Library; Zakir Husain Library, JMI and Nehru Memorial Museum and Library: An evaluative study. Updhayay, Ashok Kumar. Aligarh Muslim University, Uttar Pradesh, 2010. Guide- M Masoom Raza. 1597

The need for arranging subject headings to Sanskrit and Marathi manuscripts: A case study. Sakhare, Rajendra. University of Pune, Maharashtra, 2008. Guide- S K Patil. 1598

Entry No.

a. Catalogue Codes

A study of the compatibility of AACR2, MARK 21 and UNISIST. Shewale, Nanaji G. University of Pune, Maharashtra, 2004. Guide- A R D Prasad. 1599

Cataloguing of shared authorship: A comparative and critical account of catalogue codes. Mishra, V K. Banaras Hindu University, Uttar Pradesh, 1992. Guide- H N Prasad. 1600

Cataloguing since Cutter: A topographical and dialectical account of the theoretical and practical development of art and science of bibliographical control. Venugopal, M V. Jiwaji University, Madhya Pradesh, 1994. Guide- S M Tripathi. 1601

Treatment of authorship: A critical study of catalogue codes. Das, Asitabha. University of Calcutta, West Bengal, 2007. Guide- Pijush Kanti Mahapatra. 1602

Treatment of Indic names in AACR 2: A study. Kaushik, Devender Kumar. Osmania University, Andhra Pradesh, 1999. Guide- D B Eshwara Reddy. 1603

b. Cataloguing

Auto extraction of proper names from web texts: A case study. Sivasamy, K. University of Madras, Tamil Nadu, 2007. Guide- K S Raghavan. 1604

Document description in university libraries. Dhrubajit Das. Gauhati University, Assam, 2007. Guide- Narendra Lahkar. 1605

GENBIBCON: A generalized approach to analysis, definition and conversion of heterogeneous bibliographic database formats vol 2 additional notes and program listing. Rajashekhar, T B. University of Pune, Maharashtra, 1989. Guide- S G Mahajan. 1606

Entry No.

Prospect of automated cataloguing in the three university libraries of Assam: Based on users satisfaction under catalogue codes. Lahkar, Narendra. Gauhati University, Assam, 1998. Guide- Alaka Buragohain. 1607

Study of the peculiarities of the names of north east region of India for cataloguing. Devi, Thoidingjam Madhuri (Ms). Manipur University, Manipur, 1994. Guide- M R Kumbhar. 1608

The problems and prospects of cataloguing in Bengali: An analytical study. Ray, Sibani (Ms). University of Calcutta, West Bengal, 2002. Guide- A Dasgupta. 1609

c. Classification

An analytical investigation into the characteristics of a subject: A case study. Dutta, Bidyarthi. Jadhavpur University, West Bengal, 2008. Guide- Krishnapada Majumder. 1610

Analysis of the problems in the recognition and manifestation of the fundamental categories in inter disciplinary subjects. Gopinath, M A. Karnataka University, Karnataka, 1981. Guide- M R Kumbhar. 1611

Development of classification system for organizing literature on machine tools and production engineering. Reddy, K Ramakrishna. University of Mysore, Karnataka, 2003. Guide- M A Gopinath. 1612

Development of terminology in the field of library classification with special reference to Indian school of thought: A case study in terminology development. Prasad, K N. Karnataka University, Karnataka, 1983. Guide- M R Kumbhar. 1613

Development pattern of language lateralization among monolinguals and early late bilinguals. Balhara, Lokesh. Maharshi Dayanand University, Rohtak, Haryana, 1997. Guide- Rajbir Singh. 1614

Entry No.

Jansanchar evam pattarkarita vishay pe Hindi mein prakashit pustako ka vergikaran evam unki vishay vastu ka tulnatmak adhayan: Dashamlav vergikaran padhdhati ke vishesh sandarbh mein. Sarang, Arti. Makhanlal Chaturvedi National University of Journalism and Mass Communication, Madhya Pradesh, 2010. Guide- B S Nigam. 1615

Knowledge organization in the field of gender studies in informatics. Amsaveni, N. Annamalai University, Tamil Nadu, 2010. Guide- M Sadik Batcha. 1616

Mapping of coral reef research literature: A global perspective. Mohan, V. Annamalai University, Tamil Nadu, 2006. Guide- S Ravi. 1617

Mapping the dynamics of human nutrition. Florence, C. University of Madras, Tamil Nadu, 2002. Guide- A Amudavalli. 1618

Modes of formation of subjects and their role in information retrieval. Binwal, J C. Karnataka University, Karnataka, 1990. Guide- C R Karisiddappa. 1619

Preparation of classification schedule for Muslim theology based on Dewey Decimal Classification Scheme. Usmani, Mohammad Sajjad. University of Delhi, Delhi, 1995. Guide- Kamleshwar Nath. 1620

Structure and development of subject fields in social sciences and their implication to classification and indexing. Rama Devi, V. Karnataka University, Karnataka, 1992. Guide- C R Karisiddappa. 1621

The structure of biotechnology R & D: Co-classification based analysis of the database. Mymoon, M. University of Madras, Tamil Nadu, 1999. Guide- K S Raghavan. 1622

Entry No.

d. Classification Schemes

A knowledge representation model for management of analytico synthetic scheme: A case study of Colon Classification. Madalli, Devika P. University of Mysore, Karnataka, 2001. Guide- A R D Prasad. 1623

Comparative study of common space and time isolates with special reference to DDC, UDC, and CC for developing uniform tables for these isolates. Shah, Leena. Vikram University, Madhya Pradesh, 2000. Guide- S Kumar. 1624

Compatibility among medical classification systems: A case study in the classification of cardiovascular diseases. Seetharam, S. Karnataka University, Karnataka, 1984. Guide- M R Kumbhar. 1625

Concept of analytico synthetic scheme of classification with special reference to Ranganathan, Barbara Kyle, Farradane and Foskett: A study. Vohra, Ranjana (Ms). Panjab University, Chandigarh, Punjab, 1984. Guide- J S Sharma. 1626

Design and development of a knowledge representation model for analytico synthetic classification with special reference to medicine. Panigrahi, Pijush Kanti. Vidyasagar University, West Bengal, 1996. Guide- Ashok Basu & A R D Prasad. 1627

Design of a classification scheme for knowledge representation model in anthropology. Jana, Pijush Kanti. Vidyasagar University, West Bengal, 2001. Guide- Ashok Basu & J K Sarkhel. 1628

Development of an unified scheme of common subdivisions in the general classification systems. Asundi, A Y. Gulbarga University, Karnataka, 1983. Guide- S R Gunjal. 1629

Entry No.

Emergence of interdisciplinary subjects in science and technology in 20th century and their treatment in different classification schemes. Bhattacharya, Udayan. Jadhavpur University, West Bengal, 2006. Guide- Prabir Roy Choudhury. 1630

Evaluation of literature in cancer, its treatment in various classification schemes and proposal for special scheme of library classification. Anand, Virender Kumar. Panjab University, Chandigarh, Punjab, 1993. Guide- Ranjana Vohra. 1631

Facet analysis and depth classification of agriculture. Krishna Rao, D B. University of Delhi, Delhi, 1957. Guide- S R Ranganathan. 1632

Knowledge classification systems: Origin, growth and development. Tiwari, Brijesh. Jiwaji University, Madhya Pradesh, 1991. Guide- S M Tripathi. 1633

Organization of knowledge in general classification schemes: A comparative study of social science subjects in Colon Classification and Dewey Decimal Classification. Shenoy, Rekha (Ms). Mangalore University, Karnataka, 2002. Guide- A K Baradol. 1634

Universe of subjects and classification schemes. Kaushik, Purnima. University of Rajasthan, Jaipur, Rajasthan, 1987. Guide- Pushpa Dhyani. 1635

Use of library classification schemes in Indian libraries with special reference to Delhi. Dhyani, Pushpa. University of Rajasthan, Jaipur, Rajasthan, 1979. Guide- S N Srivastava. 1636

i. Classification Schemes - CC

Assessment of the treatment of statistical sciences in the seventh edition of Colon Classification. Pandit, A M. University of Pune, Maharashtra, 1999. Guide- S P Ganpule. 1637

Entry No.

Design and development of depth schedule on medicine (L) of Colon Classification, 7th edition. Iyengar, S Anju. Makhanlal Chaturvedi National University of Journalism and Mass Communication, Madhya Pradesh, 2009. Guide- B S Nigam. 1638

Design and development of micro schedule on physical education based on Colon Classification, Ed 6. Ramasamy, A. University of Madras, Tamil Nadu, 2001. Guide- B Ramesh Babu. 1639

Rethinking genesis and development of Colon Classification scheme and vice-versa. Sukhdev Singh. Guru Nanak Dev University, Amritsar, Punjab, 1999. Guide- M P Satija. 1640

ii. Classification Schemes - DDC

A critical study of synthesis in DDC. Kherde, M R. Sant Gadge Baba Amravati University, Maharashtra, 2002. Guide- P S G Kumar. 1641

Changing patterns and emerging trends of DDC: A study of DDC edition 16th to 20th with special reference to application of facet analysis and recent editions. Shrivastava, Rakesh Kumar. Jiwaji University, Madhya Pradesh, 1998. Guide- J N Gautam. 1642

Expansion and modification of Dewey Decimal Classification (18th edition) for classifying indological books with special reference to Indian philosophy and religion. Sharma, Pandey Suraj Kant. Panjab University, Chandigarh, Punjab, 1977. Guide- J S Sharma. 1643

Expansion and modification of Dewey Decimal Classification (20th Edition) for classifying the forestry documents. Pathania, Mohan Singh. Panjab University, Chandigarh, Punjab, 1997. Guide- Ranjana Vohra. 1644

Entry No.

e. Metadata Models

A model for harvesting metadata from divergent information sources. Amin Saiful. University of Pune, Maharashtra, 2012. Guide- A R D Prasad. 1645

A study on interoperable e governance metadata model. Sainul Abideen P. University of Pune, Maharashtra, 2012. Guide- A R D Prasad. 1646

Interoperability of metadata schema for digital repositories. Seth, Renu. University of Pune, Maharashtra, 2010. Guide- A R D Prasad. 1647

Metadata in open access context: A critical study. Bherwani, Mohini (Ms). Rashtrasant Tukadoji Maharaj Nagpur University, Nagpur, Maharashtra, 2011. Guide- M Hirwade. 1648

f. Subject Headings Lists

Compilation of a comprehensive list of subject heading on science and technology in Bengali. Mukhopadhyay, Pinaki Nath. Jadhavpur University, West Bengal, 1997. Guide- Prabir Roy Choudhury. 1649

Compilation of comprehensive list of standard subject heading on humanities in Bengali. Bandyopadhyay, Ratna. Jadhavpur University, West Bengal, 1995. Guide- Prabir Roy Choudhury. 1650

List of subject headings on social sciences in Bengali language: limitations and its solutions. Chattopadhyay, Madhab Chandra. Rabindra Bharati University, West Bengal, 2012. Guide- Pinaki Nath Mukhopadhyay. 1651

Technology: Subject heading list in Bengali language. Basu, Keya. Rabindra Bharati University, West Bengal, 2008. Guide- Pinaki Nath Mukhopadhyay. 1652

Entry No.

g. Thesaurus Construction

Bilingual thesaurus of LIS: A pragmatic and thematic approach. Giri, Smita (Ms). Rashtrasant Tukadoji Maharaj Nagpur University, Nagpur, Maharashtra, 2011. Guide- Ashwini P Paradkar. 1653

Compatibility issues in multilingual thesauri: A case study of Indian languages. Chandrakumar, V. University of Madras, Tamil Nadu, 1999. Guide- K S Raghavan. 1654

Construction of a vocabulary control tool (thesaurus) for library and information science. Kumbar, Rajendra Madhavrao. Dr Babasaheb Ambedkar Marathwada University, Aurangabad, Maharashtra, 2002. Guide- Ashwini Anand Vaishnav. 1655

Design and development of thesaurus on fashion technology. Sanjeev Kumar. Sambalpur University, Orissa, 2005. Guide- B K Choudhury. 1656

Designing of thesauro facet in soil sciences. Sharma, Arun Kumar. Jiwaji University, Madhya Pradesh, 2004. Guide- J N Gautam & Shashi Prabha Singh. 1657

Management thesaurus with special context to management training schools in Asia. Paricharak, M D. Gulbarga University, Karnataka, 1989. Guide- S R Gunjal. 1658

Natural language versus controlled vocabulary in information retrieval: A case study in soil mechanics. Rao, M M. University of Pune, Maharashtra, 1992. Guide- S G Mahajan. 1659

Thesaurus in the subject of geography with a focus to combine classified and alphabetic approaches in display. Sujata (Ms). Kurukshetra University, Haryana, 2000. Guide- N K Sharma. 1660

Entry No.

TOTAL QUALITY MANAGEMENT

A study of total quality management in central university libraries of India. Munawwar Iqbal. Aligarh Muslim University, Uttar Pradesh, 2011. Guide- M Masoom Raza. 1661

Application of total quality management to the university libraries in Punjab, Haryana and Chandigarh. Dabas, Krishan Chander. Guru Nanak Dev University, Amritsar, Punjab, 2001. Guide- Sewa Singh. 1662

Application of TQM in the libraries of some selected academic institutions in Kolkata: A comparative study. Mukhopadhyay, Chinmay. University of Burdwan, Rajbati, Bardhaman, West Bengal, 2012. Guide- Tridib Tripathi. 1663

Application of TQM in university libraries of Karnataka State. Sherikar, A G. Karnataka University, Karnataka, 2003. Guide- S L Sangam. 1664

Problems and prospects in the design and implementation of quality management system in special libraries of Kolkata. Thakur, Ranjan Singha. Vidyasagar University, West Bengal, 2010. Guide- P K Jana. 1665

Quality management practices in university libraries of Uttar Pradesh: A study. Sharma, Swadesh. Vikram University, Madhya Pradesh, 2012. Guide- Surendra Singh. 1666

Quality of information services and users satisfaction in academic libraries of Puducherry Region: An analytical study. Balasubramanian, S S. Annamalai University, Tamil Nadu, 2012. Guide- M Sadik Batcha. 1667

Quality of library and information services: A study of customers satisfaction in academic libraries. Manjunatha, K. Mangalore University, Karnataka, 2002. Guide- D Shivalingaiah. 1668

Entry No.

The influence of total quality management in information technology environment in the university libraries in Andhra Pradesh: A case study. Prathipati, Prema Chand. Sri Krishnadevaraya University, Andhra Pradesh, 2005. Guide- P Kamaiah. 1669

Total quality management (TQM) and its application in university libraries of Andhra Pradesh: A study. Konappa, D. Sri Venkateswara University, Tirupati, Andhra Pradesh, 2012. Guide- D Chandran. 1670

Total quality management in academic libraries: A case study. Bankar, Nilima Rajendra (Ms). Dr Babasaheb Ambedkar Marathwada University, Aurangabad, Maharashtra, 2006. Guide- Ashwini Anand Vaishnav. 1671

Total quality management in Kerala University Library: A case study. Nair, Bindhu P. University of Kerala, Kerala, 2008. Guide- G Devarajan. 1672

Total quality management in technical college libraries of Orissa. Behera, Sanghmitra Dal. Utkal University, Orissa, 2012. Guide- Pushpanjali Jena. 1673

Total quality management in the university libraries of Northern India. Mange Ram. Dr B R Ambedkar University, Agra, Uttar Pradesh, 2007. Guide- U C Sharma. 1674

USE AND USER STUDIES

Attitude of post graduate students towards the use of Punjabi: A comparative study of Punjabi University Library, Patiala and Guru Nanak Dev University Library, Amritsar. M Singh. Guru Nanak Dev University, Amritsar, Punjab, 1991. Guide- Jagtar Singh. 1675

Library support for technology transfer: A three group user behaviour analysis. Vengan, Ramaswamy. University of Pune, Maharashtra, 1995. Guide- V A Kamath. 1676

Entry No.

Socio-psychological study of library users. Yadav, Upendra Prasad. Tilka Manjhi Bhagalpur University, Bihar, 1984. Guide- N A. 1677

Use of optical discs databases in Iran: A study of the present situation and proposal for a desirable system. Dizaji, Ali Jalali. Panjab University, Chandigarh, Punjab, 2001. Guide- H R Chopra. 1678

Use of reference sources in university libraries in Karnataka: A study. Adithya Kumari. University of Mysore, Karnataka, 2005. Guide- V G Talwar. 1679

a. Academic Libraries

A study of library use pattern among the college students in relation to their academic achievements. Mandal, Dilip Kumar. University of Calcutta, West Bengal, 2010. Guide- Rita Sinha & Mohan Chel. 1680

A study of the use of libraries of colleges of Education in Punjab. Nirmal Singh. Punjabi University, Patiala, Punjab, 2010. Guide- Trishanjit Kaur. 1681

Critical study of the organization and utilization of libraries in higher educational institutions of Kerala. Bavakutty, M A. University of Kerala, Kerala, 1984. Guide- M S G Ammal. 1682

Library users and their use patterns in the changing environment: A study of Chandigarh college libraries. Vashisht, Meenakshi (Ms). Panjab University, Chandigarh, Punjab, 2008. Guide- Ranjana Vohra. 1683

Readers' use of the university libraries in the north eastern region with special reference to the University of Assam and Meghalaya. Barua, Meera Bala (Ms). Panjab University, Chandigarh, Punjab, 1984. Guide- J S Sharma. 1684

Entry No.

Study of the effect of library use on academic advancement of post graduate students in the M S University of Baroda. Sudame, G R. M S University, Baroda, Gujarat, 1972. Guide- T P Lele. 1685

Use of books in Punjab and Guru Nanak Dev University libraries: An evaluative study of collections in physics, botany, history and punjabi. Kulwinder Singh. Punjabi University, Patiala, Punjab, 2007. Guide- Trishanjit Kaur. 1686

Use of information resources, facilities and services by the research scholars in the university libraries in Karnataka. Gowda, Vasappa. Mangalore University, Karnataka, 2008. Guide- D Shivalingaiah. 1687

Use pattern of university libraries in Andhra Pradesh with reference to Osmania University and University of Hyderabad: A study. Sunitha, K Hanna (Ms). Osmania University, Andhra Pradesh, 2006. Guide- A A N Raju. 1688

Users level of motivation and aspiration and its impact on use of library: A study of Central Library, BHU. Parihar, Shiva. Banaras Hindu University, Uttar Pradesh, 2012. Guide- H N Prasad. 1689

b. Agriculture Libraries

Madhya Pradesh ke krishi vishwavidyalaya granthalayaon mein upyokta adhyayan: Ek servekshan. Mishra, Ashutosh. Pt Ravishankar University Raipur, Chhattisgarh, 1999. Guide- A K Varma. 1690

Use of collection and services in IARI library and G B Pant Agricultural University Library: A comparative study. Naqvi, Tanveer Haider. Aligarh Muslim University, Uttar Pradesh, 2011. Guide- Sudharma Haridasan. 1691

Use of Punjab Agricultural University Library and Haryana Agricultural University Library by post graduate students: A comparative study. Malhotra, Harpal Kaur (Ms). Panjab University, Chandigarh, Punjab, 1987. Guide- U K Tikku. 1692

Entry No.

c. Engineering Libraries

A survey and use of the resources of engineering college libraries in Punjab with a view to propose their network for resource sharing. Tahir Ahmad. Guru Nanak Dev University, Amritsar, Punjab, 2006. Guide- M P Satija. 1693

A survey of engineering college libraries and their users in Sri Venkateswara University area. Chinna Balu, B R. Sri Venkateswara University, Tirupati, Andhra Pradesh, 2012. Guide- V Pulla Reddy. 1694

Use and misuse of reading materials in engineering college libraries in Karnataka State: A study. Anandahalli, Gavisiddappa. Gulbarga University, Karnataka, 2004. Guide- N Parvathamma. 1695

d. Periodicals

A study of the statistical serials: Their development and use in the libraries of ICSSR institutions in Delhi. Jain, Praveen Kumar. University of Delhi, Delhi, 2011. Guide- R K Bhatt. 1696

Availability and use of periodicals in the field at physical sciences in University of Delhi and Jawaharlal Nehru University: A study. Singh, M P. Bundelkhand University, Jhansi, Uttar Pradesh, 2005. Guide- M T M Khan. 1697

Use of periodicals by researchers in the agricultural universities of North India: A survey and bibliographical analysis. Raza, M Masoom. Panjab University, Chandigarh, Punjab, 2003. Guide- Preeti Mahajan. 1698

Use of periodicals in chemistry, physics and botany by scientists in large size libraries of science and technology in Delhi. Jain, Sarita (Ms). University of Delhi, Delhi, 1994. Guide- J L Sardana. 1699

Entry No.

Use of periodicals in economics, political science and sociology in the libraries of Aligarh; Banaras; Delhi and Jawaharlal Nehru University. Sachdeva, Darshan Lal. University of Delhi, Delhi, 1988. Guide- P B Mangla. 1700

Use of physical science periodicals in selected university libraries of West Bengal: A comparative study. Ambia, Golam. University of Burdwan, Rajbati, Bardhaman, West Bengal, 2008. Guide- Tridib Tripathi. 1701

Use pattern of periodicals in engineering college libraries of north coastal Andhra Pradesh: A study. Usha Rani, D (Ms). Andhra University, Andhra Pradesh, 2012. Guide- P Bhaskara Rao. 1702

Utilization of journals: A survey of university libraries in Rayalaseema, A P. Sri Sarada. Sri Venkateswara University, Tirupati, Andhra Pradesh, 2011. Guide- K Padmini. 1703

e. Public Libraries

Perceptions of library users towards the relevance and improvement of public libraries in Srikakulam District. Vijayakumar, M P N. Andhra University, Andhra Pradesh, 2010. Guide- J Vijaya Kumari. 1704

USER SATISFACTION

User satisfaction in engineering college libraries in A P: with special reference to book bank facilities and services. Usha Rani, K (Ms). Sri Venkateswara University, Tirupati, Andhra Pradesh, 2012. Guide- I Chandraiah. 1705

User satisfaction in university libraries. Sudhakar Rao, V. Sri Venkateswara University, Tirupati, Andhra Pradesh, 1997. Guide- V Pulla Reddy. 1706

Entry No.

User satisfaction in Zakir Husain Library, Jamia Millia Islamia; Central Library, JNU; Maulana Azad Library, AMU: A comparative study. Keshwar Jahan. Aligarh Muslim University, Uttar Pradesh, 2012. Guide- Mehtab Alam Ansari. 1707

VANDALISM

Mutilation, misplacement, theft and loss of library reading material in the colleges of Punjab and Chandigarh. Arora, Madhuri (Ms). Guru Nanak Dev University, Amritsar, Punjab, 1996. Guide- Sewa Singh. 1708

User behavioural pattern towards theft and mutilation in the university libraries: A case study of Andhra University. Tata Rao, K. Andhra University, Andhra Pradesh, 1994. Guide- P Soma Raju. 1709

Vandalism in college libraries in Marathwada. Garad, Madhukar D. Dr Babasaheb Ambedkar Marathwada University, Aurangabad, Maharashtra, 2011. Guide- Ashwini Anand Vaishnav. 1710

WEB PORTALS

Design and development of a web portal on women in ICT. Meenakshi, B. Annamalai University, Tamil Nadu, 2010. Guide- M Suriya. 1711

Mathematical subject gateways on web resources: An analytical study. Poonkothai, R. AVVM Sri Pushpam College, Bharathidasan University, Tamil Nadu, 2009. Guide- A Ganesan. 1712

Online services of Indian government portals: A critical study. Borkar, Vikas. Rashtrasant Tukadoji Maharaj Nagpur University, Nagpur, Maharashtra, 2011. Guide- M Hirwade. 1713

Entry No.

WEB RESOURCES

An investigation on web enabling of library material in open learning system: A study. Singh, Ajay Pratap. Bundelkhand University, Jhansi, Uttar Pradesh, 2004. Guide- T A V Murthy. 1714

Use of web based resources in social sciences: An analytical study of university libraries of Haryana and Rajasthan. Satish Kumar. Mohan Lal Sukhadia University, Udaipur, Rajasthan, 2010. Guide- T D Tilwani. 1715

Use of web resources by research scholars in select institutes of J & K and Delhi. Tabasum, Maqbool (Ms). University of Kashmir, Jammu and Kashmir, 2011. Guide- S M Shafi. 1716

Web as a learning resource: A study of faculty and students perception and utilization in medical college libraries of Coastal Karnataka. Rao, Mahabaleshwara. Mangalore University, Karnataka, 2011. Guide- M V Mudhol. 1717

Web based information resources in library and information science: A study. Bharathi, K (Ms). Osmania University, Andhra Pradesh, 2011. Guide- J Yadagiri Reddy. 1718

Web resources in library and information science: A managerial approach. Barman, Badan. Gauhati University, Assam, 2012. Guide- Narendra Lahkar. 1719

WEB SEARCH ENGINES

An investigation into retrieval efficiency of Internet search engines: A comparative study. Jain, Vivekanand. Banaras Hindu University, Uttar Pradesh, 2010. Guide- H N Prasad. 1720

Effect of Indian search engines uses on retrieved and precision of information from Internet: A comparative study of select search engines on the basis of practical use by the researchers in the field of education. Tripathi, Parvat Kumar. Vikram University, Madhya Pradesh, 2012. Guide- Sonal Singh. 1721

Entry No.

Searching facilities in different search engines. Deka, Sanjib Kumar. Gauhati University, Assam, 2010. Guide- Narendra Lahkar. 1722

WEBSITES

A model for organizing information for the world wide web: A case study of fungal species. Nagarkar, Shubhada(Ms). SNDT Women's University, Mumbai, Maharashtra, 2007. Guide- Harsha Parekh. 1723

Evaluation of websites of Indian universities with special reference to library web pages. Hirwade, Mangala A (Ms). Rashtrasant Tukadoji Maharaj Nagpur University, Nagpur, Maharashtra, 2004. Guide- D Rajyalakshmi. 1724

Library websites of deemed universities in India: An evaluative study. Mallikarjun, Angadi. Gulbarga University, Karnataka, 2008. Guide- Lalitha K Sami. 1725

Web credibility of engineering college websites in Tamil Nadu: An analytical study. Narendra Kumar, A M. University of Madras, Tamil Nadu, 2010. Guide- B Ramesh Babu. 1726

Websites of scientific educational and research institution in India: An analytical study. Sonwane, Shashank Sonaji. Dr Babasaheb Ambedkar Marathwada University, Aurangabad, Maharashtra, 2006. Guide- Ashwini Anand Vaishnav. 1727

WEBOMETRIC STUDIES

Content analysis of Indian library websites: A study. Vasanth Raju, N. University of Mysore, Karnataka, 2011. Guide- N S Harinarayana. 1728

Entry No.

Evaluating Indian academic and research library websites based on web impact factor analysis. Shukla, Akhandanand. Banaras Hindu University, Uttar Pradesh, 2010. Guide- Aditya Tripathi. 1729

Indian universities on the web: Analysis of hyperlinks through the application of webometric tools and techniques. Jalal, Samir. University of Burdwan, Rajbati, Bardhaman, West Bengal, 2012. Guide- Subal Chandra Biswas & Parthasarathi Mukhopadhyay. 1730

Websites of engineering educational institutions in Tamil Nadu: A webometric study. Jeyshankar, R. University of Madras, Tamil Nadu, 2010. Guide- B Ramesh Babu. 1731

WOMEN STUDIES

a. Academic Libraries - Colleges

Critical study of women college libraries in Marathwada and Vidarbha Region. Deshpande, A R. Dr Babasaheb Ambedkar Marathwada University, Aurangabad, Maharashtra, 2010. Guide- Shakuntala S Lomte. 1732

Use of information sources in women's colleges in Gulbarga City: A study. Veeranna, Veena. Gulbarga University, Karnataka, 2007. Guide- D B Patil. 1733

b. Author

Adhunik bangla sahitya mahila rachita rachanar karamavikas, 1850-1900. Choudhury, Sanghamitra. Jadavpur University, West Bengal, 2001. Guide-A K Ohdedar. 1734

c. Bibliometric Studies

Bibliometric evaluation of publications on women in ICT from developed and developing nations. Rajeswari, M G. Annamalai University, Tamil Nadu, 2010. Guide- R Ponnu Durai. 1735

Entry No.

Women in medicine research productivity: A bibliometric analysis. Arjunan, S. Annamalai University, Tamil Nadu, 2011. Guide- M Suriya. 1736

d. Empowerment

Education and information for empowering women through public libraries with special reference to public library system in Andhra Pradesh. Rani, B A. Sri Krishnadevaraya University, Andhra Pradesh, 2005. Guide- P Kamaiah. 1737

e. Health

Design and development of integrated information system and services for women health: An exploratory community based study. Yadav, B R. Karnataka University, Karnataka, 2005. Guide- C R Karisiddappa. 1738

Status of information services and health awareness among the rural women of Sagar District: A study. Jain, Ajit Kumar. Dr Hari Singh Gour Vishwavidyalaya, Sagar, Madhya Pradesh, 2011. Guide- B P Shrivastava. 1739

Women's health information based on web resources: An analysis. Ravi Kumar, S. Mizoram University, Mizoram, 2011. Guide- S N Singh. 1740

f. Information Needs

Information needs analysis and information seeking behaviour of entrepreneurs, with special reference to women. Murari, Durga. SNDT Women's University, Mumbai, Maharashtra, 2007. Guide- Harsha Parekh. 1741

Information needs, awareness and information seeking habits of elected women representatives of local government: A study with special reference to the panchayati raj institutions in West Bengal. Seal, Deepak Kumar. University of Burdwan, Rajbati, Bardhaman, West Bengal, 2012. Guide- Subal Chandra Biswas. 1742

Entry No.

g. Library Professionals

Job satisfaction among women library professionals in university and college libraries of Punjab. Rajwant Kaur (Ms). Guru Nanak Dev University, Amritsar, Punjab, 2007. Guide- Sewa Singh. 1743

Problems and prospects of women librarians of Indian university libraries: A survey. Varalakshmi, N. Gulbarga University, Karnataka, 1994. Guide- S R Gunjal. 1744

Some personality characteristics of women librarians in Kerala. Rajam, V. University of Calicut, Calicut, Kerala, 1992. Guide- A B George. 1745

Status and job satisfaction among women library professionals: A comparative study of few eastern libraries of Eastern India. Samantaray, Moortimatee. Utkal University, Orissa, 1996. Guide- Manoranjan Mahapatra. 1746

Status of women in library and information science profession a cross country analysis. Bhanumathi, J. Annamalai University, Tamil Nadu, 2011. Guide- M Suriya. 1747

Status, occupational characteristics and satisfaction among women library professionals: A study of universities and research libraries in U P. Chauhan, Punam (Ms). Banaras Hindu University, Uttar Pradesh, 2012. Guide- Aditya Tripathi. 1748

Women professionals in libraries: A case study of Manipur. Devi, Gurumayum Padma (Ms). Manipur University, Manipur, 2007. Guide- R Lahiri. 1749

Women professionals in various libraries in Karnataka: A study. Swaroop Rani, B S. University of Mysore, Karnataka, 2002. Guide- V G Talwar. 1750

Entry No.

h. Reading Habits

Extra-curricular reading habits of women teachers in the academic institutions of Goa State: A critical study. Shivalli, M P. Sambalpur University, Orissa, 1996. Guide- R K Rout. 1751

WORK ENVIRONMENT

Organizational climate of engineering college libraries in Tamil Nadu. Panneerselvam, P. University of Madras, Tamil Nadu, 2007. Guide- Manorama Srinath. 1752

Organizational climate of university libraries. Srinath, Manorama (Ms). University of Madras, Tamil Nadu, 1987. Guide- P Gangadhara Rao. 1753

Relationship between job satisfaction and organizational climate in academic libraries in Delhi: A survey. Ram Chander. Sambalpur University, Orissa, 2011. Guide- B K Choudhury. 1754

PART III

APPENDICES

Appendix I

Universities with Number of Ph Ds Awarded

S N	*Name of Universities*	*Ph Ds*	*%*	*Rank*
1.	Allahabad University	1	0.06	44
2.	Hemawati Nandan Bahuguna University	1	0.06	44
3.	Jamia Millia Islamia	1	0.06	44
4.	Jawaharlal Nehru University	1	0.06	44
5.	University of Patna	1	0.06	44
6.	Birla Institute of Technology	2	0.11	43
7.	Gujarat University, Ahmedabad	2	0.11	43
8.	Indian Institute of Technology, Delhi	2	0.11	43
9.	Kachchh University	2	0.11	43
10.	Lalith Narayan Mithila University	2	0.11	43
11.	Maharshi Dayanand University	2	0.11	43
12.	Saurashtra University	2	0.11	43
13.	Tilak Maharashtra Vidyapeeth	2	0.11	43
14.	Bhavnagar University	3	0.17	42
15.	Madurai Kamaraj University	3	0.17	42
16.	North Maharashtra University	3	0.17	42
17.	Ranchi University	3	0.17	42
18.	Anna University, Chennai	4	0.23	41
19.	Cochin University of Science & Technology	4	0.23	41
20.	Rabindra Bharati University	4	0.23	41
21.	Babasaheb Bhimrao Ambedkar University, Lucknow	5	0.28	40
22.	Mumbai University	5	0.28	40
23.	Mahatma Gandhi Chitrakoot Gramodaya Vishwavidyalaya, Satna	6	0.34	39
24.	Makhanlal Chaturvedi National University of Journalism and Mass Communication	6	0.34	39
25.	Tilka Manjhi Bhagalpur University	6	0.34	39
26.	M S University, Baroda	7	0.40	38
27.	Shivaji University, Kolhapur	7	0.40	38
28.	Swami Ramanand Teerth Marathwada University	7	0.40	38

Table contd...

S N	*Name of Universities*	*Ph Ds*	*%*	*Rank*
29.	Mizoram University	8	0.46	37
30.	Sardar Patel University	9	0.51	36
31.	SNDT Women's University	9	0.51	36
32.	Mohan Lal Sukhadia University	10	0.57	35
33.	Pt Ravishankar University	10	0.57	35
34.	University of Jammu	10	0.57	35
35.	Bharathidasan University	11	0.63	34
36.	University of Kashmir	12	0.68	33
37.	Kuvempu University	13	0.74	32
38.	Punjabi University	13	0.74	32
39.	University of Lucknow	14	0.80	31
40.	Sant Gadge Baba Amravati University	15	0.85	30
41.	University of Kerala	15	0.85	30
42.	Aligarh Muslim University	16	0.91	29
43.	Kurukshetra University	17	0.97	28
44.	Sri Krishnadevaraya University	18	1.02	27
45.	Awadhesh Pratap Singh University	19	1.08	26
46.	Hemchandracharya North Gujarat University	19	1.08	26
47.	Manipur University	19	1.08	26
48.	North East Hill University	20	1.38	26
49.	Vidyasagar University	21	1.19	25
50.	Bangalore University	22	1.25	24
51.	Guru Ghasidas University	22	1.25	24
52.	Berhampur University	23	1.31	23
53.	Mangalore University	24	1.37	22
54.	University of Burdwan	26	1.48	21
55.	Dr B R Ambedkar University, Agra	27	1.54	20
56.	Osmania University	27	1.54	20
57.	University of Calcutta	27	1.54	20
58.	Guru Nanak Dev University	29	1.65	19
59.	Vikram University	29	1.65	19
60.	University of Calicut	30	1.71	18
61.	Bundelkhand University	31	1.76	17
62.	Sambalpur University	32	1.82	16
63.	Banaras Hindu University	33	1.88	15
64.	Dr Babasaheb Ambedkar Marathwada University, Aurangabad	33	1.88	15
65.	Dr Hari Singh Gour Vishwavidyalaya	33	1.88	15
66.	Gulbarga University	33	1.88	15
67.	Utkal University	34	1.93	14
68.	Gauhati University	38	2.16	13
69.	Jadhavpur University	43	2.45	12
70.	Sri Venkateswara University	44	2.50	11
71.	University of Mysore	51	2.90	10
72.	Rashtrasant Tukadoji Maharaj Nagpur University	51	2.90	10
73.	University of Rajasthan	52	2.96	9
74.	Panjab University	54	3.07	8
75.	University of Delhi	58	3.30	7

Table contd...

S N	*Name of Universities*	*Ph Ds*	*%*	*Rank*
76.	Andhra University	61	3.47	6
77.	University of Madras	63	3.58	5
78.	University of Pune	67	3.81	4
79.	Karnataka University	84	4.78	3
80.	Annamalai University	88	5.01	2
81.	Jiwaji University	97	5.52	1
	Total	**1754**	**100%**	

Appendix II

Alphabetical List of Subjects

S N	Subjects	Ph Ds	%	Rank
1.	Administrative Training Libraries	7	0.40	30
2.	Adult Education	4	0.23	33
3.	Area studies	3	0.17	34
4.	Automated Library Management System	24	1.37	17
5.	Bibliographical Control	14	0.80	23
6.	Bibliometric Studies	118	6.73	1
7.	Bio Bibliography	5	0.29	32
8.	Children Literature	2	0.11	35
9.	Collection	15	0.86	22
10.	Collection Development	28	1.60	16
11.	Collection Management	29	1.65	15
12.	Community Information Centres	6	0.34	31
13.	Content Analysis	2	0.11	35
14.	Cost Benefit Analysis	8	0.46	29
15.	Customer Relationship Management	3	0.17	34
16.	Development Studies	29	1.65	15
17.	Digital Libraries	11	0.63	26
18.	Digitization	9	0.51	28
19.	DRDO Libraries	3	0.17	34
20.	E Resources	52	2.96	8
21.	Expert Systems	7	0.40	30
22.	Farradane's Law	1	0.06	36
23.	Financial Management	24	1.37	17
24.	Government Documents	3	0.17	34
25.	Government Libraries	3	0.17	34
26.	Information and Knowledge Society	3	0.17	34
27.	Information Communication	15	0.86	22
28.	Information Generation	5	0.29	32
29.	Information Literacy	17	0.97	21
30.	Information Management	6	0.34	31
31.	Information Needs	69	3.93	5
32.	Information Retrieval Tools, Techniques and System	30	1.71	14
33.	Information Science	2	0.11	35
34.	Information Seeking Behaviour	94	5.36	3
35.	Information Services	73	4.16	4
36.	Information Sources	21	1.20	18
37.	Information Systems	41	2.34	12
38.	Institutional Repositories	10	0.57	27
39.	Intellectual Property	9	0.51	28
40.	International Relations	1	0.06	36
41.	Internet Resources	19	1.08	20

Table contd...

S N	*Subjects*	*Ph Ds*	*%*	*Rank*
42.	IT Application in Libraries	52	2.96	8
43.	IT Impact on Libraries	12	0.68	25
44.	IT Infrastructure Facilities	5	0.29	32
45.	Knowledge Audit	2	0.11	35
46.	Knowledge Management	2	0.11	35
47.	Law Libraries	4	0.23	33
48.	Library Administration and Management	50	2.85	10
49.	Library Associations	4	0.23	33
50.	Library Automation	21	1.20	18
51.	Library Buildings	5	0.29	32
52.	Library Catalogue	2	0.11	35
53.	Library History	8	0.46	29
54.	Library Legislation	12	0.68	25
55.	Library Management Software	15	0.86	22
56.	Library Personnel	114	6.50	2
57.	Library Policies	6	0.34	31
58.	Library Profession	6	0.34	31
59.	Library Resources and Services	21	1.20	18
60.	Library Services	51	2.91	9
61.	Library Standards	5	0.29	32
62.	Library Studies	53	3.02	7
63.	LIS Education	29	1.65	15
64.	LIS Literature	4	0.23	33
65.	Literacy Movement	4	0.23	33
66.	Literature Growth Studies	14	0.80	23
67.	Manuscripts	5	0.29	32
68.	Marketing	19	1.08	20
69.	Media Libraries	4	0.23	33
70.	National Information Centres	2	0.11	35
71.	National Information Systems	8	0.46	29
72.	Networks and Consortia	49	2.79	11
73.	Newspaper Libraries	5	0.29	32
74.	Online Public Access Catalogue	7	0.40	30
75.	Open Access Resources	5	0.29	32
76.	Organizational Effectiveness	14	0.80	23
77.	Public Libraries	11	0.63	26
78.	Public Library Movement	9	0.51	28
79.	Public Library System	15	0.86	22
80.	Publishing Pattern	5	0.29	32
81.	Ranganathan Studies	4	0.23	33
82.	Reading Habits	13	0.74	24
83.	Research Role of University Libraries	6	0.34	31
84.	Resource Sharing and Networking	34	1.94	13
85.	Role of UGC	4	0.23	33
86.	RTI Act and Censorship	1	0.06	36
87.	Scientometric Studies	49	2.79	11
88.	Technical Processing, Tools and Techniques	65	3.71	6
89.	Total Quality Management	14	0.80	23
90.	Use and User Studies	30	1.71	14

Table contd...

S N	Subjects	Ph Ds	%	Rank
91.	User Satisfaction	3	0.17	34
92.	Vandalism	3	0.17	34
93.	Web Portals	3	0.17	34
94.	Web Resources	6	0.34	31
95.	Web Search Engines	3	0.17	34
96.	Websites	5	0.29	32
97.	Webometric Studies	4	0.23	33
98.	Women Studies	20	1.14	19
99.	Work Environment	3	0.17	34
	Total	**1754**	**100.00**	

Appendix III

List of Single Supervisors

S N	Name of Supervisors	Ph Ds	%	Rank
1	A A N Raju	6	0.36	20
2	A Amudavalli	6	0.36	20
3	A B George	2	0.12	24
4	A Dasgupta	3	0.18	23
5	A Ganesan	3	0.18	23
6	A K Bandyopadhyay	3	0.18	23
7	A K Baradol	8	0.48	18
8	A K Ohdedar	2	0.12	24
9	A K Varma	10	0.60	16
10	A K Verma	3	0.18	23
11	A Neelameghan	2	0.12	24
12	A R D Prasad	10	0.60	16
13	A R Kulkarni	1	0.06	25
14	A S Chandel	3	0.18	23
15	A Tejomurty	2	0.12	24
16	A V Satyanarayana Rao	1	0.06	25
17	A Y Asundi	7	0.42	19
18	Aditya Tripathi	2	0.12	24
19	Alaka Buragohain	9	0.54	17
20	Aloke Mitra	1	0.06	25
21	Amitabha Chatterjee	2	0.12	24
22	Amritpal Kaur	5	0.30	21
23	Anuradha Mishra	1	0.06	25
24	Arvind Kumar Sharma	3	0.18	23
25	Ashok Basu	4	0.24	22
26	Ashu Shokeen	9	0.54	17
27	Ashwini Anand Vaishnav	15	0.89	11
28	Ashwini P Paradkar	3	0.18	23
29	B Anderson	1	0.06	25
30	B B Pahurkar	1	0.06	25
31	B B Shukla	3	0.18	23
32	B D Kumbhar	8	0.48	18
33	B Guha	1	0.06	25
34	B K Choudhury	7	0.42	19
35	B K Sharma	6	0.36	20
36	B K Sohoni	1	0.06	25
37	B L Joshi	1	0.06	25
38	B Mukharjee	1	0.06	25
39	B Nagappa	1	0.06	25
40	B P Shrivastava	15	0.89	11
41	B Ramesh Babu	23	1.37	4

Table contd...

S N	Name of Supervisors	Ph Ds	%	Rank
42	B S Biradar	7	0.42	19
43	B S Garg	3	0.18	23
44	B S Maheswarappa	4	0.24	22
45	B S Nigam	5	0.30	21
46	B S Swaroop Rani	2	0.12	24
47	B U Kannappanavar	4	0.24	22
48	B Vijayalakshmi	10	0.60	16
49	Baman Parida	3	0.18	23
50	Banikanta Sarma	1	0.06	25
51	Bharati Sen	2	0.12	24
52	Bhubaneswar Chakrabarti	2	0.12	24
53	Bijoynath Mukherjee	1	0.06	25
54	Bijoypada Mukherjee	1	0.06	25
55	Biplab Chakrabarti	9	0.54	17
56	Biswanath Panda	1	0.06	25
57	Brajesh Tiwari	12	0.72	14
58	C D Sharma	3	0.18	23
59	C N Rawal	4	0.24	22
60	C P Ramasesh	3	0.18	23
61	C P Vashishth	2	0.12	24
62	C R Karisiddappa	36	2.15	1
63	C Sasikala	7	0.42	19
64	C V Rajan Pillai	4	0.24	22
65	Ch Ibohal Singh	1	0.06	25
66	Chaitali Dutta	4	0.24	22
67	D B Eshwara Reddy	3	0.18	23
68	D B Krishna Rao	1	0.06	25
69	D B Patil	1	0.06	25
70	D Chandran	7	0.42	19
71	D K Veer	1	0.06	25
72	D R Deshpande	4	0.24	22
73	D Rajyalakshmi	15	0.89	11
74	D Ravinder	2	0.12	24
75	D S Aggarwal	2	0.12	24
76	D Shivalingaiah	4	0.24	22
77	Dabir Singh	3	0.18	23
78	Devika P Madalli	2	0.12	24
79	Dinesh K Gupta	3	0.18	23
80	G C Bansal	4	0.24	22
81	G D Bhargava	2	0.12	24
82	G Devarajan	6	0.36	20
83	G Krishnamoorthy	2	0.12	24
84	G Mahapatra	3	0.18	23
85	G V S L Narasimha Raju	5	0.30	21
86	Gitaben S Patel	1	0.06	25
87	H A Khan	7	0.42	19
88	H N Prasad	15	0.89	11
89	H R Chopra	13	0.77	13
90	H S Chopra	2	0.12	24
91	H S Sengar	8	0.48	18
92	Harsha Parekh	5	0.30	21

Table contd...

S N	*Name of Supervisors*	*Ph Ds*	*%*	*Rank*
93	Hemant Sharma	18	1.07	8
94	I Chandraiah	2	0.12	24
95	I K Ravichandra Rao	4	0.24	22
96	I V Malhan	7	0.42	19
97	J C Binwal	6	0.36	20
98	J K Khanna	2	0.12	24
99	J K Sarkhel	3	0.18	23
100	J L Saini	5	0.30	21
101	J L Sardana	7	0.42	19
102	J N Gautam	20	1.19	6
103	J S Sharma	10	0.60	16
104	J Vijaya Kumari	1	0.06	25
105	J Yadagiri Reddy	3	0.18	23
106	Jagtar Singh	7	0.42	19
107	K A Isaac	5	0.30	21
108	K B Kale	1	0.06	25
109	K C Das	6	0.36	20
110	K C Panda	20	1.19	6
111	K C Ramakrishne Gowda	1	0.06	25
112	K C Sahoo	11	0.66	15
113	K G Tyagi	1	0.06	25
114	K L Mahawar	5	0.30	21
115	K M Khan	2	0.12	24
116	K Navalani	5	0.30	21
117	K Padmini	10	0.60	16
118	K Ramakrishna Rao	1	0.06	25
119	K S Deshpande	6	0.36	20
120	K S Raghavan	11	0.66	15
121	K Santi Sawrup	1	0.06	25
122	K Sarada	3	0.18	23
123	K Siva Reddy	8	0.48	18
124	K Somasekhara Rao	9	0.54	17
125	K Vijayakumar	1	0.06	25
126	Kamleshwar Nath	1	0.06	25
127	Kautilya Shukla	2	0.12	24
128	Khaiser Nikam	4	0.24	22
129	Khomdon Singh	2	0.12	24
130	Kirit M Vyas	2	0.12	24
131	Krishan Kumar	7	0.42	19
132	Krishnapada Majumder	4	0.24	22
133	L Das	1	0.06	25
134	L N Verma	5	0.30	21
135	L S Chopra	1	0.06	25
136	Lalitha Aswath	3	0.18	23
137	Lalitha K Sami	3	0.18	23
138	M A Gopinath	7	0.42	19
139	M Aravinthan	5	0.30	21
140	M B Konnur	8	0.48	18
141	M Bavakutty	10	0.60	16
142	M C Nandani	1	0.06	25
143	M Chandrashekara	3	0.18	23

Table contd..

S N	Name of Supervisors	Ph Ds	%	Rank
144	M D Baby	2	0.12	24
145	M Hirwade	3	0.18	23
146	M K Bhandi	3	0.18	23
147	M K Prajapati	7	0.42	19
148	M K R Naidu	3	0.18	23
149	M L Chakraborty	6	0.36	20
150	M L Wali	2	0.12	24
151	M M Kashyap	2	0.12	24
152	M M Shah	1	0.06	25
153	M Madhusudhan	1	0.06	25
154	Manoranjan Mahapatra	8	0.48	18
155	M Masoom Raza	2	0.12	24
156	M Nagarajan	19	1.13	7
157	M P Satija	7	0.42	19
158	M R Kherde	2	0.12	24
159	M R Kumbhar	16	0.95	10
160	M R Rawtani	6	0.36	20
161	M R Riswadkar	5	0.30	21
162	M S G Ammal	1	0.06	25
163	M Sadik Batcha	4	0.24	22
164	M Suriya	17	1.01	9
165	M T M Khan	16	0.95	10
166	M V Mudhol	3	0.18	23
167	Madhuri Devi	4	0.24	22
168	Madhusudan Dubey	1	0.06	25
169	Mallinath Kumbar	1	0.06	25
170	Mangala Prasad Singha	2	0.12	24
171	Manorama Srinath	16	0.95	10
172	Mehtab Alam Ansari	3	0.18	23
173	Moses M Naga	1	0.06	25
175	N B Dahibhate	1	0.06	25
176	N B Pangannaya	5	0.30	21
177	N C Khandekar	1	0.06	25
178	N David Livingstone	1	0.06	25
179	N G Bapat	1	0.06	25
180	N Guruswamy Naidu	7	0.42	19
181	N J Deshpande	14	0.83	12
182	N K Sharma	4	0.24	22
183	N Laxman Rao	1	0.06	25
184	N N Sharma	7	0.42	19
185	N Parvathamma	2	0.12	24
186	N R Satyanarayana	24	1.43	3
187	N S Harinarayana	4	0.24	22
188	N Vedamani Manuel	1	0.06	25
189	Namita B Khot	1	0.06	25
190	Narendra Lahkar	10	0.60	16
191	Navjot Kaur	3	0.18	23
192	Neerja Verma	1	0.06	25
193	Nihar Ranjan Ray	1	0.06	25
194	Niru Hazarika	1	0.06	25
195	Nishat Fatima	2	0.12	24

Table contd...

S N	*Name of Supervisors*	*Ph Ds*	*%*	*Rank*
196	P A Gokhale	3	0.18	23
197	P B Mangla	8	0.48	18
198	P Bhaskara Rao	3	0.18	23
199	P C Pant	1	0.06	25
200	P Dakhole	2	0.12	24
201	P Gangadhara Rao	3	0.18	23
202	P Hangsing	1	0.06	25
203	P K Jana	2	0.12	24
204	P K Mishra	1	0.06	25
205	P K Panigrahi	1	0.06	25
206	P K Patil	2	0.12	24
207	P K Rath	3	0.18	23
208	P K Walia	3	0.18	23
209	P Kamaiah	10	0.60	16
210	P M Naushad Ali	2	0.12	24
211	P N Kaula	5	0.30	21
212	P Pichappan	5	0.30	21
213	P Rajarathnam Chetty	6	0.36	20
214	P Ravichandran	6	0.36	20
215	P S G Kumar	33	1.97	2
216	P Sadashivmurthy	4	0.24	22
217	P Sivaraman	3	0.18	23
218	P Soma Raju	8	0.48	18
219	P V Konnur	2	0.12	24
220	Pandey S K Sharma	4	0.24	22
221	Pijush Kanti Mahapatra	2	0.12	24
222	Pinaki Nath Mukhopadhyay	3	0.18	23
223	Pitambar Padhi	4	0.24	22
224	Prabir Roy Choudhury	14	0.83	12
225	Preeti Mahajan	6	0.36	20
226	Promila	1	0.06	25
227	Pulin Behari Barua	8	0.48	18
228	Purnima Devi	3	0.18	23
229	Purnima Kaushik	1	0.06	25
230	Purnima Mathur	2	0.12	24
231	Pushpa Dhyani	8	0.48	18
232	Pushpanjali Jena	6	0.36	20
233	Qeyamuddin Ahmad	1	0.06	25
234	R C Gupta	1	0.06	25
235	R G Prasher	5	0.30	21
236	R K Barman	5	0.30	21
237	R K Bhatt	4	0.24	22
238	R K Mahapatra	6	0.36	20
239	R K Rout	7	0.42	19
240	R K Sharma	10	0.60	16
241	R Lahiri	4	0.24	22
242	R N Mishra	2	0.12	24
243	R N Trivedi	1	0.06	25
244	R P Bajpai	3	0.18	23
245	R Ponnu Durai	4	0.24	22
246	R R Naik	2	0.12	24

Table contd...

S N	Name of Supervisors	Ph Ds	%	Rank
247	R S R Varalakshmi	7	0.42	19
248	R T D Ramesh Gandhi	1	0.06	25
249	R Vengan	3	0.18	23
250	Rajbir Singh	1	0.06	25
251	Raju M Mathew	7	0.42	19
252	Ranjana Vohra	11	0.66	15
253	Ratna Bandyopadhyay	1	0.06	25
254	Rochana Shrivastava	1	0.06	25
255	Rosamma Joseph	4	0.24	22
256	S A Vadikar	1	0.06	25
257	S Ally Sornam	6	0.36	20
258	S C Verma	9	0.54	17
259	S G Mahajan	6	0.36	20
260	S Gopalakrishnan	1	0.06	25
261	S Innasi	1	0.06	25
262	S J Verma	1	0.06	25
263	S K Patil	10	0.60	16
264	S K Srivastava	1	0.06	25
265	S Kumar	6	0.36	20
266	S L Sangam	22	1.31	5
267	S M Charan	11	0.66	15
268	S M K Q Zaidi	3	0.18	23
269	S M Mohal	7	0.42	19
270	S M Nikose	1	0.06	25
271	S M Shafi	7	0.42	19
272	S M Tripathi	13	0.77	13
273	S Mohamed Esmail	4	0.24	22
274	S N Singh	12	0.72	14
275	S N Srivastava	6	0.36	20
276	S Nakkiran	1	0.06	25
277	S P Ganpule	4	0.24	22
278	S P Narang	1	0.06	25
279	S P Satarkar	6	0.36	20
280	S P Sood	6	0.36	20
281	S R Ganpule	3	0.18	23
282	S R Gunjal	17	1.01	9
283	S R Gupta	3	0.18	23
284	S R Ijari	6	0.36	20
285	S R Ranganathan	1	0.06	25
286	S Ravi	16	0.95	10
287	S S Agarwal	2	0.12	24
288	S S Chandel	1	0.06	25
289	S S Pal	1	0.06	25
290	S Sahay	3	0.18	23
291	S Sudarshan Rao	4	0.24	22
292	Saghasen Singh	1	0.06	25
293	Sangita Gupta	2	0.12	24
294	Self Adjudication	7	0.42	19
295	Sewa Singh	10	0.60	16
296	Shabahat Husain	3	0.18	23
297	Shailendra Kumar	8	0.48	18

Table contd...

S N	Name of Supervisors	Ph Ds	%	Rank
298	Shakuntala S Lomte	5	0.30	21
299	Shalini R Urs	2	0.12	24
300	Shalini Rewadikar	2	0.12	24
301	Shamkant J Deshmukh	3	0.18	23
302	Shashi Prabha Singh	6	0.36	20
303	Shivani Sengupta	1	0.06	25
304	Shivshankar Mishra	1	0.06	25
305	Shyama Rajaram	3	0.18	23
306	Sonal Singh	7	0.42	19
307	Srinarayan Singh	2	0.12	24
308	Subal Chandra Biswas	7	0.42	19
309	Subarna Kumar Das	1	0.06	25
310	Subir K Sen	2	0.12	24
311	Sudharma Haridasan	1	0.06	25
312	Sukumar Sengupta	1	0.06	25
313	Supervisors' Name Not Available	7	0.42	19
314	Surendra Singh	3	0.18	23
315	T A V Murthy	4	0.24	22
316	T D Kemparaju	3	0.18	23
317	T D Tilwani	3	0.18	23
318	T K Oomen	1	0.06	25
319	T P Lele	1	0.06	25
320	T Rajagopal	5	0.30	21
321	T Saravanan	3	0.18	23
322	Tarun Kumar Mitra	2	0.12	24
323	Tridib Tripathi	5	0.30	21
324	Trishanjit Kaur	2	0.12	24
325	U A Thaker	4	0.24	22
326	U C Sharma	16	0.95	10
327	U K Aggarwal	2	0.12	24
328	U K Tikku	6	0.36	20
329	U N Singh	4	0.24	22
330	U P Nahle	3	0.18	23
331	Udayan Bhattacharya	2	0.12	24
332	Usha Pawan	6	0.36	20
333	V A Kamath	3	0.18	23
334	V Chandrasekhara Rao	3	0.18	23
335	V Durairajan	1	0.06	25
336	V G Talwar	13	0.77	13
337	V Jalaja	7	0.42	19
338	V K Sharma	3	0.18	23
339	V M Bhagvatkar	1	0.06	25
340	V P Khare	2	0.12	24
341	V P Rajhans	1	0.06	25
342	V Pulla Reddy	11	0.66	15
343	V T Kamble	8	0.48	18
344	V Venkata Rao	4	0.24	22
345	V Vishwa Mohan	6	0.36	20
346	Veena Saraf	5	0.30	21
347	W A Alvi	1	0.06	25
348	Y P Dubey	4	0.24	22
349	Y Venkatesha	1	0.06	25

Appendix IV

List of Joint Supervisors

S N	Name of Supervisors	Ph Ds	%	Rank
1.	A Hussain	1	0.66	8
2.	A K Anand	1	0.66	8
3.	A K Ohdedar	1	0.66	8
4.	A N Sadhu	1	0.66	8
5.	A R D Prasad	1	0.66	8
6.	A S Chandel	2	1.32	7
7.	A Sengupta	1	0.66	8
8.	Alaka Buragohain	1	0.66	8
9.	Ashok Basu	4	2.63	5
10.	Ashu Shokeen	1	0.66	8
11.	B K Sen	2	1.32	7
12.	B K Sharma	12	7.89	2
13.	B P Shrivastava	1	0.66	8
14.	B S Maheswarappa	2	1.32	7
15.	B V Rajashekhar	2	1.32	7
16.	Bijoypada Mukherjee	1	0.66	8
17.	C P Vashishth	3	1.97	6
18.	Chaitali Dutta	2	1.32	7
19.	D B Krishna Rao	1	0.66	8
20.	D S Aggarwal	1	0.66	8
21.	Daleep Singh	1	0.66	8
22.	Devika P Madalli	1	0.66	8
23.	G Bhattacharya	1	0.66	8
24.	H S Sengar	4	2.63	5
25.	Hemant Sharma	10	6.58	3
26.	Herton	1	0.66	8
27.	I V Malhan	1	0.66	8
28.	J C Binwal	1	0.66	8
29.	J K Khanna	2	1.32	7
30.	J K Sarkhel	3	1.97	6
31.	J L Sardana	2	1.32	7
32.	J N Gautam	15	9.87	1
33.	J N Satpathi	1	0.66	8
34.	J S Sharma	1	0.66	8
35.	K Nithyanandam	1	0.66	8
36.	Krishan Kumar	1	0.66	8
37.	M A Gopinath	2	1.32	7
38.	M Abu Baker	1	0.66	8
39.	M B Bankapur	1	0.66	8
40.	M L Chakraborty	1	0.66	8
41.	M T M Khan	2	1.32	7

Table contd...

S N	*Name of Supervisors*	*Ph Ds*	*%*	*Rank*
42.	Mohan Chel	1	0.66	8
43.	N M Panda	1	0.66	8
44.	N R Satyanarayana	1	0.66	8
45.	Noorul Hasan Khan	3	1.97	6
46.	P Hangsing	2	1.32	7
47.	P K Jana	2	1.32	7
48.	Parthasarathi Mukhopadhyay	1	0.66	8
49.	Pranab Kumar Chakraborty	1	0.66	8
50.	Pulin Behari Barua	1	0.66	8
51.	R G Prasher	1	0.66	8
52.	R K Rout	1	0.66	8
53.	R Lahiri	1	0.66	8
54.	R P Bajpai	1	0.66	8
55.	R Raju	1	0.66	8
56.	Rita Sinha	1	0.66	8
57.	Rochana Shrivastava	2	1.32	7
58.	S Kumar	3	1.97	6
59.	S L Sangam	2	1.32	7
60.	S M Tripathi	9	5.92	4
61.	S N Mukherjee	1	0.66	8
62.	S R Gupta	4	2.63	5
63.	S S Chandel	2	1.32	7
64.	Shailendra Kumar	2	1.32	7
65.	Shashi Prabha Singh	1	0.66	8
66.	Sonal Singh	2	1.32	7
67.	Subal Chandra Biswas	2	1.32	7
68.	Surendra Singh	2	1.32	7
69.	T A V Murthy	3	1.97	6
70.	U N Singh	1	0.66	8
71.	Veena Saraf	2	1.32	7
72.	Y P Dubey	1	0.66	8
	Total	**152**	**100.00**	

Appendix V

Details of Universities Offering Ph D Programme

S N	*Name of Universities*	*Yr of Deptt. Estd.*	*Yr of Starting Ph D*	*Universities' Website*	*Departments' Website*
1.	Aligarh Muslim University, Aligarh (1920)	1958	1990	http://www.amu.ac.in	http://www.amu.ac.in/department.jsp?did=80
2.	Andhra University, Vishakpatnam (1926)	1935	1966	http://www.andhrauniversity.edu.in	N A
3.	Anna University, Chennai (1978)	N A	2010*	http://www.annauniv.edu	N A
4.	Annamalai University, Annamalainagar (1929)	1979	1982	http://www.annamalaiuniversity.ac.in	http://annamalaiuniversity.ac.in/fact_arts.htm
5.	Awadhesh Pratap Singh University, Rewa (1968)	1968	2001*	http://apsurewa.ac.in	N A
6.	Babasaheb Bhimrao Ambedkar University, Lucknow (1994)	1997	2008*	http://www.bbau.ac.in	http://www.bbau.ac.in/SIST/DLIS/Dept_Library.aspx
7.	Banaras Hindu University, Varanasi (1916)	1942	1976	http://www.bhu.ac.in	http://www.bhu.ac.in/DLIBS
8.	Bangalore University, Bangalore (1964)	1973	1982	http://www.bangaloreuniversity.ac.in	http://www.bangaloreuniversity.ac.in/faculties/sci_dept_ library_information.aspx

* Indicates award of first Ph D by the university (Year of starting Ph D programme was not available)

S N	Name of Universities	Yr of Deptt. Estd.	Yr of Starting Ph D	Universities' Website	Departments' Website
9.	Berhampur University,Berhampur (1967)	1983	1984	http://www.bamu.nic.in	N A
10.	Bharathidasan University, Tiruchirappalli (1892)	2007	2007	http://www.bdu.ac.in/	http://www.bdu.ac.in/schools/library_information_science/
11.	Birla Institute of Technology, Mesra, Ranchi (1955)	1993	1994*	http://www.bitmesra.ac.in/	http://www.bitmesra.ac.in/cms.aspx?this=1&mid=322&cid=188
12.	Bundelkhand University, Jhansi (1975)	1986	1998*	http://www.bujhansi.org	N A
13.	Central University of Himachal Pradesh, Dharamshala (2009)	2010	2010	http://www.cuhimachal.ac.in	http://www.cuhimachal.ac.in/library_science_mcis.aspx
14.	Cochin University of Science & Technology,Kalamassey (1986) (Estd as Cochin University 1971)	N A	1991*	http://www.cusat.ac.in	N A
15.	Dravidian University, Kuppam (1997)	2009 .	2009	http://www.dravidianuniversity ac.in	N A
16.	Dr. B. R. Ambedkar University, Agra (1996)	1984	1999*	http://www.dbrau.ac.in	http://www.dbrau.ac.in/d epartment_%20of_Library_and_Information_science.html
17.	Dr. Babasaheb Ambedkar Marathwada University, Aurangabad (1958)	1979	1986	http://www.bamu.net	http://www.bamu.ac.in/dept/libsci

* Indicates award of first Ph D by the university (Year of starting Ph D programme was not available)

S N	Name of Universities	Yr of Deptt. Estd.	Yr of Starting Ph D	Universities' Website	Departments' Website
18.	Dr. Hari Singh Gour Vishwavidyalaya, Sagar (1946)	1970	1978	http://www.dhsgsu.ac.in	http://www.dhsgsu.ac.in/departwebpages.php?depart=56
19.	Gauhati University, Guwahati (1948)	1966	1987	http://www.gauhati.ac.in	http://www.gauhati.ac.in/page.php?cat=Department&id=Library%20and%20Information% 20Science
20.	Gujarat University, Ahmedabad (1949)	1964	1978*	http://www.gujaratuniversity.org.in	http://www.gujaratuniversity.org.in/web/NWD/Departments/TeachDep/Others/DLIS.pdf
21.	Gujarat Vidyapeeth, Ahmedabad (1963)	1986	1999	http://www.gujaratvidyapith.org	N.A.
22.	Gulbarga University, Gulbarga (1979)	1979	1979	http://www.gulbargauniversity.kar.nic.in	http://www.gulbargauniversity.kar.nic.in/FacSocSci/LibZInfoSci.html
23.	Guru Ghasidas University, Bilaspur (1983)	1985	1998*	http://www.ggu.ac.in	http://www.ggu.ac.in/Academic_Course_Library% 20&%20Information%20Sci.html
24.	Guru Nanak Dev University, Amritsar (1969)	1971	1987	http://www.gndu.ac.in	http://department.gndu.ac.in/department/Libinf.asp

* Indicates award of first Ph D by the university (Year of starting Ph D programme was not available)

S N	Name of Universities	Yr of Deptt. Estd.	Yr of Starting Ph D	Universities' Website	Departments' Website
25.	Hemwati Nandan Bahunguna Garhwal University, Srinagar Garhwal (1973)	1991	2009*	http://hnbgu.ac.in	http://hnbgu.ac.in/index.php?option=com_content&view=article&id=572&Itemid=972
26.	Hemchandracharya North Gujarat University, Patan (1986)	1992	2002*	http://www.ngu.ac.in/	http://www.ngu.ac.in/department/DEPT_LIB_SCI/DEPT_LIB_SCI.htm
27.	Jadavpur University, Kolkata (1952)	1964	1991*	http://www.jadavpur.edu.in	http://www.jaduniv.edu.in/view_department.php? deptid=71
28.	Jiwaji University, Gwalior (1964)	1982	1985	http://www.jiwaji.edu of-studies-library.asp	http://www.jiwaji.edu/school-
29.	Krantiguru Shyamji Krishna Verma Kachchh University,Bhuj (2004)	NA	2012*	http://kskvku.digitaluniversity.ac	N A
30.	Karnataka State Women's University, Bijapur (2003)	2007	2008	http://www.kswu.ac.in	http://www.kswu.ac.in/departments/social-science/library-science-and-information-science
31.	Karnataka University, Dharwad (1949)	1962	1974	http://www.kud.ac.in	www.kud.ac.in/content.aspx?module=dept&page=dept_LibIS
32	Kurukshetra University, Kurukshetra (1956)	1969	1988	http://www.kuk.ac.in	www.kuk.ac.in/information.php?action= show Content&L01_id=OA==& L01_direction=H&L03_id=Mzk=&L02_id=MjE= &sublevel =y

* Indicates award of first Ph D by the university (Year of starting Ph D programme was not available)

S N	Name of **Universities**	Yr of Deptt. Estd.	Yr of Starting Ph D	Universities' Website	Departments' Website
33.	Kuvempu University, Shimonga (1987)	1993	1994	http://www.kuvempu.ac.in	www.kuvempu.ac.in/ac-dpt-libsci.htm
34.	Lalit Narayan Mithila University, Darbhanga (1972)	1976	1983*	http://lnmu.inoday.co.in	N A
35.	Madurai Kamraj University, Madurai (1966)	1974	1982	http://www.mkuniversity.org	http://www.mkuniversity.org/sub_link_pg.php?id=s16
36.	Maharaja Krishnakumarsinhji Bhavnagar University, Bhavnagar (2012) (formerly Bhavnagar University 1978)	1982	2000*	http://www.bhavuni.edu	http://bhavuni.edu/library-science-dept.php
37.	Maharaja Sayajirao University of Baroda, Baroda (1949)	1956	1996	http://www.msubaroda.ac.in/	http://www.msubaroda.ac.in/arts/index.php
38.	Mahatma Gandhi Chitrakoot Gramodaya Vishwavidyala, Chitrakoot (1991)	1991	1993	http://www.mgcgvchitrakoot.com	N A
39.	Makhanlal Chaturvedi National University of Journalism and Mass Communication, Bhopal (1990)	1993	2007*	http://www.mcu.ac.in	http://www.mcu.ac.in/Departments.aspx
40.	Mangalore University, Mangalore (1980)	1981	1990	http://www.mangaloreuniversity.ac.in	http://www.mangalore university.ac.in/xampp/departments/libscience/index.htm
41.	Manipur University, Imphal (1980)	1986	1987	http://manipuruniv.ac.in	http://libinfosc.manipuruniv.ac.in/home.php

* Indicates award of first Ph D by the university (Year of starting Ph D programme was not available)

S N	Name of Universities	Yr of Deptt. Estd.	Yr of Starting Ph D	Universities' Website	Departments' Website
42.	Mizoram University, Aizwal (2001)	2002	2005	http://www.mzu.edu.in	http://www.mzu.edu.in/schools/library%20and%20information%20science.html
43.	Mohanlal Sukhadia University, Udaipur (1962)	1975	2003*	http://www.mlsu.ac.in/	http://www.mlsu.ac.in/faculty_department.htm
44.	North-East Hill University, Shillong (1973)	1985	1985	http://www.nehu.ac.in/	http://www.nehu.ac.in/Schools/Economics%20&%20Management/Library%20Science/
45.	North Maharashtra University, Jalgaon (1990)	2000	2012*	http://www.nmu.ac.in	http://nmu.ac.in/dolib/en-us/home.aspx
46.	Osmania University, Hyderabad (1918)	1959	1989	http://www.osmania.ac.in	https://sites.google.com/site/lisosmania/
47.	Panjab University, Chandigarh (1947)	1960	1972	http://puchd.ac.in/	http://libraryscience.puchd.ac.in/
48.	Pondicherry University, Pondicherry (1985)	2007	2010	http://www.pondiuni.edu.in/	http://www.pondiuni.edu.in/department/department-library-information-science
49.	Pt. Ravishankar Shukla University, Raipur (1964)	1971	1990	http://www.prsu.ac.in/	http://www.prsu.ac.in/Departments/LibraryScience/Libraryscience.html
50.	Punjabi University, Patiala (1962)	1969	1987	http://punjabiuniversity.ac.in	http://punjabiuniversity.ac.in/pbiuniweb/pages/departments/library.html

* Indicates award of first Ph D by the university (Year of starting Ph D programme was not available)

S N	Name of Universities	Yr of Deptt. Estd.	Yr of Starting Ph D	Universities' Website	Departments' Website
51.	Rabindra Bharati University, Kolkata (1962)	1985	1990	http://www.rbu.ac.in/	N A
52.	Ranchi University, Ranchi (1963)	N A	1973*	http://www.ranchiuniversity.org.in	N A
53.	Rani Channamma University, Belgavi (2010)	2011	2011	http://www.rcub.ac.in	http://rcub.ac.in/schools/school-of-applied-sciences/department-of-library-information-science
54	Rastrasant Tukadoji Maharaj Nagpur University, Nagpur (1923)	1956	1987	http://www.nagpuruniversity.org	http://www.nagpuruniversity.org/links/faculty_of_social_science/dep_libraryninfo.htm
55.	Sambalpur University, Sambalpur (1967)	1976	1979	http://www.suniv.ac.in	http://www.suniv.ac.in/Lib&InformationScience.pdf
56.	Sant Gadge Baba Amravati University, Amravati (1983)	1987	1998	http://sgbau.ac.in	http://sgbau.ac.in/SGB%20Amt%20Uni%20Website/library science.html
57.	Sardar Patel University, Vallabh Vidyanagar, Anand (1955)	1982	1996	http://www.spuvvn.edu	http://www.spuvvn.edu/academics/departments/library_information_science/

* Indicates award of first Ph D by the university (Year of starting Ph D programme was not available)

S N	Name of Universities	Yr of Deptt. Estd.	Yr of Starting Ph D	Universities' Website	Departments' Website
58.	Saurashtra University, Rajkot (1967)	1976	2010*	http://www.saurashtrauniversity.edu	http://www.saurashtrauniversity.edu/UserSideSaurashtr_Dyanamic/DepartmentView.aspx
59.	Shivaji University, Kolhapur (1962)	1965	1983	http://www.unishivaji.ac.in	http://www.unishivaji.ac.in/acdms/dptlibsc.htm
60.	SNDT Women's University, Mumbai (1916)	1961	1988	http://www.sndt.digitaluniversity.ac	http://sndt.digitaluniversity.ac/Content.aspx?ID=26489
61.	Sri Krishnadevaraya University, Anantpur (1981)	1982	1990	http://www.skuniversity.org	http://www.skuniversity.org/Department%20&%20Faculty/Social%20Sciences/Dept%20of%20Library%20&%20Information%20Science.asp
62.	Sri Venkateswara University, Tirupati (1954)	1974	1987	http://www.svuniversity.in	N A
63.	Swami Ramanand Teerth Marathwada University, Nanded (1994)	1994	1994	http://www.srtmun.ac.in/	N A
64.	Tilak Maharashtra Vidyapeeth, Pune (1987)	1984	2008	http://www.tmv.edu.in	http://www.tmv.edu.in/nehruinst.asp

* Indicates award of first Ph D by the university (Year of starting Ph D programme was not available)

S N	Name of Universities	Yr of Deptt. Estd.	Yr of Starting Ph D	Universities' Website	Departments' Website
65.	Tilka Manjhi Bhagalpur University, Bhagalpur (1960)	1971	1977*	http://www.tmbu.org	http://www.tmv.edu.in/nehruinst.asp
66.	Tumkur University, Tumkur (2004)	2005	2012	http://tumkuruniversity.in	http://tumkuruniversity.in/index.php/pg_library-and-information-science/
67.	University of Burdwan , Bardhaman (1960)	1964	1977	http://www.buruniv.ac.in	http://www.buruniv.ac.in
68.	University of Calcutta, Calcutta (1857)	1945	1972	http://www.caluniv.ac.in	http://www.caluniv.ac.in/academic/library.htm
69.	University of Calicut, Kozhikode (1968)	1978	1985	http://www.universityofcalicut.info	http://www.universityofcalicut.info/index.php?option=com_content&task=view&id=56&Itemid=133
70.	University of Delhi, Delhi (1922)	1946	1952	http://www.du.ac.in	http://dlis.du.ac.in
71.	University of Jammu, Jammu (1969)	1971	1985	http://www.jammuuniversity.in	http://www.jammuuniversity.in/departments/lib%20science/intro.asp
72.	University of Kalyani, Kalyani (1960)	1991	N A	http://www.klyuniv.ac.in	http://www.klyuniv.ac.in/lib_info_sc.html

* Indicates award of first Ph D by the university (Year of starting Ph D programme was not available)

S N	Name of Universities	Yr of Deptt. Estd.	Yr of Starting Ph D	Universities' Website	Departments' Website
73	University of Kashmir, Hazratbagh, Srinagar (1969)	1970	1985	http://www.kashmiruniversity.net	http://lis.uok.edu.in
74.	University of Kerala, Thiruvanthpuram (1937)	1961	1980	http://www.keralauniversity.ac.in	http://www.keralauniversity.ac.in/departments/dlis
75.	University of Lucknow, Lucknow (1921)	1972	1984	http://www.lkouniv.ac.in	http://www.lkouniv.ac.in/dept_lib_sci.htm
76.	University of Madras, Chennai (1857)	1960	1977	http://www.unom.ac.in	http://www.unom.ac.in/index.php?route=department/department/deptpage&deptid=45
77.	University of Mumbai, Vidyanagari, Mumbai (1857)	1944	1995	http://www.mu.ac.in	http://www.mu.ac.in/arts/library_science/profile.html
78.	University of Mysore, Mysore (1916)	1965	1976	http://www.uni-mysore.ac.in	http://www.uni-mysore.ac.in/library-and-information-science/#A
79.	University of Pune, Pune (1948)	1958	1979	http://www.unipune.ac.in/	http://www.unipune.ac.in/dept/mental_moral_and_social_science/library_and_ information_ science/default.htm
80.	University of Rajasthan, Jaipur (1947)	1960	1974	http://www.uniraj.ac.in	http://www.uniraj.ac.in/FACULTY/fac_con_librarysc.html

* Indicates award of first Ph D by the university (Year of starting Ph D programme was not available)

S N	Name of Universities	Yr of Deptt. Estd.	Yr of Starting Ph D	Universities' Website	Departments' Website
81.	Utkal University, Bhubaneswar (1943)	1981	1984	http://www.utkaluniversity.ac.in	http://utkaluniversity.ac.in/page.php?page=library-and-information-science
82.	Vidyasagar University, Midnapore (1981)	1985	1988	http://vidyasagar.ac.in	http://vidyasagar.ac.in/library_Information/dept_library_information.html
83.	Vikram University, Ujjain (1957)	1957	1976	http://www.vikramuniv.net	N A

* Indicates award of first Ph D by the university (Year of starting Ph D programme was not available)

PART IV

INDICES

A: Scholars Index

(With Entry Numbers)

B: Title Index

(With Entry Numbers)

C: Subject Index

(With Entry Numbers)

D: Single Supervisors Index

(With Entry Numbers)

E: Joint Supervisors Index

(With Entry Numbers)

F. Universities Index

(With Entry Numbers)